SWIFT and the twentieth century

Milton Voigt is assistant professor of English at the University of Utah. He received his M.A. degree from the University of California and his Ph.D. from the University of Minnesota.

SWIFT
and the
twentieth
century

MILTON VOIGT
University of Utah

Detroit 1964
Wayne State University Press

for my three sons

forever intent on subverting their father's will

table of contents

preface

This book is a study of the major developments in the critical, biographical, and textual study of Jonathan Swift in this century. Chapter I outlines the prevailing nineteenth-century images of Swift and his works, images which comprise the background of received opinion against which the distinctive twentieth-century emphases emerge. While the treatment of these twentieth-century emphases is intended to be exhaustive, the treatment of Swift studies generally is not. Studies of the minor prose and the poetry have been almost wholly excluded in favor of concentration on studies of the two major satires and of Swift the man. If this choice has resulted in some regrettable omissions (Oliver Ferguson's studies of the Irish tracts and Herbert Davis' essays on the poetry, to cite two examples), it has the advantage of focusing attention on twentieth-century responses to Swift at his most pure and complex. By illuminating these responses, this study aims at giving the beginning student of Swift an indication of the scope of, and a guide to, the world of Swift scholarship, and giving the accomplished Swift scholar a fresh look at the victories and vagaries of his colleagues, past and present.

Swift scholarship is nothing if not voluminous, and Swiftians will understand my deep gratitude to Louis A. Landa and James E. Tobin for their indispensable bibliography, *Jonathan Swift: A List of Critical Studies Published from 1895 to 1945* (New York, 1945). Professor Landa has also kindly made available to me the wealth of bibliographical information which he has gathered since 1945 and which is to be incorporated in a revision and expansion of Landa-Tobin now in preparation. Many of the studies cited in the following pages have been reprinted in the several source books of Swift criticism which have recently appeared. As citation of these reprintings would have made the footnotes yet more unwieldy than they now are, I have appended to the Notes section a guide to these helpful anthologies, with a brief indication of their contents.

I am happy to acknowledge the help I have received from friends, colleagues, and mentors. Professors George T. Wright, Kenneth E. Eble, Arthur L. Cooke, Donald Heiney, Jack Garlington, Robert E. Helbling, and the late James T. Hillhouse gave valuable advice; the University of Utah, and especially Dean Jack Adamson and Professor Harold F. Folland, gave assistance of various kinds in the preparation of the final manuscript. For encouragement and advice I am particularly indebted to Professor Robert L. Peters. Most of all I am grateful to Professor Samuel Holt Monk, who first suggested this study as a dissertation and patiently watched over its development.

Finally, I wish to thank Dr. Harold Basilius of the Wayne State University Press and Mrs. Faith Schmidt, Press editor. I was fortunate to enjoy the typing services of Mrs. V. C. Midkiff and Mrs. Carol Baer. My wife has also helped, and I am grateful.

M. V.

I

nineteenth-century
views

A remark made by Edward Dowden in a review of Leslie Stephen's *Swift*[1] reflects the oftentimes painful contortions of nineteenth-century criticism when faced with Jonathan Swift. An ideal critic of Swift, says Dowden, will be "both attracted and repelled," but must also "be able to hold his own with masculine force, while aware of repulsion within a zone of attraction and attraction within a zone of repulsion." In a discussion of nineteenth-century Swift criticism the image of human particles caught in a magnetic field is not inappropriate. A nicety of this critical strategy is illustrated in Dowden's own remarks on Swift. As critics often do, when suspended between attraction and repulsion, Dowden takes refuge in paradox: "Swift's vices were inverted virtues; his finest qualities had in them something of the satanic. His foulness was cleanliness grown rabid." Moreover, "he was a patriot who hated his country" and "a philanthropist who scorned his species." Dowden is in fact partial to paradox, and it is not surprising that in the same review he expresses a nostalgia for the romanticized and richly legendary Swift of Sir Walter Scott. Dowden regrets to find in Stephen and other late nineteenth-century biographers of Swift a "hurry to disengage the prosaic figure from the mist which magnifies it."

The "magnified" Swift of Scott was, as Pons[2] and Berwick[3] have pointed out, the result of Scott's undue receptivity to all forms of the Swift legend. Scott's *Memoirs*

3

of Jonathan Swift, D.D. (1814), because of its sheer wealth of material, is rather diffuse and contradictory, and, as a result, later Swift studies, dependent as they were upon Scott as a source, often advanced a Swift who was a living paradox. Certain critics, yielding wholly to attraction or repulsion, and consequently choosing to ignore whatever in Scott proved intractable to their view, were able—at the cost of their critical balance—to present a Swift relatively free of paradox. In Jeffrey,[4] Thackeray,[5] Taine,[6] and Lowell[7] the force of repulsion was evidently overwhelming. Fixing upon a bitterly satirical, morose, and despairing Swift, they ignored the Swift of *"vive la bagatelle,"* the genial friend and companion. Yet even in these critics, whose approach one is inclined to call "simple-minded," some elements of paradox are present, especially when their subject, whatever shifts they may have made to avoid it, proves too large for their prejudices.

Though it is true that the image of Swift as paradox in nineteenth-century criticism can be traced to the diffuse and often irreconcilable material of Scott's *Memoirs,* there is another and more significant cause for the predominance of this image: the general inability to cope with Swift. A profound uncongeniality of philosophy and temperament separated the nineteenth-century critic from Swift and his works. Only a few isolated biographers (John Forster and Henry Craik, for instance) had a concern for fact and evidence rigorous enough to enable them to transcend the limitations which this uncongeniality imposed. For the most part, critics simply threw up their hands before the enigma of Swift, disguising their failure in a catalog of paradox.

SWIFT AND THE "HUMAN FORM DIVINE"

Among the several signs of radical uncongeniality,[8] though by no means the most important, is the anxious concern shown by critics over the scatology, or as one writer termed it, "the plain-speakingness" of Swift's works. Now the ordure, filth, and other perhaps unpleasant details of Swift's writings are surely not among their

4

most important elements, yet when reading nineteenth-century criticism of Swift one is inclined to think they are composed of little else. Coleridge, early in the century, censured Swift's works "for the vast quantity of physical dirt with which they abound." [9] Concern over this aspect of Swift deepened as the century continued, becoming in the time of Victoria an intense and virtually universal aversion. One of Macaulay's famous "places" on Swift declares Swift's mind to be "richly stored with images from the dunghill and the lazar-house," [10] and Thackeray's famous advice to leave Part IV of *Gulliver* unread, offered for the first time in the 1851 lectures, was in part prompted by antipathy for the scatology and general coarseness (p. 36). Taine's reaction is particularly violent. "Swift's cruel, positive mind," says Taine, was nourished "on filth and folly" and "clings only to vileness; it will see only what is behind things; armed with sorrow and boldness, it spares no ignoble detail, no obscene word," and "compared with his, all foul words are decent and agreeable" (II, 165–66, 171). Even John Forster, the most sympathetic of Swift's nineteenth-century biographers, can offer no excuse for Swift's coarseness, finding it to be a serious blemish in *A Tale of a Tub*, a work which otherwise wins his praise.[11]

It was a simple step from exclaiming over the presence of "filth" to ascribing to it an evil influence and to Swift a malicious intent. James Russell Lowell is left "uncomfortable" by Swift's humor, which "too often impregnates the memory with a savor of mortal corruption proof against all disinfectants" (p. 188). In 1880 in his *History of the Reign of Queen Anne* John Hill Burton, the Benthamite historian and biographer of Hume, called the poems "a stinging insult" to every gentleman with "wife, daughter, or sister to cherish and protect." [12] The "horrible foulness" of the voyage to the Houyhnhnms, writes Edmund Gosse in his *History of Eighteenth Century Literature* (1889), "banishes from decent households a fourth part of one of the most brilliant and delightful of English books." [13] A characteristic exclamation is Augustine Birrell's in *Essays about Men, Women, and Books,* published in 1894. "No fouler pen than Swift's has

soiled our literature," and as a result it is a question for
Birrell "whether it is becoming to sit in the same room with
the works of this divine." He goes on to wonder in amaze-
ment "how the good Sir Walter ever managed to see him
through the press." [14] W. E. H. Lecky, in his "Biographical
Introduction" to the Temple Scott edition of the prose, found
the "coarse, revolting, and indecent imagery . . . peculiarly
unbecoming in a clergyman," and explained that Swift's "un-
rivalled power of ludicrous combination seldom failed to get
the better of his prudence." [15]

Some critics tried to explain the presence of scatological
material in Swift, and, more rarely, to excuse it. Some, such
as Lecky, blamed Swift's inability to resist a joke, however
coarse it might be. Thus Gosse explains that from Swift's
"lambent spirit of pleasantry" and "imperturbable humour
. . . nothing human or divine was safe" (p. 166). J. Churton
Collins, who compares the late poems to "the depraved and
diseased mind of Lear" when it "runs riot in obscenity and
rage," attributes the scatology "partly to misanthropy . . .
and partly to a desire to furnish dissuasives from vice." With
regard to the latter aim Collins points out that Swift was
doing "nothing more than the Saints and the Fathers of
the Church have habitually done, and with the same object,"
and notes passages in St. Chrysostom and St. Gregory "as
nauseous and disgusting as anything that can be found in
Swift." In summarizing, however, Collins de-emphasizes the
moral intent, restricting the causes of the scatological tendency to three: "Something is no doubt to be attributed to
the age in which he lived, something to his constitution, and
more to his rage against his kind. What is certain is that, as
his misanthropy intensified, his imagination grew fouler and
his filth became more noisome." [16]

This is as benevolent as the nineteenth century can be
on the subject. A more common view was that the coarseness
was a sign of actual or "incipient" [17] madness. When Collins
denied on medical authority that Swift was ever insane, one
reviewer regretted the assertion, pointing out that it "denied
to Swift's eulogists the excuse they have often urged for his

6

scurrility and filth." [18] Lowell, hardly a eulogist, explained that Swift's "diseased eye" had the microscopic quality of Gulliver's in Brobdingnag, thus partly accounting for the "loathsome obscenity" which "tainted his imagination" (p. 188), and in the same year, 1876, a writer in the *British Quarterly Review*, decrying the "utterly loathsome coarseness that stains his works," suggested that Swift's coarseness was "not that of his own or any other age," but was "the coarseness of the man himself; the suggestion of his incipient madness, or its cause, and of that alone." [19]

If nineteenth-century readers were offended by the scatology in Swift, they were outraged by what they chose to regard as his travesty of "the human form divine," or as Bulwer-Lytton called it in a line of his "The Souls of Books": "God's and man's libel in that foul Yahoo!" [20] There is hardly a stronger epithet in the Victorian vocabulary than "unmanly," yet Thackeray used it, along with "horrible," "shameful," and "blasphemous," in describing the voyage to the Houyhnhnms. After advising against reading it, he calls it "Yahoo language; a monster gibbering shrieks, and gnashing imprecations against mankind—tearing down all shreds of modesty, past all sense of manliness and shame; filthy in word, filthy in thought, furious, raging, obscene." Taking the Yahoo to be Swift's final comment on mankind, Thackeray interprets it to mean that "man is utterly wicked, desperate, and imbecile," and "is and deserves to be the slave of brutes" (pp. 35–37).

One of the leading critics of the mid-century, George Gilfillan, in praising Thackeray on Swift, seizes the occasion to add some observations of his own. "As moral monsters," he says, "Swift and that Yankee-Yahoo, Edgar Poe, must be classed together. Neither of them could believe that a race which had produced *them* had any link relating it to the divine. They saw all things and beings in the vast black shadow cast by themselves." [21] This view of Swift as Manichean, Gilfillan takes up again in an essay, "Satire and Satirists," published in 1856, in which he says that Swift "believed man to be as a whole the work and child of the devil," a notion which is "the very madness of Manicheanism," since Swift's devil reigns supreme as "the only God," not, as in orthodox Manicheanism, as merely one of two aboriginal powers. Gilfillan, as did Thackeray, takes the Yahoo to be Swift's image of man, and thus "from a Yahoo man it was inevitable to infer a demon deity." He goes on to attack those who would prove Swift a Christian, and cites as damning evidence "his perpetual and unlimited abuse of man's body and soul, his denial of every human virtue," and, most important, his belief that man was not "a fallen angel" but "a bungled brute." In view of all this, Gilfillan thinks it would be ridiculous to praise Swift's powers as a satirist, and concludes that "he was not a satirist, but a minor Satan," a heartless "monster of misanthropy," who surprised man naked and asleep, looked at him with microscopic eyes, ignored all his peculiar marks of "fallen dignity" and "incipient godhood," and reported accordingly.[22]

A more temperate ascription of diabolism to Swift makes him a rather interesting anticipation of Thomas Mann. David Masson finds in Swift what "Goethe and Niebuhr . . . agreed to call the *demonic* element," which is "perhaps the sign and source of all real greatness." But Swift's was of a peculiar sort, not of the "*super*natural" but "a demonic of the *infra*-natural—fiends and shapes of horror tugging at [his] thoughts from beneath." While Milton and Shakespeare could hear "angelic music and the rustling of seraphic wings," it was Swift's unhappier lot to be related rather to "the darker and subterranean mysteries," and therefore it might be said of Swift "that he had far less of belief in God than a belief in the Devil." [23]

Gosse too had noted a "darker side" in Swift "exemplified to excess" in the voyage to the Houyhnhnms, which, written with "the horrible satisfaction of disease" and intensified by his chronic vertigo and the loss of Stella, is the "literary expression of his rage and despair." Gosse accounts for the character of this satire by positing a mad author, or, as he puts it, someone with "a brain not wholly under control" (p. 161), which, as we have seen, is a common nineteenth-century shift. William Allingham, writing in 1867 under the pseudonym Patricius Walker, Esq., offered Swift's Yahoo image of "the human form divine" as a "test and measure of his general truthfulness," [24] and even a sympathetic critic such as the American scholar Charles Mills Gayley thought Swift had fashioned men "more filthy than they are," and then, "with most virtuous intent," threw filth at them.[25]

The best summary of the period's reception of Part IV of *Gulliver* is found in a frequently reprinted essay, Rev. John Mitford's "Life of Swift," which first appeared in 1833 as the Introduction to the Aldine edition of the poems. The voyage to the Houyhnhnms, writes Mitford,

> is the one that has been received with the least approbation of the public, and, perhaps, exhibits the smallest talent and judgment in the author. Of all the creations of his fancy it is the most improbable; and it is filled with such a fierce indignation against the frailties and vices to which our nature is so prone; it betrays such a bitter misanthropy; it indulges in such a fiendish mockery of the degraded species, and holds up such hideous representations of the loathesome depravity of our sins, while it renders its satire more effective by drawing through it the richest vein of ridicule and the most pointed wit, that persons of delicate and refined taste have been hurt by its grossness, and those of more severe and religious feelings have marked it with that moral disapprobation which rejects a work so wide in its temper and feeling from the spirit of Christianity. It must certainly be allowed that the picture, in all its nauseating details and its frightful impurities, is overcharged; that the colors are not sufficiently subdued, and that the representation of beings so thoroughly brutalized and degraded, by exciting disgust and horror, destroys the effect which it was intended to produce.[26]

Amidst this chorus of anguish over Swift's "gross libel on human nature" [27] were a few dissenting voices. Hazlitt, in his *Lectures on the English Poets* (1818), declares that the view of human nature taken in *Gulliver's Travels*—not Gulliver's view, that is, but Swift's—is "such as a being of a higher sphere might take of it," this in the sense that Swift has exposed imposture, "has torn the scales from off his moral vision," leaving "nothing solid, nothing valuable," nothing but "virtue and wisdom." Mocking the Swiftophobes, Hazlitt exclaims, "What a libel is this upon mankind! What a convincing proof of misanthropy! What presumption and what malice prepense to shew men what they are, and to teach them what they ought to be!" Swift's intention is "to tear off the mask of imposture from the world; and nothing but imposture has a right to complain of it." Hazlitt goes on to attack directly the "quacks in morality" who "preach up the dignity of human nature" and "pamper pride and hypocrisy with the idle mockeries of the virtues they pretend to, and which they have not: but it was not Swift's way to cant morality, or anything else; nor did his genius prompt him to write unmeaning panegyrics on mankind!" [28]

But Hazlitt's purple passage, one fears, is merely Swiftophobia reversed, representing, more probably, a difference of taste and not a closer reading or more sensitive interpretation than that offered by Swift's detractors. The view of human nature from a "higher sphere" sounds disturbingly like the Houyhnhnm view of the Yahoo, which can hardly be equated with Swift's view of man or of the human condition. It is probable that Hazlitt, like so many other critics, took the Yahoo to be Swift's image of man, Swift's device, in Hazlitt's words, "to shew men what they are." Hazlitt is sound in his analysis of those elements of the satire which he chooses to discuss—Gulliver's making off with the Blefuscu fleet, the character of Glumdalclitch—but these are from the early voyages and are of an elementary sort. One wishes he had dealt more closely with Part IV, for instance with the Houyhnhnm threading the needle or with the Houyhnhnm widow's excuse for her lack of punctuality.

In the nineteenth century close and sensitive readings of works such as *Gulliver* were not in fashion; to find anything at all resembling a truly critical approach to the fourth voyage one must go to the correspondence pages of *Academy* for August 18, 1883. There a letter from one Thomas Tyler, a biblical scholar and editor of Shakespeare's sonnets, suggests that the brief and scanty criticisms devoted to *Gulliver's Travels* are inadequate and that such a work deserves "extended dissertations." Tyler cites Stephen's purely biographical rejection of the last two voyages— "wrung from him in later years, after a life tormented by constant disappointment and disease" [29]—as an example of the inadequate criticism from which Swift suffers. He goes on to disagree with Craik's view of the Houyhnhnms as "the negation of all human attributes" [30] while agreeing with Stephen that the land of the Houyhnhnms may be a "delineation of an ideal commonwealth" in which conduct and polity are "perfectly in accord with reason." But here Tyler differs with Stephen and other critics: he says that Swift advances this utopian picture with "no practical aim," that is, that Swift "was not writing for the universal improvement of mankind." The Houyhnhnms, in other words, are not to be taken as paragons worthy of emulation; indeed, Tyler points to the Houyhnhnm widow and to what is said of conjugal and parental love as instances of subtle absurdity usually neglected in criticism of the last voyage. Tyler concludes with a perceptive comparison of Houyhnhnm and Yahoo:

> As the life according to original and essential human nature, the life of the Yahoos, is exhibited as revolting, so the life according to perfect reason—that of the Houyhnhnms—is set forth as impracticable and even absurd. There is no hope for mankind neither on the one side nor the other. And thus the 'Voyage to the Country of the Houyhnhnms' becomes the fullest expression of the fundamental pessimism. We may dislike the foundation; but on it the whole building firmly rests. [31]

As a poet or as an example of "the poetic temperament" there was hardly a place for Swift in the nineteenth century. Anna Jameson, who, in 1829, could not resist the temptation to include Stella and Vanessa in her *Loves of the Poets,* begins her discussion with an awareness of her presumption. "It is difficult to consider Swift as a poet," she says. "So many unamiable, disagreeable, unpoetical ideas are connected with his name, that, great as he was in fame and in-

11

tellectual vigour, he seems as misplaced in the temple of the muses as one of his own yahoos." [32] Poetry, as understood for the most part in the nineteenth century, was a rite to be performed in a "temple of the muses," and then only with proper sanctity and dedication.

An American critic, Henry T. Tuckerman, discussing Swift's claim to poetry in the *Southern Literary Messenger* for 1849, pointed out that "the term 'poet' has now more than a technical meaning" and is "used to designate a certain species of character and tone of mind." In fact, it is "often applied to those who have not written verse and, perhaps, never written at all." Tuckerman cites some qualities "now regarded as essential to the office of poet," in particular, "a deep sense of the beautiful and intimate relations with the human and the divine, arising from earnestness of feeling and spirituality of perception." It hardly needs saying, as Tuckerman does, that "in these Swift was singularly deficient." Even Swift's prose is evidence for Tuckerman, who notes that "the flow of words never accidentally becomes rhythmical from the loftiness of the sentiment," and adds that "no poet could habitually write such prose," so "utterly destitute" of "glow" and "kindling expressions." He is as disappointed as Mrs. Jameson in the "love verses," in which "there is not a trace of genuinely amatory feeling," a deficiency which will be apparent if we compare them with Petrarch, Barry Cornwall, Mrs. Norton, "or any other sincere votary of the tender passion." It is no wonder then that "as a rhymester, the higher level of taste condemns him to neglect." [33]

Taine pursues much the same argument, identifying poetry, first of all, with that "involuntary music in which thought wraps itself" and which "hides ugliness and unveils beauty." "Here, as elsewhere," says Taine of Swift, "he is most unfortunate" (II, 160). Taine acknowledges a certain "truth and force" in such "prosaic subjects" as *Cadenus and Vanessa* and *Verses on the Death of Dr. Swift,* and even grants him "greatness of invention and audacity" (II, 163), but he cannot consider Swift a poet. "All poetry exalts the mind," he explains revealingly in commenting on *Verses on the Death of Dr. Swift,* "but this depresses it; instead of concealing reality, it unveils it; instead of creating illusions, it removes them." Swift was rather "an artisan, strong of arm, terrible at his work and in a fray, but narrow of soul." Taine cannot offer a line of his which "indicates a genuine sentiment of nature" because "he saw in the forest only logs of wood, and in the fields only sacks of corn." Poetry was "too fine to be grasped by those coarse hands," and in *A Description of the Morning,* poetry is "a queen travestied into a rough country girl" (II, 162–65). Swift was, Taine concludes, "excluded from poetry . . . by the clearsightedness and narrowness of his common sense" (II, 177).

Lowell thinks it "misleading to talk of the poetry of one whose fatal gift was an eye that disidealized" (p. 174) and "who had done more than all others together to strip life and human nature of their last instinctive decency of illusion" (p. 194). De Quincey notes "the meanness of Swift's nature and his rigid incapacity for dealing with the grandeurs of human spirit, with religion, with poetry," [34] while Churton Collins thought that Swift's mode of thinking could only "paralyse the wings of the soul" (p. 250). Saintsbury finds that poetry, "in its strict and rare sense, Swift seldom or never touches," though he grants that *The Last Judgment,* if authentic, may be a genuine example.[35]

Many critics recognized that an esthetic and ethical gulf separated them from Swift and from the age which had given the *Tale* and *Gulliver* such immediate and high acclaim. Some thought it to be a simple difference of taste or culture. Others, more ambitious but no less confident, saw the gulf as a sign of progress. The clearest statement of this latter view, a view often tacit but nonetheless pervasive in the period, is found in Jeffrey. His famous review in 1816 of Scott's edition of the works begins by noting "the considerable change which has taken place in the world of letters . . . by which the wits of Queen Anne's time have been gradually brought down from the supremacy which they had enjoyed, without competition, for the better part of a century." There can be, Jeffrey suggests, "but two possible solutions for phenomena of this sort": either "our taste has degenerated," or "its old models have been fairly surpassed." The former he quickly dismisses, apparently *pace* Jeffrey on Wordsworth *et al.*, because "national taste" is, "of all faculties, that which is most sure to advance and improve with time and experience," and "the general taste of every successive generation is better than that of its predecessors." There are, he grants, "little capricious fluctuations," but "the great movements are all progressive."

The Queen Anne wits, as a result, "have been eclipsed by those of our own time," and they have "no chance of ever regaining the supremacy." This is not to be wondered at, for the earlier writers had only "their judgment and industry to stand on" and were recommended more by "the fewness of their faults than the greatness of their beauties." Their poets "had no power or greatness of fancy—no pathos, and no enthusiasm." As philosophers, the wits had "no comprehensiveness, depth, or originality." Though they are "neat, clear, and reasonable," they are at the same time "cold, timid, and superficial" (I, 158–60).

Thackeray too had noted the gulf and, when glancing at Gay's ballads and his *Beggar's Opera* in the lecture on Steele, exclaimed, "Contrast these with the writings of our present humourists! Compare those morals and ours—those manners and ours!" In the same lecture, displaying again the same insensitivity to irony which enabled him to find in *A Modest Proposal* Swift's "want of feeling" and "rage against children," Thackeray offers the *Polite Conversation* as a reliable picture of eighteenth-century society. "Fancy the moral condition of that society," says Thackeray, "in which a lady of fashion joked with a footman, and carved a great shoulder of veal, and provided besides a sirloin, a goose, hare, rabbit, chickens, partridges, blackpuddings, and a ham for a dinner for eight Christians" (pp. 80, 106). Thackeray goes on in this vein, and one hopes that the perfect quiet which is said to have reigned over his lectures was broken here by a saving titter. In the lecture on Swift, which was first in the series, Thackeray, in a discussion of Swift's various criminal characteristics, charitably pointed to the age as one in which criminality was common, when "public society was in a strange disordered condition" and "morality was lax," when men as well as old beliefs and institutions "had lost their moorings and gone adrift in the storm" (p. 19). Though Swift was "a highwayman" and was in other respects culpable, some explanation can be discovered in the age itself, when highwaymen were common and people were indiscreet at dinner.

William Allingham, writing in 1867, asserts that "there is but poor nourishment for the soul in any part of Swift's writings," which are the products of an age whose literature was "in its whole result . . . rather poor and thin, however elegantly simple and clear in its turns of expression" (p. 652). In an essay on Pope dated 1871 Lowell indicts the age for what he considers to be its lack of principle, a time "when men could be Protestant or Catholic, both at once, or by turns, or neither, as suited their interest, when they could swear one allegiance and keep on safe terms with the other." Its morality "was the morality of appearance, of the side that is turned toward men and not toward God. The very shamelessness of Congreve is refreshing in that age of sham." This lack of principle in the age Lowell quickly detects in Swift, one "who aspired to the mitre," yet "could write a book [36] whose moral, if it had any, was that one religion was as good as another." "It was impossible," Lowell concludes, "that anything truly great, that is, great on the moral and emotional as well as the intellectual side, should be produced by such a generation." [37]

In 1880 John Hill Burton, following Jeffrey's theory of progress in the arts, declared that progress had made satire itself, not merely Swift's, a victim of technological unemployment. In a discussion of the offensiveness of Swift's works, the defects of which "are of a nature not to be palpably discussed in an age of decorum like the present" (III, 274), Burton goes on to account for the change of taste. "In the present day, what might be called the plain-speakingness of such literature would not be tolerated; and yet we have managed to cleanse ourselves of a vast load of impurities," which "plain speaking and scolding" had sought in vain to eradicate. The credit for this singular success belongs to "that sanitary science which is still in its strong youth," and which "with a purity and dignity" can "approach all things without contamination or the uneasy sense of disgusting." What has "long been so in the sphere of the anatomist and the physiologist" will soon be so elsewhere. "The sanitary engineer is replacing the scavenger and the nightman, and a single decisively expressed proposition in the report of some sanitary philosopher will do more in the cause of cleanliness and health than the immortal taunts of the greatest of our satirists" (III, 276). Consequently Burton "does not envy" Swift's "hangman's duty of administering the lash" in such lines as

> Corinna, pride of Drury Lane,
> For whom no shepherd sighs in vain,

though he grants Swift a "consummate adroitness" in the execution. He grants too, rather disarmingly, that "sanitary science" has not as yet enjoyed many triumphs on Drury Lane, whose interior "is said to be" not at all improved since the time of Swift, which seems to suggest "a dead level of brutality and viciousness" beyond the cure even of sanitary science (III, 280).

Churton Collins, whose "sympathetic" biography, published in 1893, was an amplification of two earlier articles, censures the eighteenth century for its enthusiastic reception of *Gulliver*. Its very applause of such a work confesses its moral character, for "at no period distinguished by generosity of sentiment, by humanity, by decency, by any of the nobler and finer qualities of mankind, could such a satire as the satire of which the greater part of *Gulliver* is the embodiment have been universally applauded." The apolog of *Gulliver* "would scarcely have passed without protest in the Rome of Petronius," yet the Queen and the Princess of Wales "were in raptures with it" (pp. 213–14). Swift's popularity during his lifetime was as much a puzzle to nineteenth-century critics as were Swift's works.

SWIFT AND RELIGION

If Swift was not allowed the delicate sensibility of the poet, it is not surprising that he was denied the religious sensibility as well. Ample evidence of this deficiency was found in *A Tale of a Tub*, especially as it was read primarily as a biographical rather than a literary document. Too often critics, underestimating the difficulty or the importance of the literary problem, brushed it aside in order to deal with what they thought more challenging or engaging, the *Tale* as a biographical document, especially the *Tale* as a key to Swift's religious beliefs. Craik stands virtually alone in the century in his willingness to treat the *Tale* first of all as a work of literary art. Whatever judgments of a biographical character he offers with respect to the *Tale* are firmly grounded in the careful and perceptive reading he gave to the work. Craik was more careful than any other critic to make the important distinction between Swift and the fictional Grubstreet author who "writes" the work, and his discussion also rightly emphasizes what other critics failed to see, that the satire on abuses in learning weighs far more heavily in the work than the satire on abuses in religion. As a result he rises above the common nineteenth-century argument over the religious or irreligious character of the work, and stresses rather the breadth of the satire, which "expresses the whole range of the author's mind," "reaches far beyond the accidents of ecclesiastical controversies," and "pursues human nature and routs it out from all its subterfuges and disguises" (pp. 102–6).

The argument over the religious or irreligious character of *A Tale of a Tub*—and, by inference, of Swift—continued a discussion begun upon the original appearance of the *Tale*. Critics took several stands, often dependent upon their own religious and philosophic convictions. The most common reaction to the *Tale* is one which Leslie Stephen called "the prudery of the tea table," the reaction of Archbishop Sharpe and Queen Anne, whose horror over the "irreverence" of the *Tale* is said to have kept Swift from being regarded as properly a Christian, and thus contributed to the charges of atheism, scepticism, and hypocrisy brought against him. This interpretation of the *Tale* derives primarily from a failure to distinguish Swift from the "modern writer" who is its pretended author. Swift is ridiculing modern scepticism, unenlightened science and pedantry, even irreverence itself, in the *person* of his Grubstreet author. By missing the thread of irony in this way—or, more properly, by discovering it only intermittently—readers mistakenly tend to identify Swift with the objects of his ridicule. The degree of detachment which the *Tale* demands of its readers is considerable, and it is not surprising to find it suffering from chronic misinterpretation. Thus Lowell's assertion, previously quoted, that the moral of the *Tale* was that "one religion was as good as another," is the result of associating rather than dissociating Swift and his fictional author, a habit which leads Lowell to quote a passage from the *Tale* and then gravely ask of it whether it "be of so penetrative an insight as it is apt to suppose;" the answer, of course, is no. Or again, in a curious mixture of misreading, lugubriousness, and desperate paradox, Lowell asks, "How should he be happy who had defined happiness to be 'the perpetual possession of being well deceived' and who could never be deceived himself?" (*Function of the Poet*, pp. 187–88). Lowell, typical of nineteenth-century critical practice, expected literature to be as straightforward as he was himself.

The fatal tendency to read Swift's mock author as Swift is flagrantly present in Edmund Gosse, who in his *History of Eighteenth Century Literature* is uncertain "whether Swift wrote or only proposed to write" the facetious treatises which the Grubstreet author lists on the flyleaf and threatens to publish. Gosse also takes as Swift's the author's confession that he found his "Common-Place-Book fill much slower" than he had reason to expect, explaining that this "probably" means "the sprightly flow of inspiration in 1696–97 dried up for the time being before he had done more than sketch his

General History of Ears and his *Critical Essay upon the Art of Canting*" (pp. 143–44). It would be absurd to speculate on Othello's activities at Aleppo, and monstrous to speak of Shakespeare's doings there, yet that is the equivalent of what Swift criticism of this sort attempted to do—and, it must be added, in fairness to the nineteenth century, occasionally still does. Later, in his *Short History of Modern English Literature* (1897), Gosse characterizes the *Tale* as "a long gibe at theology," and consequently "it is not surprising that no bishopric could be given to the inventor of the Brown Loaf and the Universal Pickle." Gosse thinks it little use for Swift to explain away his mockery by declaring it to have been employed in the Anglican cause, for "the damning evidence remained that when he had the sacred garments in his hands he had torn away, like an infuriated ape, as much of the gold fringe as he could." The common reversion to a purely biographical explanation takes an interesting form in Gosse, who asserts that Swift, "without any design of impiety, . . . knew not how to be devout" and "always, by instinct, saw the hollowness and the seamy side." [38]

An earlier reading of the *Tale* by De Quincey in 1847 prompted that critic to censure Swift's "*astonishment* at a religious princess refusing to confer a bishopric upon one that had treated the Trinity, and all the profoundest mysteries of Christianity, not with mere scepticism and casual sneer, but with set conscious merriment and farcical buffoonery." Reverting to biography, De Quincey proceeds confidently, pointing out that Swift was in "a state of constitutional irreligion," the result of "a vulgar temperament." To Swift, people differed "not by more and less religion," but by "more and less dissimulation" (XI, 14–15). Taine finds the *Tale* to be "the satire of all science and all truth, and asks, "What church and what creed are not involved in his attack?" (II, 166). Lecky, in the Temple Scott edition (1897), asserts that those who "have read and understood" the material on the aeolists, the brown loaf, and the mutton, "will not greatly wonder at the scruples of the queen" (I, xxvii). Masson summed up the matter charitably in 1854: "Despite all that

Swift could afterwards do, the fact that he had written this book left a public doubt as to his Christianity" (*Three Devils,* p. 250).

A slightly more moderate variation of the view that the *Tale* is irreligious comes from a rationalist's misreading. Leslie Stephen advances the same assertions of irreligion, but spares us some of the spleen against Swift. Stephen's *History of English Thought in the Eighteenth Century,* published in 1876, declared the *Tale* to be "the keenest satire against all theologians," and six years later in his biography for the English Men of Letters Series, Stephen granted at least prudence to the "tea-table" attitude of Archbishop Sharpe and Queen Anne, arguing in effect that to laugh at the *Tale* is to laugh with Voltaire, and to laugh with Voltaire is to be irreligious. Whatever might be his expressed intention, says Stephen, Swift was "sublimely unconscious" that his arguments could redound against his own beliefs and values (*Swift,* pp. 43–45). Stephen had recognized in his earlier work that Swift professed orthodoxy and was a sincere partisan of the Established Church, but he felt at the same time that it would "be an insult to that fiery intellect to suppose that his official defense of the Thirty-nine Articles represents a very vivid belief." [39] Stephen's analysis of Swift's religion is basically the popular nineteenth-century notion, that Swift was not in any sense sincerely religious, but practiced instead a form of what De Quincey called "dissimulation."

Non-religious, rather than irreligious, motives were ascribed to Swift to account for this dissimulation. Lowell's phrase for Swift's religion is "ceremoniously decorous" (*Function of the Poet,* p. 198)—as opposed to Forster's assertion that Swift was devout. Masson compared Swift to a liberated Brahmin who yet desired "to maintain Brahminism as a vast, pervading establishment in Hindostan." Thus Swift is accorded a purely political interest in "that fabric of bishoprics, deaneries, prebends, parochial livings, and curacies, which ancient belief had first created and put together" (p. 250). Along with Stephen, the biographers writing in the latter part of the century—with the exception of Forster—take essentially this position.[40] But while Stephen saw Swift's orthodoxy as a mere mask, "no more part of Swift than his bands and cassock," Thackeray saw a Swift "poisoned" by his cassock and "strangled in his bands." Stephen's Swift, less disturbed theologically than Thackeray's, sees through the "shallow optimism" of his time, but lacks "the speculative power to endeavor to remould the ancient creeds" (*Eighteenth Century Thought*, II, 373–74).

At the end of the nineteenth century two critics denied the alleged irreligion of the *Tale*. Saintsbury, in his *Short History of English Literature* (1898), said, "It may be peremptorily asserted that irreligion is neither intended nor involved in it." Saintsbury explains that polemics between sects habitually disregarded the religion which underlay their enemies' beliefs as well as their own, and the danger latent in such polemics "was not seen till long after Swift's death" (pp. 530–31). Thus the "irreligion" of the *Tale* is an historical anomaly, not properly present at the time of its first appearance, but presumably genuine for readers of later periods. In a similar argument, G. P. Moriarty in his *Dean Swift and His Writings* (1893) grants that Swift's intention was, as he declared it to be in his "Apology," to satirize abuses in religion and learning but argues that the work is weakened by Swift's "extraordinary indifference to human susceptibilities," a fault which "occasionally blunts the edge of Swift's satire" and is "nowhere so marked" as in the *Tale* (p. 45). Historical process and human weakness both explained and excused misreadings of Swift's work.

SWIFT THE MAN

If the nineteenth century's notions of propriety were outraged by Swift's scatology, if its benevolent, perfectibilitarian view of human nature was mortally insulted by *Gulliver's Travels*, if its peculiar demands on the poetic sensibility found Swift sorely wanting as a poet, if its solemn piety failed to grasp Swift's reticent and tactical religion, yet the nineteenth century did bequeath something of value to succeeding generations of Swift students. Its interest in mystery, especially in mysterious affairs of the heart, indeed, its interest in biography generally, made Swift a focus of almost constant biographical attention. The nineteenth century produced several important studies culminating in the monumental achievements of Forster and Craik.

Scott's *Memoirs of Jonathan Swift, D.D.* shows the strong fascination with the private life of Swift which was characteristic of the century. Swift the Dean of St. Patrick's, the public man, takes second place to Swift the private man of mystery. The latter was explained as much as possible in the light of the traumas which the public man suffered. Under this approach Swift emerges as a kind of highly vocal, even eloquent, Heathcliff. The poverty and dependence of his early years, the "indignities" suffered at Moor Park under Sir William Temple, the disappointments of his political career, produce the morose, vindictive satirist dying an exile in Ireland "like a poisoned rat in a hole." This is the figure we meet in Jeffrey, Macaulay, Thackeray, Taine, and in the large body of periodical criticism of the period. Sometimes the more speculative critics give the image a larger psychological dimension, which by turns made him the victim from his unhappy youth of an unnamed but ominous "means of assuaging desire," [41] one who suffered from "the excesses of a secret habit," [42] who, because of a "cold temper," [43] "was not susceptible . . . of any passion stronger than friendship" [44] and, indeed, "had ceased to be a man." [45] The great achievement of rigorous and thorough Swift biography in the nineteenth century lies in the disciplining of such flights of fancy and in the recovery of a Swift bearing some relation to available evidence.

A partial corrective to Scott was a study done in 1820 by W. Monck Mason, *The History and Antiquities of the Cathedral Church of St. Patrick*, a sizable section of which is devoted to Swift.[46] Mason turns a sceptical eye on the mass of Swift legend and tries to prune away the spurious. His grounds for rejection, as Craik later showed (*Life*, pp. 523–30), are not always defensible, but there is no doubt that the Swift criticism of the period stood greatly in need of Mason's sort of scepticism. Mason denied the charge of political apostasy made by Swift's detractors, pointing out that Swift was consistently a High-Church Tory who for a while embraced Whig principles in government, one for whom the mere party labels were not of primary consideration. Mason's most significant departure from prevailing opinion, however, is his refusal to accept the alleged marriage to Stella, which he rejects as based primarily on hearsay evidence of an unreliable sort. Scott took up Mason's arguments on this matter in footnotes to his second edition (I, 234–38), but maintained his original opinion that a token ceremony had taken place.

In May and August of 1847 in the *Dublin Quarterly Journal of Medical Science* there appeared an article by Dr. W. R. Wilde, the father of Oscar Wilde, in which the question of Swift's "insanity" was taken up and reviewed in the light of the soundest medical opinion of the time. This study, for the most part the product of very careful scholarship, was revised and expanded in 1849 and published under the title *The Closing Years of Dean Swift's Life.* Though there are some curious lapses from its generally careful examination and presentation of evidence,[47] Wilde must be credited with correcting some of the irresponsible allegations of Swift criticism and with helping to expose a pseudo-scientific approach to Swift—the then popular phrenology.[48] With regard to the sometimes alleged insanity of Swift, Wilde finds that "up to the year 1742 Swift shewed no symptom whatever of mental disease, beyond the ordinary decay of nature," and that "toward the end of that year the cerebral disease under which he had so long laboured, by producing effusion, &c., destroyed his memory, and rendered him at times ungovernable in his anger, as well as produced paralysis. . . . But that Swift was either mad in middle life, or mad or imbecile in later years, as tried and tested by the meaning and definition of these terms, . . . has not been proved" (pp. 71–74).

John Forster lived to write only the first volume of what would surely have been, even now, the most detailed and exhaustive biography of Swift. Indeed, the attention to detail shown in the existing volume (*The Life of Jonathan Swift*, 1875) is generally regarded as excessive, since only a partial, fragmented picture of its subject is able to emerge. Rigorous and thorough Forster was, however, and of the several misconceptions of Swift listed in the Preface—"that he was an apostate in politics, infidel or indifferent in religion, a defamer of humanity, the slanderer of statesmen who had served him, and destroyer of the women who had loved him" (I, v)—Forster was able to deal in some measure with all but the last, which, because Volume I covered only the years until 1711, was a matter reserved for later consideration. Forster's most important correction of the nineteenth-century image of Swift was his careful refutation of the charge of political apostasy advanced in its most influential forms by Jeffrey and Macaulay. Forster's argument is essentially that of the neglected Monck Mason, that Swift's political position was from the first informed by High-Church principles, and on this score he never misrepresented himself to the Whigs. Dealing as he does with the early years, Forster is also able to correct some of the misconceptions, largely the work of Courtenay and Macaulay, regarding Swift's life at Moor Park. "Universal as is now the practice of associating Temple's house with Swift's greatest misery, this is decidedly not the impression to be derived from himself. There is nothing that is not on the whole kindly and grateful in his memories of it" (I, 89).

Forster's preparation for his great work involved his bringing to light a great deal of manuscript material, much of it previously unpublished or, if published, misprinted. Forster restored the text of the hitherto misprinted later portions of the *Journal to Stella* and printed the restored passages in an appendix. He had the use of over 150 previously unpublished letters, and he is further to be credited with having discovered Swift's *Holyhead Journal,* later printed by Collins in *The Gentleman's Magazine* (June 1882) and reprinted by Craik in an appendix to his *Life of Jonathan Swift.*

After the death of Forster the manuscript materials which he had amassed were deposited as the Forster Collection in the Victoria and Albert Museum in South Kensington. Craik had the use of this material in the preparation of his *Life,* which, first published in 1882, remains to this day the standard biography. No less thorough than Forster in essential matters, Craik brought to his work a fine critical intelligence which revealed itself in his analyses of Swift's literary talent as well as in the mustering of biographical fact. Under his hand the horrendous image of Swift which still stalked the century was given its most decisive blows, yet Craik avoids eulogy and does not blink the less creditable elements of his subject's character when they are revealed in well-authenticated incidents and actions. Craik tends to over-use—and misapply—the phrase "bitter cynicism" with regard to Swift, but it must be added that the Swift who emerges from his biography is clearly less cynical than world-weary, tinged with a melancholy which Craik at one point suggests is similar to that of Lucretius. That Swift is not in fact conceived of as a cynic is evident throughout, for Craik carefully documents Swift's exertions in behalf of the various causes which engaged his attention until his faculties failed him.

In the same year, somewhat in advance of Craik, appeared the English Men of Letters Series *Swift,* by Leslie Stephen. Although it presents no new material, this study is a valuable introductory work. Unfortunately, Stephen's approach, like Craik's, inclines to the lugubrious, with the result that a somewhat too solemn and melancholy figure emerges. No biographer has as yet successfully drawn out from the shadows the more genial, fun-loving side of Swift. Stephen, a modest but straight-laced rationalist, was unable to achieve any genuine sympathy with his subject. He finds, for instance, *A Modest Proposal* to be "fearful to read even now" (p. 165), and confesses that the joke of the *Bickerstaff Papers* does not strike him "as of very exquisite flavour" (p. 59). However, Stephen's handling of evidence enjoys the careful austerity of his point of view, prompting him to leave open the question of the marriage to Stella with the confession that "even biographers are not omniscient" (p. 144).

The old ghost of Swift the political apostate is surely laid when Stephen asserts of Swift that "few men have ever adhered more strictly to the principles with which they have started" (p. 74).

In the last decade of the century three more works on Swift appeared. The most important of them was Churton Collins' *Jonathan Swift: A Biographical and Critical Study* (1893), a lively, very readable, but strangely inconsistent study. It was written ostensibly to correct "the injustice of the popular estimate of Swift," which held "that he was a gloomy and ferocious misanthrope, with a heart of stone and a tongue of poison; that, if not exactly a libertine, he revelled in impurity and filth; that he was an apostate in politics, a sceptic in religion, and a tyrant in private life; that he wrought the ruin of two women who passionately loved him, and that he paid the penalty for his inhumanity and selfishness by an old age of unutterable misery" (p. 11). Collins' was a worthy aim, but one for which his profound lack of sympathy with Swift made him singularly unsuited. Collins' medicine is often worse than the disease. In trying to suggest Swift's special superiority and self-confidence, Collins makes him offensively imperious. The popular estimate, according to Collins, had made Swift "a sceptic in religion"; Collins makes him "professionally orthodox." The popular estimate made Swift "a tyrant in private life"; Collins makes him a bully. By contrast, his judgments on the late poems make many Swiftophobes appear flatterers. On the other hand, Collins justly emphasizes Swift's generosity to friends and even opponents, while he rightly damns the early pindarics, to which Craik had shown undeserved kindness, later praising them in his volume of selections.

The "mystery" in James Hay's *Swift: The Mystery of His Life and Love* (1891) is one advanced before and since, namely, that Stella was the natural daughter of Sir William Temple, a mystery which helps to save Swift in Hay's eyes from charges of "sexual anesthesia." G. P. Moriarty's volume, *Dean Swift and His Writings* (1893), professes to be a reaction against "certain modern writers" who, in seeking to correct "the sombre and somewhat inaccurate" picture in Thackeray and Taine, "have all but tried to raise the Dean of St. Patrick's to the rank of a saint and a hero" (pp. iii–iv). The unidentified "modern writers" are presumably Stephen, Craik, and Forster. Only the work of the latter, however, approaches in any sense what Moriarty chooses to call "whitewashing." Moriarty's rather thin and halting study can hardly be regarded as the strong or significant reaction the author intended. Whatever picture of the Dean it intended to advance is lost in the mass of expurgated but undigested passages from the works and correspondence. But Moriarty's attempt to bolster the old image of Swift is a sign that that image is now beginning to totter, and thinking of that is like thinking of an empire falling.

II
textual criticism

The air of mystification which accompanied the publication of almost all of Swift's works, joined with a certain indifference which Swift sometimes showed toward his literary ventures, has presented vexing problems to Swift's recent editors—who, it must be said at the outset, have been the first of his many editors to realize and face up to the immense difficulties involved in determining the canon and arriving at reliable texts. When manuscripts pretending to be by "Lemuel Gulliver," "M. B. Drapier," "Simon Wagstaff," or anonymous Grubstreet hacks are delivered to printers by unknown messengers or by persons claiming to be "Richard Sympson," "T. N. Philomath," or even by known friends of Swift such as Mrs. Barber, it is already a problem, occasionally a simple one but not always, how such works are to find their way into the canon of Jonathan Swift. When the mysteriously delivered manuscripts—and others less mysteriously delivered—appear in print with numerous gross errors of the press, edited and mangled by publishers understandably fearful of their ears, and when these texts in turn appear in further editions with accretions, deletions, and alterations (many clearly spurious, but others having a sort of manuscript authority, though not, of course, the authority of the original manuscripts, most of which, it seems, have been systematically destroyed), then another and far more vexing problem is created: that of determining an authoritative text. That we can now read with any sort of assurance the works of Jonathan Swift is a miracle of textual scholarship for which Swift's editors and textual critics as well as analytical bibliographers deserve our sincere gratitude.

EDITIONS

Virtually no textual criticism of Swift's work was done before the twentieth century, and the passage of time made the task that much harder. The Temple Scott edition of *The Prose Works of Jonathan Swift, D.D.*, whose twelve volumes appeared during the years 1897–1908 (republished 1900–1914), was the first important edition of Swift since that of Sir Walter Scott, whose 1814 edition in nineteen volumes, including prose, verse, and correspondence, was reprinted with additional material in 1824 and again in 1883. In textual fidelity and authenticity the Temple Scott edition was a considerable improvement over its all too generous and uncritical predecessor, but work in the field of analytical bibliography soon rendered much of it out of date. William Ernst Browning, in his two-volume edition of the *Poems* (1910), largely perpetuated the canon and texts as presented by Sir Walter Scott and preserved in the Aldine *Poetical Works* (1833) and its reprints. Browning's was the first collected edition to print from Forster's several manuscript discoveries. Another decade passed before truly rigorous textual study began.

The results of thorough study of all the early editions and manuscript sources first appeared in the handsome editions published by the Clarendon Press. These include A. C. Guthkelch and D. Nichol Smith's *A Tale of a Tub* (Oxford, 1920; 2nd edition, 1958), Herbert Davis' *The Drapier's Letters* (Oxford, 1935), Sir Harold Williams' three-volume edition of the *Poems* (Oxford, 1937; 2nd edition, 1958) and his two-volume edition of the *Journal to Stella* (Oxford, 1948). A new collected edition of the prose, a project interrupted by the war but now nearing completion, is the Shakespeare Head edition of *The Prose Writings of Jonathan Swift* (Oxford), edited by Herbert Davis (and cited hereafter as "HD," followed by volume and page numbers). Volume I, containing *A Tale of a Tub* and other early works, was published in 1939, and all but one of the projected fourteen volumes have since appeared. The Clarendon Press volumes had each offered extensive notes giving detailed and very valuable material of an historical, biographical, or textual nature. Davis, choosing to avoid a needless repetition of these notes, confines background material to introductions, an arrangement which he explains was "adopted out of consideration for those who may prefer to read what Swift wrote, undisturbed by comment, reference, or textual trivialities" (HD, I, vi). Following Williams' example in the *Poems,* Davis admits only well authenticated works, printing doubtful pieces in appendices and excluding without comment the many items which have been proved spurious or have never been distinguished with evidence in their favor. Davis, like Williams, shows particular care in dating each item, printing the works as far as possible in chronological order.

The volume of *Unpublished Letters of Dean Swift,* edited by G. Birkbeck Hill and published in 1899, was a valuable supplement to the correspondence in Sir Walter Scott's edition. Both Scott and Hill were superseded with the appearance between 1910 and 1914 of the six-volume edition of *The Correspondence of Jonathan Swift* by F. Elrington Ball. This edition remains standard, but must now be supplemented with A. Martin Freeman's *Vanessa and Her Correspondence with Swift* (London, 1921), which contains letters and verse which came to light during World War I, and D. Nichol Smith's *Letters of Swift to Ford* (Oxford, 1935). The latter volume, which gives all the extant Swift-Ford correspondence, including fifty hitherto unpublished letters and several poems found in the Ford papers, is an unusually revealing record of Swift's literary, political, and personal life. A new and doubtless definitive five-volume edition of the letters, edited by Sir Harold Williams, is soon to be issued by the Clarendon Press.

TEXTS

Of the many textual and editorial problems faced by Swift's editors, and faced too in a host of studies in books and learned journals, only a few of the more significant can be taken up here, but these few will in some measure suggest the intense and fruitful activity in the recent textual study of Swift.

The first to ascertain and locate a number of Swift's rare editions was Stanley Lane-Poole, whose modest pioneer study in the analytical bibliography of Swift, *Notes for a Bibliography of Swift*, appeared in the *Bibliographer* in 1884 and was reprinted in a limited edition of twenty-five copies.[1] A more thorough and still very helpful list is W. Spencer Jackson's "Bibliography of Swift's Works," which appeared in Volume XII of the Temple Scott edition in 1908.[2] H. Teerink's *A Bibliography of the Writings in Prose and Verse of Jonathan Swift, D.D.* (The Hague, 1937) attempted to list all the printed works of the Swift canon, including European translations and works attributed to Swift, and gave special attention to analysis of the miscellanies and collected editions. However, because of his methods of description and reference, in which he departs from standard practice, and because of the numerous omissions and oversights and the inclusion of doubtful and supposititious works as genuine, Teerink's volume is inadequate and misleading. Of considerable value bibliographically are the two descriptive catalogs of printed books and manuscripts exhibited in 1945 on the two hundredth anniversary of Swift's death. One, compiled by John Hayward with the assistance of Harold Williams and Lord Rothschild, describes the extensive exhibit in the Old Schools of the University of Cambridge, the other, by Autrey Nell Wiley, describes the exhibit of items from the Aitken, Wrenn, and Stark collections at the University of Texas.[3] Important bibliographical studies dealing specifically with *Gulliver's Travels* are those of Lucius L. Hubbard, *Contributions Towards a Bibliography of Gulliver's Travels* (1922),[4] and Harold Williams, in his 1926 edition of Gulliver.[5] Both of these will be discussed more fully later.

Swift's early masterpiece, *A Tale of a Tub,* appeared anonymously in 1704 along with *The Battle of the Books* and *The Mechanical Operation of the Spirit.* Though never publicly acknowledged by Swift, and questioned—though only in conversation—by Dr. Johnson, the work is undoubtedly genuine and has been, in fact, one of Swift's less troublesome works from the editorial point of view.[6] Nineteenth-century editors, including Temple Scott, were inclined to credit Hawkesworth's claim in 1755 that his edition of that year had independent textual authority based on a "corrected copy." A. C. Guthkelch and D. Nichol Smith, however, in their 1920 edition of the *Tale,* demonstrated conclusively that the changes in Hawkesworth's edition were of no importance (pp. lxx–lxxi). Their text is based directly on the fifth edition of 1710, the first to include the "Apology" and the set of supplementary footnotes, and is corrected with the editions of 1704 and 1705. Davis, in the Shakespeare Head *Tale of a Tub,* follows Guthkelch and Nichol Smith in choosing to print from the fifth edition and in using the earlier editions [7] to correct his text.[8]

A far more difficult problem is presented by the text of *Gulliver's Travels,* which appeared already mangled and corrupt in its first edition. The first edition and the three octavo editions which quickly followed were not properly distinguished from each other until the important work of Hubbard and Williams appeared in the 1920's. At the close of the nineteenth century, when G. Ravenscroft Dennis was preparing a *Gulliver* for the Temple Scott *Prose Works,*[9] he had to labor under the limited bibliographical knowledge of his time regarding the early editions. Yet his critical spirit in facing his task was markedly different from the critical indolence of previous editors, who were content for the most part to follow the "established" texts of Hawkesworth or Scott.[10] When not complacent, editors tended to be cavalier about textual fidelity. W. Cooke Taylor, for instance, in a luxurious and in some respects scholarly edition of *Gulliver*,[11] felt no compunction about changing the first sentence of almost every chapter so as to accommodate the elaborate pictorial initial letters which had been prepared for a French edition. Needless to say, Taylor supplied no critical apparatus to indicate "variant" readings. There were also, of course, many silently expurgated editions of *Gulliver* in the nineteenth century. Taylor's edition, it must be added, is not among these.

Dennis based his text on Charles Ford's interleaved large paper copy of the first edition with Swift's corrections supplied in Ford's hand. It is now agreed that this approach to the text of *Gulliver* is the most reliable means of approximating the text of the original manuscript, which was of course precisely what Dennis was attempting to do. Ford's large paper copy was, as Hubbard and Williams later showed, a true first edition—in fact, a late issue of that edition in which a few errors had been corrected in the press, and thus offered the least corrupt text as far as printer's errors were concerned. Ford's corrections were meant to restore the text to manuscript fidelity,[12] first by making over one hundred verbal and typographical changes, second by supplying correct readings for several passages which Motte, the publisher, had edited or materially revised out of fear of offense, particularly offense to Walpole and the Hanoverian dynasty. None of the more extensive corrections were embodied in any of the Motte editions; most of them are first found in the 1735 Dublin edition published by George Faulkner as part of a four-volume edition of *The Works of J.S., D.D., D.S.P.D.* The rescuing of this Faulkner edition from the disrepute into which it had fallen as the result of charges of piracy and untrustworthiness is the most important single development in the twentieth-century textual study of Swift's works.

The rehabilitation of Faulkner's edition is largely due to the researches of Lucius L. Hubbard and Harold Williams, who were the first to suspect that the Faulkner edition of *Gulliver's Travels* (and to this Williams later added the other volumes of the *Works* published in 1735) was not a piracy.

There were several indications that the Faulkner edition was an authorized, or at least "semi-authorized," edition which had, in fact, enjoyed some measure of supervision by Swift himself, in many instances extending to authorized revision. One indication was the appearance, original with Faulkner, of almost all of the major corrections of Ford's interleaved *Gulliver*. A second was the publication, also original with Faulkner, of Gulliver's letter to his cousin Sympson. But the third and more telling indication—one which, it must be added, did not go unchallenged—was the presence in the 1735 *Gulliver* of numerous original alterations, which, as Williams argued, "are frequently of a character unlikely to have been made by the printer or by Swift's friends," and "strongly suggest authoritative revision" (Introduction, *Gulliver*, ed. Williams, pp. xlvii, xlix n.). On the basis of this evidence, Williams claimed that the 1735 text was the latest coming from the hand of Swift, and thus the best on which to base an authoritative text.

Although the introduction to Williams' 1926 edition of *Gulliver*, prepared for the First Edition Club, sets forth in detail all the arguments for the authority of Faulkner's edition, the Williams edition is not based on a 1735 text but on Motte's text of the first edition, occasioned by the two hundredth anniversary of its appearance. The first twentieth-century text of *Gulliver* to be based on the 1735 edition was published in the Nonesuch *Swift*, edited by John Hayward, in 1934. The new developments in Swift bibliography gave weight to Hayward's claim, set forth in his Introduction, that *Gulliver* was there rendered in "a more exact and reliable text than any that has been published in the last two hundred years." [13] Faulkner partisans readily admit that the 1735 text omits some of Ford's corrections and contains many printer's errors. Consequently Hayward, Williams, and later Davis, who used the 1735 text for his Shakespeare Head *Gulliver*, use Ford's copy and collate with the Motte editions in order to correct their text.

A reaction to the Faulkner ascendancy began in 1938 with the publication of A. E. Case's edition of *Gulliver's*

Travels, whose text was based on Motte's first edition, corrected with the Ford copy. Case presented in detail his arguments for adopting this procedure in *Four Essays on "Gulliver's Travels,"* published in 1945. The first of the four essays argued his preference for a recension approximating the text of the manuscript delivered to Motte in London in 1726, a manuscript described by Case as the culmination "of a six-year period of inspired creation and detailed revision." After comparing the variants between Motte and Faulkner, and disagreeing with Hubbard and Williams about their character and significance, Case concludes that though some of Faulkner's variants may have come from Swift's pen, "it is impossible to identify them," and thus the 1735 text is to be regarded as "a composite and relatively untrustworthy piece of editing," given, at best, only "perfunctory" attention by Swift.[14]

Most critics addressing themselves to the problem sided with Hubbard and Williams. They felt that statements made in the Swift-Ford correspondence, the greater part of which had appeared in the Nichol Smith edition of 1935, placed Swift's positive role in the 1735 edition beyond any doubt. Reviews of Case in 1945 and 1946 showed a preponderance of critics, including Davis, Quintana, Sherburn, and of course Williams, inclined to favor Faulkner. One exception was R. F. Jones.[15] Quintana, accounting for the now dominant attitude favoring the 1735 text, pointed out that since Case calls for a text "depending in part on editorial reconstruction, . . . the Faulkner text will still be preferred by Swift editors intent on avoiding such reconstruction." [16]

Despite critical preference for Faulkner, texts of *Gulliver* in popular editions continue to appear based on Motte, with the letter to Sympson added from the 1735 edition. Carl Van Doren, for instance, in the Viking Portable *Swift* (1948), prints a *Gulliver* which "restores the lost original so far as possible on the basis of the corrections furnished by Swift to Charles Ford." Van Doren adds that "since the Faulkner text includes a good many demonstrable errors due, it seems, to careless editing and printing, and omits one considerable passage in Part III apparently out of fear of further prosecution, the Motte-Ford text is here preferred." [17]

Williams' Sandars Lectures in Bibliography, delivered in 1950, were published as *The Text of "Gulliver's Travels"* in 1952. Here the claims for the authority of the Faulkner edition were again reviewed, along with the several differences with Case, and a further corroborative argument, one which had been briefly advanced earlier by both Williams and Davis,[18] is set forth in detail. The text of *Gulliver*, Williams argues, is not an independent problem, but part of the larger question of the authority of all four volumes of the 1735 edition, of which *Gulliver* was merely the third. The other volumes, no less than does *Gulliver*, show signs of the author's revision. The greater part of Swift's autograph corrections in copies of the 1727–32 Swift-Pope *Miscellanies* appears for the first time in print in the 1735 volumes, and Williams adds "that major alterations, rearrangements, and revisions, are difficult to explain except as his work; and that minor corrections, which are few in number, have every appearance of being those of an author and of no one else." [19]

The debate continues. A review by William B. Todd in *The Library* occasioned a reply by Williams, a rejoinder by Todd, and a second reply by Williams, in the course of which all the old ground was again covered, Todd taking essentially the position of Case.[20] Another reviewer, writing in the *Times Literary Supplement,* questioned Williams' assumption that Swift's autograph corrections in the *Miscellanies* were made before rather than after 1735, pointing out that at least one marginal comment, the "now deaf 1740" in Swift's hand, is unquestionably later than 1735. Williams' reply, accompanied by a rejoinder,[21] pointed out that "now deaf 1740," being Swift's comment on a reference to deafness in a birthday poem to Stella, is not to be related to the numerous items having the clear design of correcting the text. Williams further argued that there would be no conceivable reason for Swift, after 1735, to transcribe the Faulkner variants into the miscellany volumes.

The twentieth-century textual quarrel is an interesting

revival of the one waged in the eighteenth century between Faulkner and Hawkesworth, who was an editor of Motte's successor, Bathurst. While the eighteenth-century battle was in a sense "won" by the Motte forces, who succeeded in discrediting the Faulkner edition and establishing their own text at the head of the tradition extending through the nine-teenth and into the twentieth century, the twentieth-century battle, by all signs, especially the pervasive importance of the Faulkner edition in the Shakespeare Head *Prose Writings,* seems to have fallen the other way.

That the textual discussion has in fact reached a new stage is indicated by the growing inclination to emend Faulk-ner freely when it is used as a copy-text. Davis, for instance, in the Shakespeare Head *Gulliver,* has some eleventh-hour misgivings over twenty-one readings in which he had, mis-takenly he now thought, followed the copy-text. Finding it too late to alter his text, Davis calls attention to these in his notes, indicating a preference for readings from earlier texts (HD, XI, 285–86). This discussion has been carried forward and clarified in recent statements by Irvin Ehren-preis. While granting the presence of Swift's hand in, for instance, Faulkner's edition of *Gulliver,* Ehrenpreis urges, nonetheless, the use of Motte's first edition as copy-text, as its authority for accidentals (spelling, punctuation, capitali-zation, etc.) and for forms (contractions, endings, moods, etc.) seems to be stronger than that of Faulkner, where ec-centricities of grammar and pointing seem to have crept in. For substantive changes, that is, changes of sense, Ehren-preis favors emending the copy-text with Faulkner supple-mented by the Ford copy. Ehrenpreis seems justified in his confidence that this approach avoids an error to which the Faulkner partisans were prone, "printing from what is right in general and wrong in particulars." [22]

The same wariness toward the Faulkner edition appears in Herbert Davis' approach to establishing the text of *The Drapier's Letters,* which he edited for the Clarendon Press in 1935. Davis fully supported Williams' view regarding the au-thority of the 1735 edition and noted too the presence in the five letters reprinted by Faulkner of certain alterations which "indicate definitely that the revision was made by Swift himself." But he felt that it was "safer . . . to hesitate before accepting it as the only authoritative text, and as entirely superseding the text of the separate letters, originally printed by Harding." [23] Davis also pointed out that Harding's texts, being closer to the controversy, have "definite historical interest." For the first five letters, then, Davis prints Harding's texts, supplying variants from the 1725, 1730, and 1735 editions at the bottom of the page. Letters VI and VII, which first appeared in the 1735 edition, are printed from that text, as is *An Account of Wood's Execution.* The importance of the 1735 edition as evidence in determining canonical works is illustrated in Davis' assurance that everything in Faulkner's fourth volume, which contained *The Drapier's Letters* and other tracts relating to Ireland, "is certainly Swift's work" (p. lxxiv).[24] Thus Davis duly prints the *Presentment to the Grand Jury* and *An Account of Wood's Execution,* along with the *Seasonable Advice* and the seven letters, as authentic works.

For the Shakespeare Head *Drapier's Letters,* which appeared in 1941, Davis follows his edition of 1935 in all matters regarding the canon,[25] but there is a major textual difference between the two Davis editions. In the first volume of the Shakespeare Head edition Davis had indicated one of the aims of that edition would be "to provide a text of the works giving, not the earliest form either of the written manuscript or first printed edition, but the final corrected and revised versions which appeared during Swift's lifetime" (HD, I, v). Consequently in Volume X, *The Drapier's Letters,* Davis uses the 1735 edition as his copy-text for *Seasonable Advice, An Account of Wood's Execution,* and all seven of the letters, correcting his text with the earlier editions and supplying variants in a textual apparatus. Many of the variants show that in 1735 Swift was inclined to omit some of his less creditable arguments, while strengthening and emphasizing others having to do with his quarrel with the notion of Ireland's "dependency" upon England. At such points one suspects that the Swift of 1735 was perhaps less the Drapier than the Irish Patriot concerned about his reputation. This is said with no intention of questioning Davis' text, which is eminently sound throughout and, in the light of the aims of the Shakespeare Head edition, beyond question. Students of Swift will rather applaud the propitious eclecticism which produced in 1935 and 1941 two distinct texts, neither of which is itself eclectic.

The textual history of the *Journal to Stella* is a checkered one, involving both editorial blundering and unflagging pursuit of accuracy and thoroughness. The work of modern editors was dubiously lightened when, in the eighteenth century, Deane Swift, a cousin of the Dean of St. Patrick's, after translating and transcribing to his own satisfaction thirty-nine letters, comprising well over half of the *Journal,* published them in his edition of 1768 and then, apparently, destroyed the originals.[26] Consequently, for letters II to XL a modern editor, as Harold Williams has said with admirable restraint and resignation, "can but take his text from Deane Swift" (I, iii). The remaining twenty-five, letters I and XLI to LXV (with the exception of LIV, which is missing), have been available to editors since Hawkesworth deposited them in the British Museum after his edition of 1766; but prior to Forster's painstaking work on the originals, the results of which were published in his *Life of Jonathan Swift* (1875), only John Nichols, for his *Supplement to Dr. Swift's Works* (1779), gave the manuscripts any measure of attention. The numerous blottings, illegible words and passages, the constant abbreviations, and the "little language" in which the *Journal* is written, have made its editing a uniquely difficult task. Craik, Williams, and others have felt that Forster's important work on the *Journal* was marred "by a too painful nicety of interpretation" [27] and by an "unwillingness to admit defeat" which led him sometimes to rely on "sheer guesswork" (Williams, *Journal to Stella,* I, liii). Forster's careful scholarship, however, did inaugurate a new phase of close textual scrutiny which has since produced four important editions [28] and several significant studies.

Each of the four editions of the *Journal* draws, in its own way, upon the holographs, so far as they are preserved. In 1897, Frederick Ryland, editing the *Journal* for the Temple Scott edition, printed two letters, I and XLI, as faithful examples of the originals. In the other letters Ryland conventionalized the spelling, punctuation, and capitalization, and supplied all abbreviations in full. The edition of G. A. Aitken (1901) also offered a conventionalized text, but with collations of the readings in Forster and Ryland. J. K. Moorhead's edition for Everyman's Library (1924) sought to provide a reproduction of the originals within the limits permitted by an ordinary font of type. Moorhead's success in his endeavor can be attributed to a combination of meticulous care and good judgment. The Clarendon Press edition of the *Journal*, edited by Harold Williams, appeared in two handsomely printed, richly annotated volumes in 1948. Williams offers a text faithfully reproducing the originals, but chooses to avoid insignificant orthographic peculiarities. The little language is rendered "as closely as it can be deciphered without any expansions or modifications in favor of uniformity" (I, lix); capitalization is conventionalized; and undecipherable words or passages are not guessed at, but indicated with marks of elision, with the conjectures of other editors supplied in footnotes. Williams' copious and invaluable notes clarify the many obscurities, references to contemporary figures and events.

In 1937 Émile Pons published an interpretative essay on the *Journal to Stella* involving considerable analysis and interpretation not merely of the little language, but also of the blots, erasures, and calligraphy of the manuscripts.[29] Pons challenged the common view that most of the erasures and other obliterations were made at a later date by Swift or by someone else. He argued that these erasures, obliterations, and pen strokes which encircle rather than delete are part of Swift's original "text" and are devices used to tease the ladies or to hide a secret meaning known only to Stella and himself. The crossings-out and blots, furthermore, Pons regarded as indicative of emotional tension, evidence of which is the greater frequency of blots and scorings in the passages of tender feeling. The particularly heavy blotting over two instances of the word "rife" led Pons to his most important conclusion, that the phrase "deelest rife" is not, as all commentators before and since have had it, "dearest life," but rather "dearest wife," and thus is a hidden, intimate, passionate acknowledgment of the mysterious relationship which Pons wished to illuminate.

Williams takes up these conjectures in the Introduction to his edition (1948), calling them "an ingenious and interesting contribution to the reading of the manuscript," but registers some strong objections to reading "wife" for "rife," especially the difficulty which this entails when Swift addresses both Stella and Dingley, as he does on 1 March 1711–12: "Nite my two deelest Rives MD" (I, liii–lv). Williams' essay, "Deane Swift, Hawkesworth, and *The Journal to Stella*," [30] published in 1945, carefully reviews the editorial history of the *Journal* and defends the editorial methods of Deane Swift against the detractions of Forster (*Life of Swift*, I, 406–7), Ryland (*Journal to Stella*, ed. T. Scott, II, xviii), and Aitken (*Journal to Stella*, ed. Aitken, p. vi).

A thorough discussion of the meaning and interpretation of the little language, avoiding the idiosyncrasies of Pons, was offered by Irvin Ehrenpreis in an article in *Studies in Philology* in 1948. Ehrenpreis rightly stresses that the little language is phonetic and not orthographic, though he seems disinclined to associate it, as do most critics, with a form of baby talk. The various formations derived from replacement, omission, and reduplication of letters are set forth in detail, with the suggestion that Swift's distortions "fit the linguistic concepts of assimilation, dissimilation, and metathesis." The more common forms are given a gloss insofar as they admit of translation. Having established this solid foundation, Ehrenpreis goes on to demolish the "ingenious fantasy" of Pons, concluding that the " 'little language' remains what it always has been: not a unique insight into Swift's passion, but an endearing sidelight on a great man's character." [31]

In 1954 Roland M. Smith offered some learned support

for Ehrenpreis' analysis of the little language. Smith found in Edward Lhuyd's *Archaeologia Britannica* (1707), a weighty tome on linguistics, an account of sound-changes which coincided with those common in the *Journal*. By assuming that the little language had its inception when Swift "pored over" the pages of Lhuyd, Smith attempts to discredit the notion, apparently an unpalatable one to some scholars, that baby talk had some influence in its formation.[32]

CANON

A most pressing task facing twentieth-century Swift studies has been the need to establish the canon. Many eighteenth- and nineteenth-century editors sought to enhance their work by adding new pieces, and this habit, uncritically pursued, left the body of Swift's work increasingly difficult to define. The canon of Swift's prose is now in process of redefinition in the Shakespeare Head edition, and Herbert Davis, its editor, has gone on record outside the pages of his edition on the problems involved in this endeavor.[33] While Davis is inclined to regard publication in the 1735 edition as evidence favoring authenticity, he guards against being unduly swayed by such evidence. Thus in the Introduction to Volume IX, *Irish Tracts 1720–1723 and Sermons*, Davis considers the evidence "very strong" in favor of Swift's authorship of *The Wonderful Wonder of Wonders* and *The Wonder of All the Wonders*, both of which appeared in *Miscellanies, the Third Volume* (1732) and in Volume I of Faulkner's edition; yet Davis, prompted in part by the doubts of other critics, places these pieces in an appendix with others "Probably written by Swift" (HD, IX, xvii–xix, 281–87). On the other hand, the *Swearers Bank*, a work generally accepted as Swift's, is relegated to the Appendix and printed as "Attributed to Swift," because, as Davis explains in his Introduction (HD, IX, xix), no positive evidence, such as reference to it in correspondence or appearance in authorized editions, could be found in its favor. Perhaps the most important exclusion is *A Letter of Advice to a Young Poet*, which Davis prints in an appendix after noting in his Introduction both adverse internal evidence [34] and the absence of favorable external evidence (HD, IX, xxiv–xxvii). Louis Landa, who writes an introduction to the sermons, thoroughly reviews the textual history of *The Difficulty of Knowing One's Self*, previously accepted as genuine by Swift's editors, and concludes in the light of both internal and external evidence that *The Difficulty* is a doubtful attribution. It is printed in the Appendix (HD, IX, 103–6). Eleven sermons, adjudged to be genuine, appear in the text proper.

The Present Miserable State of Ireland, originally raised to the canon almost purely on the basis of its title, is wholly rejected by Davis (HD, XII, xv; and "The Canon of Swift," pp. 128–29). Evidence from the correspondence serves to exclude *The Right of Precedence between Physicians and Civilians* (*Letters to Ford*, p. 87; HD, IX, xxv–xxvi; and "The Canon of Swift," p. 128), as it does also in the case of *The History of John Bull*, which Teerink had argued, with little success, to be genuine.[35]

The authenticity of *The History of the Last Four Years of the Queen*, which had been questioned by Dr. Johnson, Stanhope, and Macaulay, and advanced on internal evidence by Craik and Temple Scott, was placed beyond doubt by Williams' discovery in 1935 of the Windsor Manuscript with Swift's autograph corrections and his endorsement, "written at Windsor 1713." [36] The text in the Shakespeare Head edition is based on this newly discovered manuscript. Swift's corrections are followed, with the earlier readings and other variants given in the textual apparatus.

Serious attempts to define the canon of Swift's poetry date from the appearance of F. Elrington Ball's *Swift's Verse: An Essay* (London, 1929). Ball was aware of the immensity of the problem, and the modest title given his work suggests its preliminary nature. Taking up the verse in chronological order, Ball also attempts to supply exact dates of composition. His perusal of the doubtful items ascribed to Swift from *The Whimsical Medley* (first advanced by Barrett, *Essay on the Earlier Part of Dean Swift's Life*, 1808, but questioned even by Scott and forcefully rejected by Forster) and from transcripts in a copy of Hayward's *Almanack* (advanced by W. R. Wilde, *The Closing Years of Dean Swift's Life,* 1849) were important contributions to discussions since carried forward by Williams. While many attributions advanced or seconded by Ball, such as *Jove's Ramble, On the Burning of Whitehall,* and the *Ode on Science,* have since been set aside, other attributions, including several which were original with Ball, have been substantiated. These latter include *The First of April, A Panegyric on Dean Swift, The Life and Genuine Character of Doctor Swift, A Letter from Dean Swift to Dean Smedley,* and *The Bank Thrown Down,* all of which were later printed for the first time in a collected edition—*The Bank Thrown Down* with some hesitation—by Williams in 1937.

Davis, writing in *The Book-Collectors' Quarterly* in 1931,[37] minutely examined the several early editions of *Verses on the Death of Dr. Swift,* including copies with manuscript corrections and additions. He discovered that the first edition, under the drastic editing of Pope and William King (of St. Mary's Hall) was actually a patch-work composed of only part of the manuscript carried to London by King, plus lines interpolated from *The Life and Genuine Character of Doctor Swift,* a work which hitherto had been taken to be, as Swift himself claimed, a poor imitation of *Verses on the Death of Doctor Swift.* Davis went on to substantiate Ball's allegation that *The Life and Genuine Character* was an authentic work, written, published, and disowned by Swift in his customary spirit of mystification.

An important piece of research by Sidney L. Gulick, Jr.,[38] published in 1933, demonstrated that though *The Day of Judgment* was accepted on insufficient grounds in 1775 when it was taken from Chesterfield's *Letters to His Son* and added without question to the canon of Swift, it is nonetheless a genuine work. The poem, Gulick shows, was not printed with Chesterfield's *Letters* until the fourth edition in 1774. Prior to this it had twice appeared in periodicals, first in the *St. James Chronicle* (9–12 April, 1774), and later in the *Monthly Review* (LI, July, 1774, 25), from which it was copied and given its proper place accompanying Chesterfield's letter to Voltaire of 27 August 1752. Why the poem was left out of the first three editions of the *Letters* and how it came to appear in the *St. James Chronicle*,[39] we do not know; but Gulick offers sufficient evidence to identify the tenuously transmitted poem which we now have with the one referred to in the letter to Voltaire, a poem which Chesterfield claimed to have in the original manuscript in Swift's hand.

In the Clarendon Press edition of the *Poems* (1937) Williams drew upon the work of these and other scholars and, adding his own tremendous labors, produced a work which is a model of scholarly editing. Of the approximately 400 poems which had been ascribed to Swift, not including riddles, epigrams, and the like, Williams distinguishes some 250 genuine items as against 150 attributions adjudged to be doubtful, demonstrably unjustifiable, or written by another hand. While Williams regarded the task of trimming and pruning the canon as of primary importance, he was by no means reluctant to include original attributions if the evidence warranted doing so. Besides those poems mentioned above which Ball had originally advanced and which Williams was able to accredit, *To Mr. Harlyes Surgeon* (printed from Swift's holograph), certain *"jeux d'esprit"* from the Scriblerus manuscript, *The Character of Sir Robert Walpole*, *Verses to Vanessa*, and three poems from the Holyhead Journal, are all printed for the first time in a collected edition. The prize inclusion, however, is Williams' recovery of the lost ode, *To the King on His Irish Expedition*, found in the rare and neglected fourth volume of *Miscellanies* printed by Samuel Fairbrother in 1735. This poem fits the description of a "pindarique" ode on King William which Swift is known to have written, as the hitherto accredited ode in quatrains, *Ode to King William on His Successes in Ireland*, does not. Williams presents all the evidence for the poem from the Fairbrother volume (*Poems*, I, 4–6), and his claim, modestly advanced, has apparently found unanimous acceptance. It has been further substantiated on internal grounds argued skilfully by Irvin Ehrenpreis.[40]

Among poems excluded from the canon with certain misgivings and printed as "Poems attributed to Swift" are *Jack Frenchman's Lamentation, The Tale of a Nettle, A Poem on Rover, Blue Skin's Ballad,* and *The Puppet Show.* Strong evidence against *The Puppet Show* in a letter to Ford dated 15 April 1721 (*Letters to Ford,* p. 91) puts it seriously in doubt, but "a possibility that Swift played some part in its composition" prompts Williams to retain it in the Appendix. The *Tripos* and the pieces from Hayward's *Almanack* are firmly rejected, as are several attributions formerly accepted as Swift's on grounds of their appearance in a "well-known disguised hand," which Swift is alleged, without foundation, to have used on occasion.

Careful scrutiny of manuscripts enabled Williams to emend and augment the text of *Vanbrug's House, The History of Vanbrug's House,* the early version of *Baucis and Philemon, In Pity of the Emptying Town,* and *The Author upon Himself,* and to bring to light new and important facts regarding several poems. *The Problem,* for instance, we now know satirized the Earl of Romney and not, as had been previously thought, Lord Berkeley, a piece of intelligence which releases Swift from some of the odium which that poem had formerly shed on him. Of somewhat less moment was the information, discovered in Orrery's annotations in his own copy of the *Remarks,* that *Daphne* and *Death and Daphne* were written to Lady Acheson and not to Laetitia Pilkington. Insofar as possible Williams furnishes for each poem its date, place of writing, and mood or occasion of its composition.

Williams examines all texts of any value, records variants at the bottom of the page, and prints, in all but one instance, from the text which he regards as most authoritative. His one departure from this habit is his printing, for good reasons, a recension of *Verses on the Death of Dr. Swift.* When manuscript versions exist in Swift's hand (or in the hand of Stella or Ford) these take precedence over printed texts. In the absence of a manuscript, Williams favors a first edition, though in several instances he sets aside unauthorized first editions in favor of later editions showing signs of authorial supervision. This practice is in keeping with the editorial principle observed in the Shakespeare Head edition, of regarding the latest text coming from Swift's hand as the authoritative one. The principle, in almost all instances carefully followed by Williams, forces him in one case to print a text which on grounds other than purely textual, can be regarded as questionable. Williams passes over the first edition of *Cadenus and Vanessa,* published in London by Roberts in 1726, in order to print from the text in the 1727 *Miscellanies.* But the miscellany text of *Cadenus and Vanessa* is edited, very likely by Swift himself, on purely discretionary grounds, resulting in the alteration or cancellation of lines in which the passion of Vanessa is strongly suggested. The situation is not unlike the differences between the early and late texts of *The Drapier's Letters,* in which the kind of authority lost as the result of revision remains questionable. Williams' edition, textually grounded on the soundest principles and offering all the variant readings, performs the truly valuable function of laying bare these and other knotty problems which face future editors.[41]

III

a tale of a tub

All present-day students of Swift's masterly early work, *A Tale of a Tub* (1704), owe special thanks to A. C. Guthkelch and D. Nichol Smith. Their edition (1920; 2nd ed., 1958) of the *Tale* and its companion pieces, *The Battle of the Books* and *The Mechanical Operation of the Spirit*, furnishes not only an admirably edited text, but also a thorough presentation of such important matters as Thomas Swift's role in the composition, the circumstances of publication, the textual authority (with a list of all early editions), the alleged sources, and the chronology of composition. For all these matters Guthkelch and Smith's introduction remains the best and most easily accessible discussion. The substance of Guthkelch's earlier articles [1] is assembled here, and the earlier discussions of sources advanced by such students as "Indagator" (1814) and Churton Collins (1893),[2] René Macé (1721), and Voltaire (1756) [3] are surveyed and answered. In a series of appendices Guthkelch and Smith supply texts of such related works as Wotton's *Observations upon the "Tale of a Tub,"* the spurious continuation of the *Tale* entitled *The History of Martin*, Curll's *Complete Key to the "Tale of a Tub,"* as well as extensive notes on the "dark authors" touched upon in Swift's work.

Swift's own statement in the "Apology" [4] and internal evidence indicate that the greater part of the *Tale* was composed in 1696 or earlier, the "Dedication to Somers" and "The Bookseller to the Reader" having been added between 1702 and 1704. Guthkelch and Smith take Swift's statement to indicate that the sections of allegory were largely completed early, perhaps as early as 1696, and that the various digressions were added the following year. Thus Guthkelch and Smith support the generally held view that the composition of the *Tale* is to be associated with Swift's stay at Moor Park in 1696–97,[5] though they do not rule out the possibility that certain rough drafts may have been made as early as Swift's undergraduate days at Trinity College. Because of its close connection with Richard Bentley's first *Dissertation on the Epistles of Phalaris* (1697) and with Boyle's "victory" over Bentley in his *Examination* (1698), the composition of *The Battle of the Books* can be placed with reasonable confidence in 1697–98.

Along with the Guthkelch and Smith edition of the *Tale*, the year 1920 also saw the appearance of two background studies which placed the quarrel of the ancients and the moderns in an altogether new light. Earlier students had regarded the quarrel as a trivial diversion of seventeenth-century literati.[6] Now R. F. Jones in "The Background of *The Battle of the Books*"[7] and Anne Elizabeth Burlingame in *"The Battle of the Books" in Its Historical Setting* (New York, 1920) identified it as a stage in the much larger controversy between the sciences and the humanities extending from the time of Montaigne and Bacon to our own day. Jones's work in this area illuminated the scientific attitude, the idea of progress, and the impact of these on sensibility in the seventeenth and eighteenth centuries. C. M. Webster, taking up the *Tale's* place in the history of ideas, puts the *Tale* and the *Mechanical Operation* in a tradition attacking Puritan enthusiasm, especially the Puritan tendency to confuse flesh and spirit in a kind of teetotalling dionysianism.[8]

Much twentieth-century comment has perpetuated the nineteenth-century conviction that the *Tale* is a sacrilegious work. This interpretation is often the result of confusing Swift's intention with the intention of its pretended author, a modern Grubstreet hack. Thus W. A. Eddy finds sacrilege in the *Tale* once he assumes that passages of the Grubstreeter's self-analysis refer to Swift himself. "Already in 1697," wrote Eddy, confusing vaporizing and vertigo, "he [Swift] diagnosed his malady: 'I myself, the author of these momentous truths, am a person whose imaginations are hard-mouthed, and exceedingly disposed to run away with his reason, which I have observed from long experience to be a very light rider, and easily shook off; upon this account my friends will never trust me alone.'"[9] J. Middleton Murry, Swift's most recent biographer, for similar reasons found the *Tale*'s "spirit of irreverence all-pervasive: indeed, a much more potent 'universal pickle' than Lord Peter's—a universal disintegrator."[10] Yet a far better critical grasp of the work did not keep Paul Elmer More (1915)[11] from a similar judgment. After glancing at "the sublime and refined point of felicity, called the possession of being well deceived," More concluded, "It is not strange that the reputation of this book should have overshadowed him through life, deterring those in power from placing him in a position of authority over the higher illusions of society" (pp. 118–19). The revised judgment which has emerged strongly in the past two decades required both a firm critical grasp of the *Tale* as a work of literary art as well as a new sense of the nature and ground of "the higher illusions of society."

Émile Pons, whose weighty study[12] of Swift's early years appeared in 1925, found in the *Tale* a peculiarly modern ambivalence toward the higher illusions of society. Too intent on connecting elements of the *Tale* with Swift's early experience—especially his regrets, disappointments, hatreds—Pons often lost sight of the disjunction between Swift and his persona and concluded that the interest in hermeticism, the clothes philosophy, even the allegory, was Swift's own (pp. 335, 372, 375). Consequently we often find Pons responding simultaneously to the pathos of the Grubstreet author and to the brilliant unmasking of the satirist, antithetic though these often are. Biographical criticism, particularly strong in the twenties, often led Pons to trace satirical animus to biographical sources, as when the unmasking of Lord Peter's follies before his brothers becomes the unmasking of Swift's false friends and enemies (p. 345). For Pons, the *Tale* was still primarily the biographical document it was for so many nineteenth-century critics.

In "The Irony of Swift" (1934) [13] F. R. Leavis, practicing the close explication which came to be associated with the *Scrutiny* critics, raised in a new way the old questions of intention, meaning, and effect. With the same disdain for philosophy which elsewhere brought him to differences with George Santayana and René Wellek,[14] Leavis quoted copiously from the "Digression on Madness" and demonstrated the innocent reader's involvement in the Grubstreeter's argument. Leavis' technique, essentially the same as that of many a "new critic" on this side of the Atlantic, is simply to recount his adventure with a masterpiece. Leavis' engagement with the *Tale* is at first a shocked and then a jaundiced one. Leavis rightly apprehends that Swift's irony—unlike Gibbon's, which invites the reader into its confidence—is hostile to the reader and offers no easy positives to encourage his complacency. Leavis concludes that in the *Tale* Swift indulges his compulsion to destroy, and that what we get in the *Tale*, as in Swift's other writings, is "the most remarkable expression of negative feelings that literature can offer—the spectacle of creative powers (the paradoxical description seems right) exhibited consistently in negation and rejection" (p. 86). While one can quarrel with Leavis' conclusions, the return to a close scrutiny of the text was a step toward the rediscovery of the *Tale* as literature.

The want of a positive in the *Tale* is for Rossi and Hone (1934) [15] also a shortcoming. "By making Clothism ridiculous, by laughing at it as at a very foolish account of things, Swift himself takes away value from his satire; makes it, as it were, ill-fitting" (p. 120). Rossi and Hone even see the negative and hostile character of the satire reflected in its anonymous authorship, for "a blow from the void is most efficacious, and the author laughs twice, once at his foes, and then at his readers" (p. 118). Rossi and Hone did not find Anglicanism, however, to be among the objects of Swift's laughter. They point out that upon its appearance the *Tale* was ascribed to several men of undoubted orthodoxy—Smalridge and Atterbury, for instance—indicating that contemporary readers were not incapable of seeing beneath whatever sacrilege lay on the surface of the work. Rossi and Hone, like Nichol Smith [16] the following year, denied any intent or effect of sacrilege in the work, seeing in it rather, at least in its religious dimension, a strategic attack on the enemies of Anglicanism, especially dissent and Roman Catholicism.

It was not until 1936, with Quintana's *The Mind and Art of Jonathan Swift* (London and New York, 1936; reprinted, London, 1953) that the results of twentieth-century historical scholarship were brought to bear effectively on the *Tale* and its companion pieces. The studies by Jones and Burlingame enabled Quintana to identify the place and emphasize the importance of the *Tale* and the *Battle* in the quarrel between the ancients and the moderns, between the polite learning of the gentleman and the new science of the projector. The work of Crane and Lovejoy enabled Quintana to explore the hostility to various forms of irrationalism and enthusiasm reflected in the *Tale* and the *Mechanical Operation*. Quintana offered some helpful suggestions on the form of the *Tale*, but he is rather more thorough and satisfying when dealing with the mind of his subject than with his art. Too often Quintana reverts to the manner of the impressionist, a manner in which he is not happy. The satire of the *Tale*, for instance, is described as "an insinuating lethal gas compounded of irony, parody, and implication," with the last element "refined to its deadliest degree; like some giant in *Gulliver's Travels* bending over a body of water and aimlessly stirring it with his finger, the satirist sets in motion a veritable maelstrom, whereupon with the utmost casualness he propels his tiny victims towards the devouring whirl. Beyond this, indirection cannot go" (p. 88). However, elsewhere Quintana treats the formless, digressive character of the *Tale* more rigorously and explains it correctly as part of Swift's parody of modern habits of thought and composition.

Quintana overstates Swift's relentless rationalism, which

is admittedly a palpable theme, though not an unqualified one, in the *Tale*. The Grubstreeter's distaste for reason and its consequences is clear enough in his candid comment on "the sower and the dregs" which reason has for its portion, and it is indeed relentless reason, or what he understands of it, against which he sets himself in the "Digression on Madness." If the *Tale* were a less complex work, one might be safe in assuming, as Quintana seems to here, that what the Grubstreeter rejects, Swift unequivocally acclaims. While Quintana shows some misgivings in placing Swift on the side of rigorous reason and "moral realism"—misgivings prompted apparently by their inconsistency with Swift's anti-intellectualism, his distrust of speculation, his commitment to common sense (which embraces many "common forms")— these misgivings are dismissed on the ground that "the search for moral truth beneath the concealments of false appearances not only did not constitute intellectual aberration but was the prime function of reason" (p. 96).

George Sherburn has claimed that Swift's technique is exposé, not attack.[17] It is true that much of the difficulty over "positives" and "point of view" can be overcome by carefully noting precisely what is exposed. Under exposure in the "Digression on Madness" is the complacent modern conviction that a "sublime and refined Point of Felicity" is achievable simply through denial of reason (even where it is "certainly in the right") and acceptance of appearances. The cheery optimism which has dominated so much of criticism and philosophy since Swift's time, and which has been all too confident that "Felicity" is both achievable and worth achieving, has made it difficult for readers to see that the passage offers small comfort to the probing activities of reason. The limits of reason are also under exposure, but we become aware of these limits only while observing the author-persona as, in a skilfully controlled comic passage, he tries his hand at metaphysics, something in which he is out of his depth. It is the classic comic situation of "an ass with the lyre," in which the fun derives from the incongruous assurance with which the ass handles an instrument he knows nothing about. Having gained confidence from a bout with imagination and memory, the latter of which Hobbes had called "decaying sense" and which the modern consequently disdains for being "the Grave of Things," the Grubstreeter now proceeds to solve the problem of substance and quality. We are told that the qualities, which "dwell or are drawn by Art upon the Outward of Bodies," are far preferable to that "good for Nothing" which "pretended Philosophy" (that is, reason), by "cutting, and opening, and mangling, and piercing," claims is beneath the surface. That whatever is beneath the qualities is not worth knowing, the modern author has proved to his own satisfaction on the evidence of the flayed woman and the anatomized beau, two "Corporeal Beings" whose *"Outside"* he found to be "infinitely preferable to the *In."* Thus he has a metaphysical as well as an ethical preference for appearance as against reality. The exposé reminds the reader that reason too has its limits and that "material substance" was for Locke and others in the late seventeenth century an "I-know-not-what."

Herbert Davis in 1938 [18] emphasized, as did Quintana earlier (*Mind and Art,* p. 68), the seventeenth-century character of the *Tale:* "a sort of finale, a superbly exuberant and reckless finale, triumphantly summing up all the heroics and extravagances of seventeenth-century thought and art, . . . a caricature of the most prominent features of a century of baroque art" (p. 277). Leavis had noted the "metaphysical" character of its wit (*The Common Pursuit,* p. 78); Davis in *The Satire of Swift* (New York, 1947) more fully explored its essentially parodic relation to seventeenth-century writers, including Dryden and Sir Thomas Browne (pp. 29–35).

Miriam Kosh Starkman in *Swift's Satire on Learning in "A Tale of a Tub"* (Princeton, 1950) attempts to sort out the various antipathies discernible in the satire, especially in the satire on false learning and pedantry, which, by concentrating on the religious allegory and abuses in religion, critics had too often passed over. Mrs. Starkman, placing the *Tale* against the contemporary movements of ideas in science, philosophy, and belles-lettres, finds underlying the various

movements against which Swift set himself the single ingredient of modernity, that is, the itch for innovation. The
experimental science of the Royal Society, the resurgent
epicureanism and materialism, the system-building of Descartes, the faith in progress which led to denigration of the
ancients, even the religious embroidery of Lord Peter, that
is, of Roman Catholicism, all are related, in Mrs. Starkman's
account, to the modern spirit of innovation. While her materials are sometimes forced, her study does supply a generally accurate picture of the major currents of thought reflected in the *Tale*.

On the *Tale* as a work of art Mrs. Starkman is less successful. Too often she forgets her own strictures against confusing Swift with his persona, taking as Swift's own, for instance, all of the ideas in the Preface favoring personal or
ad hominem satire as against general satire of types. Sup-
porting this misreading with the notion that Swift's satire
is personal simply because the text is sprinkled with names
of actual people, she argues that "Swift went directly against
the spirit of Renaissance satire in approving, as he does both
theoretically and in actual practice in *A Tale of a Tub*, 'ad
hominem' satire like that of Aristophanes, and in depreciating
the value of innuendo, suggestion, exaggeration, and satire
of types rather than of individuals" (p. 127). There are, of
course, abundant examples of *ad hominem* satire in Swift—
Mr. Collins, William Wood, and Jeremy Partridge come
readily to mind—and doubtless some passages of the *Tale*
can be taken as "private taxing." But the *Tale* as a whole
transcends whatever particular references it makes. To call
it *ad hominem* satire is to see only a few of its trees. A mis-
guided attempt to find a hidden "symmetry" and "balance"
in the relative positions of digressions and sections of allegory
(pp. 131–46) also reflects an inadequate understanding of
Swift's control over his persona and thus of the nature of the
Tale's artistic form.[19]

Two quite recent explorations of Swift's antipathies reflected in the *Tale* are Ronald Paulson's *Theme and Structure
in Swift's "A Tale of a Tub"* (New Haven, 1960) and Philip

Pinkus' "A *Tale of a Tub* and the Rosy Cross" (1960).[20] Both studies attempt to find an archetypal antagonism in the *Tale* by which, the authors feel, the work achieves its unity. Paulson relates the *Tale* to Irenaeus' patristic attack on the heresy of Gnosticism. Pinkus chooses an hermetic heresy much closer to Swift's own time: Rosicrucianism. Taken together, these studies re-emphasize and make abundantly clear Swift's undoubted hostility toward the dark authors of the hermetic tradition. But the unity Paulson claims for the *Tale,* depending as it does upon "a strikingly periodic order of parallel and balanced sections, subjects, and characters: a logically arranged encyclopedia of Gnostic sufficiency" (p. 233), turns out to be as wooden and mechanical as Starkman's. Paulson, moreover, in his relentless pursuit of Gnosticism in controlling images, finds little that is not grist for his mill. Thus, under the image of the crowd—"the conformation into which moderns instinctively fall" (p. 221) and which has its "prototype" in Irenaeus' "picture of heresy growing out of heresy" (p. 146)—Paulson herds the jostling fat man, "the Nation of Criticks" (p. 215), "the 'vast flourishing body' of modern writers," numerous wits, bedlamites, aeolists, even Peter, Martin, and Jack hurrying away from their father's bedside (p. 221). If Paulson's long discussion of crowds were to suggest that in his treatment of man in the mass Swift shares something with Breughel and Hieronymus Bosch, perhaps especially the latter's grimness, one might readily assent; but Paulson's purpose is to draw contrasts whenever possible between the organic harmony of traditionally oriented—especially orthodox Christian—bodies, and the wilful and disorganized antics of self-sufficient Gnostics. Great comedy is thus reduced to something distressingly sodden, and one is inclined to borrow from Leavis, from whose point of view Paulson is only imperfectly liberated, and say that while the orthodox Christians may have all the organicity, the Gnostics evidently have all the fun and games. Under the circumstances it is no great surprise when Paulson finally chooses sides and, with a patronizing glance at what he takes to be Swift's *Weltanschauung,* falls in with

Leavis, Blake, the Gnostics, and whales with bloodshot eyes
—the side that has, he thinks, all the "penetrating perception" (p. 233).

But the critics who are guilty of the gravest misconceptions of the *Tale*—those, for instance, who see in it only
irreligion or nihilism [21]—tend also to regard the anonymity
of the work, when they pay it any thought at all, as nothing
more than a device Swift used to protect himself, a form of
literary cowardice. The strongest corrective to such critical
shortsightedness is provided by the numerous rhetorical
studies of the *Tale* which have appeared since 1951. The first
of these is "Swift's *Tale of a Tub*: An Essay in Problems of
Structure" (1951),[22] by Robert C. Elliott. The formal excel-
lence which Quintana and others have admired in the *Tale*
makes it more susceptible to Elliott's rigorous Jamesian approach than is *Gulliver*, to which Elliott later turned his attention. Elliott's term for the pretended author, or persona,
of the *Tale* is *ingénu*, and, as the "compositional centre" of
the work, this *ingénu* "is a kind of distorting lens through
which all of the wildly diverse materials of the *Tale* must
pass. As they emerge from the influence of his personality,
they are twisted, inverted, awry. They are, in short, structured, but structured in such a fashion that the reader must
supply, in the lens of his own mind, the proper correction"
(pp. 446–47). This is the key insight of recent rhetorical
criticism of Swift. It has done much to free Swift criticism
from the old bogey of the flailing, angry satirist and to free
the close analysis of Swift's text from such misconceptions as
hampered the work of, for instance, Leavis and Starkman.

Harold Kelling's analysis in "Reason in Madness: *A Tale
of a Tub*" (1954),[23] is less Jamesian. At times Kelling is distressingly intent on finding in the *Tale* "the conventional form
of an oration." Kelling distinguishes such elements as the
exordium and partitio, but finds it necessary to go outside
the *Tale* proper, to the *Mechanical Operation of the Spirit*,[24]
to locate the peroration (pp. 199–200 and footnote). Kelling's
thesis, that the *Tale* is an oration against rhetoric and at the
same time an example of good rhetoric," is rather bland if the

word "oration" is not taken too literally, and, indeed, Kelling spends only a few pages of this lengthy article in pursuit of the false fire of the Grubstreeter's "oration." Far more interesting is Kelling's discussion of "reason" as understood by representative Anglicans, a discussion which leads Kelling to the meaning and implication of reason as used in the "Digression on Madness." He finds Leavis and Elliott in error in assuming that the reader is faced with an either-or between the complacent acceptance of appearance and the corrosive probing of reason, "the satirist's private conclusions that things are rotten below the surface" (pp. 213–14). Kelling argues that for the Anglican—such as Robert South and Isaac Barrow, and, by implication, Swift—reason offered not "sour and dregs" but "contentment." Though he escapes the either-or which tripped up Leavis and Elliott, Kelling, in part by failing to see the passage as a bumbling discussion of epistemology, invokes from outside the work a concept which perilously resembles the complacent felicity of the modern. For Kelling, "reason" as it is used in the *Tale* appears finally to be an amalgam of common sense and good judgment operating upon the materials of sense. It is what enables the reader to recognize the extreme views and virtual madness of the Grubstreet author and all others who, by delusive— that is, bad—rhetoric, seek to impose their ideas on others.

Rhetorical criticism is, like historical and biographical criticism, in quest of Swift's positives. Rhetorical criticism of satirical works seems to have an inescapable biographical dimension: the meaning of a satirical work is thought to reside less within the work itself than in the author's intention, which, on the basis of the work alone, most often needs to be inferred or intuited. How far afield those inferences and intuitions can go, the diverse interpretations of such a work as the *Tale* will attest. Though much present-day criticism of the lyric and of the novel studiously avoids all concern with intention, choosing to regard the work as autonomous, no critic of the *Tale* appears willing to view it apart from Swift's intention, a reflection of the assumption that the meaning of a satire is indistinguishable from the author's intention. Restoration comedies, it has been said, can be moral holidays in a "utopia of gallantry," but satires, unashamedly didactic, appear tied, all too abjectly, to their authors' ethics. Just as the satirist is assumed to be committed to a set of ideas which control his satire, so the reader too, insofar as he becomes involved in the work, becomes aware of, and very likely involved in, the same commitment.

The historical critics of Swift's satires attempted to locate that commitment by triangulation of biographical, historical, and literary evidence. The degree of their success ought not to be underestimated. Rhetorical critics of the *Tale* have been most successful when they have drawn freely upon the resources of such scholarship. Their primary aim is, of course, to set forth and illuminate the form of the work, yet none have been content to rest there. The same nagging questions about the satirist's positives and values persist to trouble them, and none have claimed that all of these could be readily found within the work itself. The indirection of satire, the need that many of its informing values be intuited, makes advisable—if not inevitable—the continued use of the crutch of extra-literary triangulation.

Where Kelling's triangulation yielded the simple positive of Anglican reason and its promise of "contentment," other recent critics have warily stressed the complexity, subtlety, and elusiveness of Swift's positives. Evading with Kelling the trap of the either-or, Martin Price in *Swift's Rhetorical Art* (New Haven, 1953) is typical of the best recent critics in his refusal to be content with simple positives. "The *Tale* points throughout," he asserted, "to a middle way that lies between opposed forms of corruption. Reason is always a balance between extremes of refinement and superficiality or, as we might put it, idle curiosity and naive credulity" (p. 80). Very close to Price in his emphases and conclusions is Kathleen Williams in *Jonathan Swift and the Age of Compromise* (Lawrence, Kan., 1958). On the great crux of the *Tale,* the "Digression on Madness," Miss Williams notes that Swift has maintained "a delicate balance between two unacceptable extremes, using each extreme as a temporary satiric standard by which to discredit the other." The positives, on the other hand, lie "in what he [the Grubstreeter] has left out in his exhaustive survey of the situation, in the compromise solution of unrefined reason, the 'common Forms,' human centrality, and good sense" (pp. 121–22).

John M. Bullitt's dissection of Swift's satirical techniques in *Jonathan Swift and the Anatomy of Satire* (Cambridge, Mass., 1953) notes examples in the Grubstreeter of what Bergson called "the mechanical encrusted on the living." Any falsified view of reality, mechanically imposed, such as the Grubstreeter's constant tendency to take the figurative literally or to "convert an allegory or metaphor into a literal interpretation" is "to act mechanically without reason" (p. 136). Price had come to similar conclusions regarding Swift's intention in such passages: "False wit can lead us wherever we want to go; reasoning by analogy can, in the hands of a fool or a sophister, be used to reach any conclusion" (pp. 92–93), a view expressed also by William Bragg Ewald in *The Masks of Jonathan Swift* (Oxford, 1954). Ewald noted the Grubstreeter's tendency "to rely more on extravagant analogies than on careful logic" (p. 19). The comedy, then, is presumably the grotesquerie of mechanical thinking and acting; the gracefulness of true reason and rational activity would be immune to ridicule.

Quintana in *Swift: An Introduction* (London and New York, 1954) responded to the new interest in rhetorical criticism as well as to his own plea in "Situational Satire" [25] for a closer analysis of Swift's satires as works of art. Quintana refines upon the criticism of the personae or masks and produces, at least for the *Tale,* complications hitherto unheard of. He distinguishes no less than six separate personae in the *Tale:* (1) "the one who is writing the *Apology,*" traditionally considered to be Swift writing in his own person; (2) " 'the author' referred to therein"; (3) the bookseller, who writes "The Bookseller to the Reader" and also signs the "Dedication to Somers;" (4) the modern author of the digressions; (5) "the latter's *alter ego,* the historian," who writes the sections of allegory; and (6) "the satirist," who "appears on the

stage only briefly but without whom the others would lose
their meaning in the satiric comedy being enacted" (pp.
54–55, 60–61). Critical analysis here becomes mere hair-
splitting. To be sure, Swift in his own person speaking in
the "Apology" needs to be distinguished from the bookseller and the Grubstreet hack, but only in a grammatical
sense is he distinguishable from the person referred to
there as "the author." To suggest otherwise is to raise the
interesting but surely not germane question of the discon-
tinuity of personality. Nor is there any purpose in di-
viding the Grubstreeter into "modern author" and "historian," unless one were to go on and distinguish the other
selves of this singularly various personality: virtuoso, projector, true critic, bedlamite, etc. His kaleidoscopic character contributes to his comedy.[26] In positing the sixth mask,
"the satirist," Quintana perpetuates a misapprehension which
had troubled earlier critics such as F. R. Leavis and R. C.
Elliott, who found it difficult to account for the occasional
flashes of truth or "insight" in the Grubstreeter's otherwise
absurd posturings except as the result of a deliberate trick or
a slipped mask. Elliott felt that in such a passage as the one
describing the "serene peaceful state of being a fool among
knaves" one could see "Swift momentarily drop the strings
controlling the *ingénu*, thrust him aside, and lash out directly
from his own hatred of the glitter of false appearances" (p.
452). Quintana, evidently loath to permit such an inartistic
intrusion by Swift himself, assigns the passage—a "dead
centre" of the *Tale's* satire (p. 65)—to person number six,
"not Swift, but . . . a satirist—perhaps we should say he is
the satirist" (p. 55). The passage—and others like it—is more
easily accounted for as an irony resulting from the persona's
occasionally speaking better than he knows. Elsewhere the
comedy offered by the persona resides mostly in his spectacle
of folly; here, in these passages of truthful or sensible coinci-
dence, the persona remains in character, and the irony is that
he stumbles only accidentally on these *bons mots*, the truth
of which he rather less than perfectly understands. Swift, like
Erasmus, knew well that drunkards, children, and fools could

speak truth.[27] Quintana glances at Erasmus' Folly occasionally, but leaves unexplored the striking similarities of technique and effect which make her a highly illuminating analog of Swift's Grubstreeter.[28]

Twentieth-century critical and scholarly attention to the *Tale* and its related works, though it has found new ways in which to disagree, has at the same time achieved a common ground of agreement whose limited area is not an adequate index to its value. Besides defining the work's position in the history of ideas, recent criticism has made possible a clearer apprehension of the *Tale* as a work of art. Without claiming that Swift, its author properly so called, was a serene and aloof intelligence presiding over his puppets with detached disdain, recent criticism has firmly set aside both the atheistic mocker of mysteries and the bitter and angry satirist with whom earlier criticism had chosen to associate the work. While the intention of the author remains an important question in current critical probing of Swift's satirical works, few recent critics of the *Tale* have been willing to equate it with a particular set of literary, philosophical, and religious antipathies or with a complementary set of so-called positives.[29] Compounded of these, it transcends them in artistic statement. Recent criticism has had much to say about the character of that statement, yet such matters as the role of parody in the *Tale*, the precise *Tendenz* of its ironies, the nature of the Grubstreeter's intention and the limits of his (as distinct from Swift's) responsibilities in the work, could bear further discussion.[30]

IV

gulliver's travels

That *Gulliver's Travels* remains a classic for the twentieth as for the nineteenth century is attested by the number of its twentieth-century editions (over two hundred by a recent count) and by the prodigious flow of criticism which it continues to inspire. For a book that has become a children's classic, *Gulliver* has given rise to an amazing array of adult-level studies, analyses, refutations, and appreciations. We can bring the variety of twentieth-century responses to *Gulliver* into focus by beginning with that scientifically inspired concern for *Gulliver's* sources, a form of criticism which flourished at the turn of the century and which for a time was synonymous with scholarship.

SOURCES

If studies of the sources of *Gulliver's Travels* have not always brought a more complete understanding of Swift's work, it must be allowed that the more rewarding of these studies made no such promise. Rather, they were intended as modest contributions to the larger task of understanding which "lay ahead." This important phase of literary scholarship, now suffering a not wholly deserved disrepute, grew from a conviction popular in nineteenth-century Germany that literary—no less than social and natural—phenomena, being moments in a larger process of change and growth, could be understood only as a phase of evolutionary development from stimulus to response, early groping to later discovery, inchoate matter to final synthesis. Thus *Gulliver's Travels* was to be understood as a development from a complex of origins. These origins were primarily literary, though other influences were to be traced, particularly those revealed in biographical and historical research. When early students of Swift's sources, aware apparently of the immensity of their task, proceeded with what was manifestly an inadequate or even nonexistent understanding of the work whose literary relationships they sought to establish, a certain modesty was only proper. The meaning and character of the work were to be examined by a method which was by definition piece-meal. As time went on, amidst many false starts and wide disagreements, certain literary and philosophical relationships were established. These relationships contributed to our knowledge of literary and cultural history and of Swift's place in it.

There had been interest in the sources and predecessors of *Gulliver's Travels* long before the pursuit of indebtedness became scientifically earnest. Orrery, Scott, Monck Mason, and others had commented on the question of *Gulliver's* sources before 1868, when Canon E. H. Knowles made what must have seemed an auspicious discovery. In *Notes and Queries* for that year,[1] he asked whether anyone had previously called attention to Swift's use of a passage in Sturmy's *Compleat Mariner* (1669), a passage which appeared in *Gulliver* almost verbatim as the description of the storm early in the voyage to Brobdingnag. Few subsequent researchers have been able to point to parallel passages with similar certainty. Knowles's discovery was perhaps an unfortunate example for later students, who were led to search for just such merely verbal parallels or parallels of incident or narrative. Source hunting of this type, so often futile and inconclusive when applied to Swift, led to a yet more mistaken type of study, of which Borkowsky's "Quellen zu Swifts *Gulliver*" (1893) [2] is a good example.

Borkowsky, ostensibly working in the best tradition of *Quellen Studien,* was actually more interested in destroying what he considered to be Swift's undeserved reputation for originality than in establishing Swift's literary relationships. Offering Sturmy and other parallel passages as evidence, Borkowsky apparently hoped to demonstrate that Swift was as dependent upon his sources as Coleridge was upon German philosophers. Indebtedness to More's *Utopia*, Rabelais, Denis Vairasse d'Alais' *L'Histoire des Sévarambes* (1677–79), Gabriel de Foigny's *La Terre australe connue* (1676), and especially Cyrano de Bergerac's *L'Histoire comique de la lune* (1656) was asserted, and relevant passages were compared. For the indebtedness to Cyrano—which had been noted as early as Orrery [3] and more extensively analyzed by Henry Wilson [4]—Borkowsky relied largely upon the more judicious study by Hönncher,[5] which had appeared in *Anglia* in 1888. Though Borkowsky's purpose was primarily to analyze Swift's sources, he also asserted Swift's authorship of *A Voyage to Cacklogallinia* (1727), a desperate conjecture not strengthened by its being based wholly upon a German translation of the work.

Several discussions of sources appeared in the decade following G. Ravenscroft Dennis' edition (1899) of *Gulliver*, the introduction to which included a succinct summary of *Gulliver*'s sources as understood at the turn of the century. In the same year a more detailed review was offered by Paul Thierkopf, *Swifts Gulliver und seine französischen Vorgänger*. An American study, Max Poll's *The Sources of "Gulliver's Travels*," appeared in 1904, followed in 1906–7 by yet another collation and summary of source criticism, Pietro Toldo's "Les Voyages merveilleux de Cyrano de Bergerac et de Swift et leurs rapports avec l'oeuvre de Rabelais." Toldo, besides dealing with Rabelais and Cyrano, took up Swift's relationship to Lucian, More, and Campanella, and pointed out numerous parallels with *The Arabian Nights*, particularly its story of Hassan-al-Bassri, which includes a visit to a land of giants.[6]

William Alfred Eddy's *Gulliver's Travels: A Critical Study*,[7] generally regarded as definitive on the sources, appeared in 1923. Eddy, unlike his predecessors, pursued his research in the light of an explicit but mistaken interpretation of Swift's work, derived primarily from a misconception of Swift's intention. Eddy, seeing that *Gulliver* was in many ways similar to the imaginary voyage of philosophic intent, especially well-represented in French literature,[8] classified it with that genre. He set about to establish systematically the literary relationships between *Gulliver* and other members of its class. However, the parallel passages and the similarities of incident and "conception" which he discovered in works such as Cyrano's *L'Histoire comique de la lune* and *L'Histoire comique du soleil* were merely superficial, for Swift was parodying incidents, conceptions, and especially the *Tendenz* of a tradition to which he was altogether hostile. The French philosophic voyages, of which Cyrano's are good examples, satirized civilization and Christianity in order to glorify natural man, natural "society," and natural, or deistic, religion. Eddy failed to perceive that if Swift used Cyrano and the tradition of the philosophic voyage, he did so to subvert the tradition, not to extend it.[9]

Eddy's misconception of *Gulliver* was not wholly disastrous to his purpose, but it sometimes leads him to dubious decisions on Swift's indebtedness to other works. Thus he contemptuously rejects Churton Collins' assertion that "several strokes for the Yahoos were borrowed from the *Travels* of Sir Thomas Herbert," [10] pointing out that Herbert's "is a dull book" and that Swift's low opinion of the work, recorded on the flyleaf of Swift's own copy, "does not indicate that Swift caught much inspiration from the reading" (p. 66, nn. 73–74). The "inspiration," if one wishes to call it that, which Swift "caught," is of the same order as that which Swift caught in another connection from Anthony Collins' *Discourse of Freethinking*, which, surely, is a "source" for Swift's parody of it, rendered into "Plain English . . . for Use of the Poor."

When discussing the possibility of a connection between *Gulliver* and Segrais' *L'Isle imaginaire* (1658), Eddy sets Segrais aside on similarly questionable grounds. Eddy finds that Segrais' work, which includes a republic of dogs, is not a sincere representation of cultivated animals; it is a burlesque, a deliberate parody of ideal commonwealths. Segrais felt the want of logic and truth in the exaggerated virtue and wisdom attributed to remote peoples by travellers. Why not as well, he implies, attribute utopian government to a race of dogs? Consequently we have represented a Republic of Dogs, but one which is ostensibly a joke. It is not to be supposed that the traveller really discovered these dogs, and the reader is not asked to credit their remarkable virtues. I take it there is a genuine distinction here. The Houyhnhnms are of course fictitious, but the fiction is a serious one. Swift implies that their life is a model one, better than man's (pp. 182–83).

Having missed the ridicule of the philosophic imaginary voyage as a genre, Eddy proceeds to miss the subtle ridicule of the utopias this genre depicted.

The shortcomings of Eddy's work are more than offset by its exhaustiveness. Of the works credited as sources by his predecessors, Eddy chooses to set aside Vairasse, Foigny, More, Godwin, and Herbert, while retaining Lucian, Philostratus, Rabelais, and Cyrano. Eddy justifies some of his rejections of earlier assertions of indebtedness on the ground that the parallels of idea and incident are not peculiar to the alleged source, but are common to the utopian voyage as a genre (pp. 66–67, nn. 74, 77–78)—an argument which suggests that Swift, not content with what he called "hints," was drawing, with truly prodigious grasp, upon the tradition as a whole. Following up a conjecture by E. N. S. Thompson,[11] Eddy suggests indebtedness to Tom Brown's *Amusements Serious and Comical* (1700) for several experiments in Lagado. He persuasively argues Swift's indebtedness to Lucian's *Voyage to Heaven* for the device of inspecting objects from a great height, and to the *Dialogues of the Dead* for the undesirability of immortality embodied in the Struldbrugg episode. Eddy finds in Cyrano's second romance, *L'Histoire comique du soleil,* which he analyzes more thoroughly than previous researchers had, adequate precedent for the alleged scathing denunciation of mankind in the voyage to the Houyhnhnms. An important discovery is Swift's probable use of d'Ablancourt's French translation of Lucian,[12] especially d'Ablancourt's continuation of the *True History*, which adds visits to "l'île des animaux . . . quelle était environée de celle des géans, des magiciens, et des pygmées." Most of the traceable similarities of narrative structure or of incident present in other imaginary voyages, Eddy has laid bare.

Eddy is lured away from the imaginary voyage and his preoccupation with purely literary sources when he fails to find a literary source for the "one fundamental idea" of the voyages to Lilliput and Brobdingnag. He defines this idea as "the relativity of human life and its values," and he traces it to Berkeley's *A New Theory of Vision* (1709). Here again, if a relationship exists at all, it is an extremely tenuous one. Lemuel Gulliver might conceivably draw upon relativist theory in order to point his moral or adorn his tale, as he does when exclaiming over the perspicuity of philosophers, who "undoubtedly . . . are in the right when they tell us that nothing is either great or little otherwise than by comparison" (II, i; HD, XI, 71),[13] but this is not to say, as Eddy does, that Swift in such instances is writing a tract in favor of relativism and that among the philosophers "undoubtedly in the right" is Swift's friend, George Berkeley.[14]

Two reviews of Eddy's work praised its exhaustiveness within the limits set but stressed the need for going beyond those limits. Émile Pons quarreled with Eddy's rough handling of some of his predecessors (especially Borkowsky) and with his dismissal of Swift's alleged indebtedness to More, Foigny, and Vairasse [15]; but he was enthusiastic over Eddy's discovery of Swift's indebtedness to d'Ablancourt, though he found Eddy's analysis of this literary relationship less full than he had hoped for.[16] Pons regarded Eddy's distaste for the Houyhnhnms and the fourth voyage generally as a result of the inadequacy of Eddy's critical method and urged the use of biographical and psychological methods for the solution of the complex critical problem of the fourth voyage. A. W. Secord, also looking beyond relationships in the literary genre, regretted that Eddy, though willing to discuss Berkeley, Sturmy, and Herbert, none of whom wrote imaginary voyages, neglected native sources and traditions, especially authentic voyages.[17] Secord is inclined to accept Eddy's account, as far as it goes, of *Gulliver*'s sources, though he objects to Eddy's rather equivocal handling of Holberg's *Journey of Klimius to the World Underground.*[18]

Secord's suggestion that Gulliver owed much to authentic voyages was proved sound when studies by R. W. Frantz and Willard Bonner appeared in the thirties. Frantz, in "Swift's Yahoos and the Voyagers" (1931),[19] an article distinguished as much for its thoroughness as for the restraint of its conclusions, traces almost all the disagreeable traits of the Yahoos to accounts of monkeys and savages in books of authentic travel by Dampier, Herbert, Wafer, and others. Placed alongside Gulliver's description of the Yahoos, the morbidly sensational passages in these accounts seem to out-Swift Swift in their disgustingness and filth. They are at the same time a striking contrast to descriptions of "noble savages" common in imaginary voyages and less frequent in accounts of authentic voyagers. While Frantz's study considerably strengthens Collins' claim for Swift's use of Herbert, its importance lies primarily in its demonstration of a general relationship between the authentic voyages and *Gulliver,* whose comedy derives partially from its elaborate pretense of authenticity.

A review of the major conclusions regarding Swift's sources up to 1932 appeared in Harold Williams' *Dean Swift's Library* (Cambridge, 1932), a valuable catalog and description of books owned by Swift, based on two manuscript lists, the original sale catalog (1745), and Williams' own extensive knowledge of Swiftiana. This volume was apparently in the press before account could be taken of Frantz's study on the voyagers, and it preceded by several years other important developments in source studies of *Gulliver.* Among these is Willard Bonner's useful book on the vogue of travel literature in the early eighteenth century, *Captain William Dampier: Buccaneer-Author* (Stanford,

1934). Dampier, whom Gulliver claims as a "cousin," was the foremost voyager and explorer of his time, the late seventeenth and early eighteenth centuries. His scrupulously kept journals, written often under severe hardship and, on at least one occasion, preserved for the eyes of civilization by being sealed in a bamboo cane, stimulated the unprecedented rage for travel books. Henry Deunting, a Grubstreet writer, exploited it by preparing a volume entitled *The Travels of the Holy Patriarchs, Prophets, Judges, Kings, Our Saviour Christ, and His Apostles, as They Are Related in the Old and New Testament: With a Description of the Towns and Places to Which They Travelled, and How Many English Miles They Stood from Jerusalem* (p. 62). The feverish preparation of travel books led some authors to curious shifts of composition. Authentic voyagers were not above heightening their material with flights of imagination. Pseudo-travellers were, of course, even more reliant upon imagination, when they weren't plagiarizing authentic accounts or the works of their fellows. Fraudulent travel accounts (a classic hoax in the history of England, George Psalmanazar's pose as a Formosan and his subsequent *Historical and Geographical Description of Formosa,* 1704, is a hoax which bears some relation to Gulliver itself [20]) were welcomed by the eighteenth-century public, which, as Bonner points out, was "travel-crazy."

It was this taste and the ways it was met which Swift in his own way sought to exploit. There is abundant evidence that he was deeply read in travel literature.[21] Bonner's chapter on Swift's relation to Dampier makes all the obvious connections, including Swift's use of Dampier's unceremonious, factual style, and his spoofing with Dampier's nautical jargon, a mode of literary borrowing which Davis has called "Swift's regular practice, something which varies between parody and imitation, and provides him with the roles of Bickerstaff, Drapier, and Gulliver," and in Dampier's case, "lends him the very speech of this plain, serious and honest seaman with eager curiosity and notable gift for veracity." [22]

Ricardo Quintana in *The Mind and Art of Jonathan*

Swift (1936), glances sceptically, as did Williams, at the methods and results of the source study of *Gulliver* (pp. 296–303). His penetrating discussion clarifies and summarizes whatever of value had thus far emerged from this approach to Swift's work. He takes issue with Gilbert Chinard,[23] who saw a source for *Gulliver* in Baron de Lahontan's *Dialogues curieux entre l'auteur et un sauvage de bon sens qui a voyagé* (1702), a *libertin*, primitivist work. Quintana points out that the striking parallels which Chinard noted are merely superficial, for if Swift used Lahontan at all, "he took over from the *libertin* not the barest shadow of the latter's real meaning." In Lahontan, for instance, the gentle and virtuous savages attribute some of the evils of civilization to civilized man's use of salt. This is precisely the kind of environmentalist nonsense that would draw Swift's fire, and when he has Gulliver declare his own liberation from salt, claiming that he knew of "no Animal to be fond of it but Man" (IV, ii; HD, XI, 216), this manifest absurdity was meant to speak for itself.[24] The technique here is, in Davis' words, "something . . . between imitation and parody," but we must take care not to regard it as mere imitation.

Because the voyage to Laputa, often called the least successful of the travels, resisted early attempts to discover its sources, some critics concluded that its weakness derived from Swift's having relied on personal idiosyncrasy instead of source material.[25] This view became untenable when, in 1937, Marjorie Nicolson and Nora Mohler[26] presented their remarkable discovery of Swift's use of the *Philosophical Transactions* and other publications of the Royal Society for all but two of the projects in the Grand Academy. Not a mere catalog of parallel passages, Nicholson and Mohler's article also deals with Swift's design and technique in appropriating, with peculiar fidelity, his source material: "For the most part, he simply set down before his readers experiments actually performed by members of the Royal Society, more preposterous to the layman than anything imagination could invent and more devastating in their satire because of their essential truth to source." Alterations, when present, extend at most to ridiculously combining two experiments or carrying an experiment "one step further—and the added step carries us over the precipice of nonsense" (p. 322).

In another article Nicolson and Mohler examine the derivation of the Flying Island. They find its origin, like that of the projects of the Grand Academy, in contemporary science, particularly in the dipping needle and terrella of William Gilbert. In addition to its part in the allegory of English-Irish relations, the Flying Island is a parody of the numerous and fantastic flying machines which appeared in the science fiction of Swift's day, the imaginary extra-terrestrial voyage. Of this genre Miss Nicolson has more to say in her admirable study, *Voyages to the Moon* (New York, 1948) [27] which illuminates, among other things, Swift's relation to the genre.

R. W. Frantz returned to *Gulliver*'s sources in 1938 with "Gulliver's 'Cousin Sympson,'" [28] in which he conclusively demonstrated Swift's use of a hitherto unnoticed source, *A New Voyage to the East Indies* (1715). Frantz suggested that "William Symson," the pretended author of this imaginary—and largely plagiarized—travel book may have had some connection with Gulliver's equally fictitious cousin, "Richard Sympson." [29] The parallel passage noted by Frantz, evidently the source of Gulliver's description of Lilliputian and other writing habits, supersedes a less similar passage in *L'Histoire des Sévarambes* which Borkowsky had pointed out.[30] Swift, as always, makes of his source something different if not wholly new: to the three kinds of writing described in Symson, including the predecessor of "aslant from one Corner of the Paper to the other, like Ladies in England," Swift adds yet another method, "from down to up," solemnly ascribed to "the Cascagians" (I, vi; HD, XI, 41).

In 1941 John R. Moore [31] argued for yet another *libertin* voyage as a source for *Gulliver*, Tyssot de Patot's *Voyages et aventures de Jacques Massé* (1710), and in doing so challenged Eddy's assertion that individually the realistic imaginary voyages, of which Tyssot's is an example, had no

significance as forerunners of *Gulliver,* since "no direct relation to any of them can be traced" (Eddy, p. 29). Moore
notes a great many resemblances, none very convincing, such
as Massé's and Gulliver's both being ship's surgeons, Swift's
and Tyssot's disapprobation of war, fire-fighting in Swift and
Tyssot (in both, alarms are sounded and ladders are used),
and the presence in Tyssot of a strange animal which appears
to be a cross between a Houyhnhnm and a Yahoo. Moore
recognizes that Swift and Tyssot were philosophically uncongenial, but except for his comment that the conclusion
of Gulliver's exploit as fireman seems an "almost conscious
burlesque" of a corresponding passage in *Massé,* Moore
leaves unexplored whatever tactical relation Gulliver might
have to *Massé.*

The last two decades have seen a falling off of source
studies on *Gulliver,* perhaps in part because of the feeling
that the task is essentially completed, and in part because of
an awareness, reflected in the studies of Nicolson and
Mohler, Bonner, and Frantz, that Swift's satire can best be
understood when placed against broad traditions rather than
particular works. While there is a great deal of the topical
and the particular in *Gulliver's Travels,* its literary satire, no
less than its political, is by no means limited to isolated
skirmishes.

Somewhat outside the main stream of source studies is
Margaret R. Grennan's exploration of Swift's possible use of
Irish folklore in the first two voyages, "Lilliput and Leprecan:
Gulliver and the Irish Tradition" (1945).[32] Unsympathetic to
suggestions that the Lilliputians are related to Ctesius' "horrible grubs" and to the pygmies, Miss Grennan seeks to trace
their "charm" and "humanity" to the Irish leprechaun tradition. Miss Grennan, aware of the obvious objections to her
argument, claims that Lilliput "owes much of its charm to
Swift's partial surrender to a spirit not entirely his own," that
"perhaps, in spite of himself, the native speech went deep
into the unwilling consciousness of the Dean," and that these
uncongenial elements were "retained by a disapproving but

retentive memory." This is as close to invoking "the deep well of unconscious cerebration" as Swift source-seeking has ever come.

The direction of Miss Grennan's work indicates, perhaps, that students of Swift's sources have taken to heart Harold Williams' caveat to "the restless discoverer of source books" whose "eager search in hidden corners for similarities of phrase or narrative may easily become a mistaken pastime." How easily we have already seen. Our knowledge of Swift's use of Sturmy, for instance, welcome though it may be, does not alter the value, aptness, and perspicuity of Scott's note on the passage ("This is a parody upon the accounts of storms and naval manoeuvres frequent in old voyages and is merely an assemblage of sea terms, put together at random.")—written a half-century before Knowles's discovery—a note which remains its best comment.[33] Nonetheless, a proper understanding of Swift's literary relationships tells us a great deal about the intent and character of the satire, its relation to its traditions, and, in the fullest Aristotelian sense, its nature.

NONSENSE WORDS

The diminishing of interest in *Gulliver's* sources has been counterbalanced by a surge of interest in the sources of the imaginary languages which Gulliver encounters, and masters, in his several travels. The value of studying these languages is dubious at best. All such studies proceed on the questionable assumption that Swift has hidden a decipherable meaning in words such as *Brobdingnag, Lengro Dehulsan, Tolgo Phomac, Grildrig, Glumdalclitch,* and the host of others. The startlingly mild apprehensions of most glossographers quickly evaporate once the chase is on. Harold Kelling recognizes "that Swift might scorn the pedantry of such an investigation,"[34] and Paul Odell Clark pauses to protest the conjectural nature of his findings before launching into his petulant, exhaustive, usually scriblerian "*Gulliver* Dictionary."[35] Swift used "the Anagrammatick Method" in at least two instances: *Tribnia* and *Langden*—which occur, no doubt designedly, in a passage given over to the discussion of "the Anagrammatick Method"—are indeed "Britain" and "England." But one may still doubt, as did Harold Williams when noting Morley's anagrammatic gloss of *Brobdingnag*,[36] whether Swift "intended to expose himself to the penetration of 'a man of Skill in this Art.' "[37] To this art recent research has added others, more esoteric, such as the art of detecting—and penetrating—assimilation, dissimilation, metathesis, macaronism, reduplication, reversal, substitution, and other alleged disguises behind which meanings lurk.

In a series of studies on the imaginary languages commonly found in the utopian voyages, Pons (1930–32)[38] offered valuable background material for students of Swift's fictional tongues. Unfortunately, no subsequent study of the invented words in *Gulliver* has compared Swift's "languages" with the utopian languages customarily offered as "improvements" over the modern European as well as ancient tongues. Indeed, all of Gulliver's comments on language might well be studied in the light of this tradition, a tradition to which Swift was attracted as cats are to mice. Pons's later study, "Rabelais et Swift à propos du Lilliputien,"[39] while it successfully and valuably relates Swift's words in Lilliput to the *jargons* in Rabelais, leaves something to be desired in this regard.

The first of the more recent studies of the outlandish names and words in *Gulliver* was that by Kelling in 1951, "Some Significant Names in *Gulliver's Travels*." Kelling wisely avoids imputing esoteric sources to the invented words and warns against finding any elaborate systems in Swift's word manipulations, pointing out that "Swift's ingenuity is not likely to be bound by any system or systems" (p. 776). Kelling views each word as a separate problem, though he does note repeated use of reversal and substitution of letters, the latter of which he traces to the little language in the *Journal to Stella*. A word with a system all its own is *Lindalino*, in which Kelling notes that the "double *lin*" and the Irish word *da*, meaning "two," indicate "Dublin," a happy conjecture which the context supports. Other conjectures are more elaborate. *Houyhnhnm,* which Gulliver tells us means "Perfection of Nature" in its etymology, Kelling renders as *manni voc,* an approximation of the Latin for "speaking horses," which he is able to find in the word by means of reversal, substitution, and omission. The gloss of *Ranfu-Lo,* which takes us by a devious route to a poem by Palladas in the *Greek Anthology,* is admittedly farfetched, and remains, in effect, "breeches," as Gulliver himself tells us. *Nardac,* the title the Lilliputians bestow on Gulliver and of which he is so proud, is more rewarding; Kelling suggests German *Narr,* "fool," and *doch,* "still," or "then," giving us the title, "still a fool," which has in its favor at least its comic effect.

Paul Odell Clark's ostensibly conjectural *"Gulliver* Dictionary" was apparently completed, except for footnotes, before the appearance of Kelling's article. Unlike Kelling, Clark finds in the languages a systematic and pervasive use of several techniques of distortion, chief among which are those found in the little language of the *Journal to Stella.* Using as a kind of guide Ehrenpreis' analysis [40] of the substitutions common in the *Journal,* Clark constructs a frequency chart (p. 595) of consonantal substitutions in *Gulliver,* and goes on to distinguish "other techniques in Swift's repertory of deception," including the several techniques mentioned above. While Clark insists that "there is nothing esoteric about the code" and that "a similar table of exchanges Swift could easily have derived from any of a number of grammars," he thinks it "doubtful that Swift needed to consult [such] authorities directly: his interest in anagrams and like verbal games, his friendship with Sheridan, the little language itself—all these conclusively indicate that we need not hesitate in ascribing the development of such a code as this to Swift" (p. 598).

Of the glosses given in Clark's dictionary only a few can be mentioned here. *Hekinah Degul,* the exclamation sounded several times by the Lilliputians upon their discovery of Gulliver, is rendered in a relatively simple translation relying wholly on similarities of sound, as "What in the Devil." *Tolgo*

Phomac, the Lilliputian battle cry, is tentatively rendered, with understandable embarrassment, as "Let go vomit." *Borach Mivola,* which Clark calls "one of the finest examples of Swift's deliberate playfulness and experimentation with sound patterns," has, he asserts, undergone reversal and other systematic jumbling in order to hide the Latin *volat cibor(i)a,* "He hurls the drinking cups." Clark traces *ciboria* to Horace's *Carmina,* II, vii, which, as does *Gulliver* at this point, involves prodigious draughts. Gulliver tells us *Lengro Dehulsan* means essentially "Untie him." Clark finds that the code and Gulliver do not agree, the code yielding rather "Run from the wild man" or "Run from the devil man," depending upon the disposition of *Dehul.* The reason for the discrepancy between Gulliver and the code is that "Gulliver was not then too well acquainted with the Lilliputian tongue and misrepresented the actual meaning" (p. 601). Clark views *Lindalino* as an augmented anagram for "Ireland," but he gives it a secondary gloss as "Dublin," which agrees with Kelling's treatment of the word.[41]

A perceptive and potentially valuable point made early in the article is left undeveloped in the dictionary. Clark suggests that Swift "causes Gulliver (and us, his readers) to say things we are all unaware of; yea, even *to say the thing that was not.* This is an old cheat. A common practical joke, reported about American soldiers and Koreans, is to teach strangers to greet others with obscene vulgarisms in the belief that they are being excessively polite. This is what Swift does to us" (p. 599). If for the moment we may set aside the ill-advised pronoun "us," hoping that we need not willingly choose to be among Swift's victims, this observation on Swift's technique seems apt. One looks in vain, however, among Clark's translations for its application and illustration. If Gulliver's Brobdingnagian name, *Grildrig,* which Clark is satisfied he has "translated sensibly in relation to the code and context of the *Travels,*" is, as he says, "Girl-thing" or "doll," one may yet prefer the comedy of Gulliver's own straight-faced gloss—"the Word imports what the Latins call *Nanunculus,* the Italians *Homunceletino,* and the English

79

Mannikin" (II, ii; HD, XI, 79). Indeed, Gulliver's explanation *is* comedy, while the translation in Clark's dictionary, except in some irrelevant, scriblerian way, is not.

Roland M. Smith's attempt to show that Swift's source for the little language was Edward Lhuyd's *Archaeologia Britannica* (1707) has already been mentioned in connection with the textual problems of the *Journal to Stella*. The same article goes on to argue that the distortions found in the *Journal* and traceable to Lhuyd are also present in the nonsense names in *Gulliver*.[42] Smith, like Kelling and Clark, finds that Swift used the further distortions of reversal, reduplication, etc., "to guard the secrets of his coinages" (p. 195). In one instance Smith emends the text, choosing to fall in with the suggestion in the letter to Sympson that *Brobdingnag* throughout the book was a misspelling and should have been *Brobdingrag*. By reversal, *Brobdingrag* yields *garg-nid-borb*, the first and last elements of which appear in Lhuyd: "*Garg: Austere, fierce, cruel,* &c.," and "*Borb: Fierce, cruel, severe.*" *Nid*, the middle element, is taken to be "Swift's disguise for English *and*." These then combine to make up a redundant epithet at least occasionally appropriate to the breed.

Smith generally approves of Kelling's findings, though he cautions against uncritical use of Dinneen's *Irish-English Dictionary* (1927), upon which Kelling had occasionally relied, Smith urging instead the use of Lhuyd's *Dictionary*, which is the tenth and last part of the *Archaeologia*. Kelling's explanation of *Glumdalclitch* ("enormous nurse," from French *grand* and Latin *altrix*), however, he regards as "a series of desperate guesses," and argues instead for reversal: "Glum=mulg, 'butt' or 'shapeless lump' . . . dalc=clad, 'clutching hand' + litch = chil'(d)!" but adds that "as these elements do not appear in Lhuyd or Begley [*English-Irish Dictionary* (1732)], one should not stake his life on the belief that Swift had all or even part of this interpretation in mind" (p. 185).[43] In a "Supplementary Note" Smith takes issue with Clark, who, by his "failure to take Swift's Irish background into account" and by ignoring "the likelihood that Swift drew upon Irish words as sources," "has built himself a house of glass from which he can ill afford to throw stones at Pons and Kelling" (p. 196). The whir of flying stones and the tinkling of glass continue to be heard, however, especially in a recent angry exchange between Clark and Smith,[44] which prompts one to conclude that we are as far as ever from a solution of these vexing problems.

POLITICAL SATIRE

Credit for illuminating the political satire in *Gulliver's Travels* falls largely to two scholars, Sir Charles Firth and A. E. Case. For his "The Political Significance of *Gulliver's Travels*" (1919) [45] Firth had the use of the then unpublished Swift-Ford correspondence (which also contains crucial evidence on the dates of composition for each of the voyages).[46] On the topical political satire in *Gulliver* Firth's conclusions have met with mixed reactions. While his identifications of Flimnap as Walpole and Skyresh Bolgolam as Nottingham have received wide support, his explanations of Reldresal, Munodi, the Yahoos, and Gulliver himself have been challenged by Case in the notes to his edition of *Gulliver* (1938) and in *Four Essays*. Firth identifies Reldresal as Lord Carteret, Case identifies him as Charles Viscount Townshend; likewise Munodi, whom Firth identified as Lord Middleton, Case finds rather to be Oxford. Rejecting as too topical and particular Firth's association of the Yahoos with "the savage old Irish," a view which Eddy had supported in his Oxford Standard edition of *Gulliver*,[47] Case says that Swift "had set up a larger canvas: his atelier was Ireland, his model England, his portrait that of Western Civilization" (*Four Essays*, p. 123). Firth had seen in some of Gulliver's experiences in Lilliput the political history of Swift and Bolingbroke during and after the reign of Queen Anne. Case, on the other hand, found here nothing of Swift's own political experience, but rather that of Oxford and Bolingbroke. This leads Case to a major disagreement with Firth over Gulliver's offense as fireman. Firth, following Sir Walter Scott, J. F. Waller, W. C. Taylor, and G. Ravenscroft Dennis, took the incident to represent Swift's indiscretion in publishing *A Tale of a Tub*. Case finds the incident rather an allegorical representation of the Peace of Utrecht, the fire itself then being the War of the Spanish Succession. The peace policy of Oxford had, of course, been extremely unpopular in some quarters, and it is said that Oxford, in negotiating with the queen for the peace, had offended her several times by appearing drunk in her presence. Case agrees with the generally held view that Flimnap represents Walpole, but he prefers to regard the first voyage, at least in its topical implications, as a defense of the Oxford-Bolingbroke ministry and only incidentally as an attack on the Whigs (p. 80).

Irvin Ehrenpreis in a recent article [48] largely supported Case on these matters but disagreed regarding the relative importance of Bolingbroke and Oxford in the Lilliputian allegory. Ehrenpreis minimized Oxford's role, arguing rather for the predominance of Bolingbroke: "By 1721, after all, it was not Oxford who wanted defending: he had been discharged from his impeachment in 1717, and he acted a free role in the House of Lords until his death in 1724—well before the completion of *Gulliver's Travels*. Bolingbroke, meanwhile, having fled to France in 1715, remained attainted and in exile until 1723; and he never regained his seat in the House of Lords" (pp. 88–89).

"Political Theory in *Gulliver's Travels*," [49] by Z. S. Fink, is an examination of some of the positive political ideas expressed in *Gulliver* and associated with Swift. Swift held the "gothic" state, in which power was divided among kings, nobles, and commoners, to be England's only check against tyranny. Fink points out, that the source of this idea is not gothic (nor, as some might think, Whig), but classical; Swift found its most perfect expression in the Roman Republic at its best. Swift had enunciated the principles of this sort of mixed government in the *Contests and Dissensions in Athens and Rome* in 1701. The frequent strictures in *Gulliver* against the chaos and destruction of rule by party and faction are another expression of this same ideal, which Fink describes as "the tradition of the partyless state dear to the hearts of the classical republicans of the Puritan era and their Renaissance predecessors" (p. 157). Brobdingnag, for instance, is a partyless state, and the Brobdingnagian king laughingly asks Gulliver whether he was a Whig or a Tory. Similarly, the hostility to standing armies, clearly expressed in the voyage to Brobdingnag, reflects fear that the accumulation of power represented by a standing army would upset the balance of power in the state. A citizens' army is less prone to this abuse, and so we find in the modified utopia of Brobdingnag the establishment by common consent of a militia, but only after a long period of strife, presumably the result of earlier experimentation. Fink also takes up deteriorationism, an essential theme in the conservative cast of *Gulliver*. Fink traces the several instances in the work where societies have degenerated from earlier, more excellent stages, such as the seemingly utopian sixth chapter of the first voyage, and the Brobdingnagian king's observations on European manners and customs, in which he discerned "some Lines of an Institution, which in its Original might have been tolerable, but these half erased, and the rest wholly blurred and blotted by Corruptions" (II, vi; HD, XI, 116). For Swift, disruption from within was more of a threat to the stability of the state than disruption from without.

These and other conservative elements of *Gulliver* are given close and lively attention by George Orwell in his "Politics vs. Literature: An Examination of *Gulliver's Travels*," published posthumously in *Shooting an Elephant and Other Essays* (New York, 1950, pp. 53–76). Orwell is aware of the gulf separating his own hopeful liberalism and, as he puts it, "the reactionary cast of Swift's mind" (p. 57), and though this open political hostility leads to some curious judgments, it is not as disastrous critically as might be expected. Orwell's observations on the totalitarian character of public opinion in Houyhnhnmland—"less tolerant than any system of law" (p. 66); on the "dreary" Houyhnhnms themselves, whose "reason" he finds to be in effect a "death wish" (p. 69), and for whom we can feel at best only "dislike" (p. 68); and on Swift's "extraordinarily clear pre-vision of the spy-haunted 'police state,' with its endless heresy-hunts and treason trials" (p. 62), carry the peculiar weight and force of one great satirist commenting upon another, though the separation between them—both historical and political— was wide. Orwell's habit of translating Swift into twentieth- century political terms and associating him with various nineteenth- and twentieth-century rightists, such as W. H. Mallock and Ronald Knox, has been commented on by Quin- tana (*Swift: An Introduction,* pp. 28–31). Nonetheless, Or- well's description of Swift's "vision" in *Gulliver* as "the Chris- tian attitude, minus the bribe of a 'next world' " (p. 75) is surprisingly similar to some recent and considerably more sympathetic interpretations of Swift—interpretations which, however, would not be likely to agree that Swift's is "a world-view which only just passes the test of sanity" (p. 76). Yet it is precisely this vision, given the artistry of its expres- sion in *Gulliver,* for which Orwell values the work, declaring that in it "enjoyment can overwhelm disapproval, even though one clearly recognizes that one is enjoying something inimical" (p. 73). For Orwell, *Gulliver* apparently satisfies what I. A. Richards has called an appetency.

GEOGRAPHY

The old gentleman, of whom Arbuthnot tells, who went to his map to look for Lilliput, was probably the first in a tradition of serious students of the geography of *Gulliver's Travels.* In the mid-nineteenth cen- tury Swift's chaotic, error-filled geography was exposed in *Notes and Queries* by Augustus De Morgan,[50] but it was only in this century that critical attention produced exhaustive studies of this matter. Case's 1938 edition of *Gulliver* stimu- lated this attention by pointing out that the geography of the work could be made quite reasonable and credible once two "printer's errors" were corrected. Thus, if the location of Lilliput were changed from northwest of Van Diemen's Land (Tasmania) to north*east,* and the latitude left as the text gives it, 30° 2′ S, Lilliput could then be moved out from the interior of Australia into the open sea. The hapless mapmaker employed by Motte to illustrate the first edition, faced with such erroneous information, had no choice but, as Case later put it, "ruthlessly" to erase Australia from the map. The other error, which occurs in the first chapter of the voyage to Laputa, mislocates the point at which Gulliver was seized by the pirates. In order to make the geographical data of the voyage consistent and permit a reasonable location for Laputa, Case emends the reading of the text from 46° N 183° E to 20° N 145° E. Once these two errors are corrected, the Gulliverian geography, Case promises, will fit reasonably, if not neatly, into the known world of the eighteenth century. Case presented a more thorough and documented exposition of this argument in "The Geography and Chronology of *Gulliver's Travels*," in *Four Essays* (1945), where he also supplied a "Gulliverian Hemisphere," a composite map of the charts and information found in the early editions, but emended and modified in the light of his conclusions.

Case's argument did not settle the question. Quintana, reviewing *Four Essays* in 1947, thought that while "Swift never devised in his own mind as clear-cut and consistent a map as Case implies," nonetheless Case had "disposed of once and for all" the theory "that the hopeless confusion of the geographical details in the *Travels* is part of the satire." [51] But John R. Moore was less convinced. In "The Geography of *Gulliver's Travels*" (1941),[52] Moore called Swift's geography "incredible" and posed three possible explanations: "(1) that Swift intended an extravagant burlesque on the voyages, or (2) that he was ignorant of geography, or (3) that he intended a burlesque and knew too little to carry it out accurately." Moore seems to waver between the second and third explanations. He demonstrates the incredibility of the geography by pointing out that Brobdingnag contains three times the area of North America, forty times that of Alaska (with which it had been associated by Bonner [*Dampier*, p. 176]), and just under one half the total land area of the world.

The map used by the mapmakers as a basis for the charts in the Motte edition was convincingly identified by Frederick Bracher [53] in 1944 as "A New and Correct Map of the Whole

World" (1719), by Herman Moll. Besides making further conjectures on the identities of Motte's mapmakers and the difficulties they faced in dealing with the geographical data offered by the text, Bracher comments on the significance of the geography in the interpretation of the work. Agreeing with Moore on Swift's "errors" and "carelessness," Bracher finds that Swift's treatment of geographic details not only "provides additional evidence of his contempt for natural, as opposed to moral philosophy" but also reveals his disdain for "the kind of knowledge embodied in maps, voyages, and geographical works" (p. 73), a judgment which Louis Landa,[54] in an otherwise favorable comment on Bracher's findings, considered to be an overstatement. Bracher concludes that the maps provide a kind of supplementary comedy which Swift had no reason to discourage. The too credulous reader will be "bewildered and irritated" by the geographical inaccuracies, and Swift, as Bracher points out, would enjoy this sort of "bite" just as he did the story about the Irish bishop who said that *Gulliver* "was full of improbable lies, and for his part, he hardly believed a word of it" (p. 74).

On the meaning of Swift's jumbled geography, critics continue to limit themselves to wary comments. George Sherburn, reviewing *Four Essays* in 1946,[55] refuses to come down on either side. In one paragraph he indicts Swift for errors and carelessness, suggesting that critics who praise Swift's "simplicity and clarity of style" ought to be embarrassed by his handling of geography, in which so many details are "grossly and complexly inconsistent"; in another paragraph he recognizes the possibility that in the geography "Swift is burlesquing voyage-writing," and here the word "faults" appears hedged round with quotation marks.

HISTORY OF IDEAS

The study of the history of ideas, so important in eighteenth-century studies generally, has played a major part in Swift studies, and especially in studies of *Gulliver*. Lucius W. Elder's "The Pride of the

Yahoo," [56] which appeared in 1920, was the first critical work of this century to approach *Gulliver* by way of the history of ideas. Elder takes Gulliver's final execration on pride as an occasion for exploring the grounds on which pride was condemned during the Renaissance and Enlightenment. Elder confines himself to the social and psychological effects of pride, to pride as a passion in individual men, and he finds Swift's treatment to be typical of his time. The Yahoos are irrational because they are creatures of passion, including the passion of pride; the passionless Houyhnhnms extol reason and are free of pride. This interpretation of the fourth voyage, similar to the one common among nineteenth-century critics, remained dominant in the early twentieth century and can be found in such important critics as Firth, Eddy, F. R. Leavis, Basil Willey, Case, and the early Quintana.

The first strong challenge to the prevailing view came in 1926 when Theodore O. Wedel, using the history of ideas as evidence in his "On the Philosophical Background of *Gulliver's Travels*," [57] attempted to explain the widespread misunderstanding of *Gulliver* from 1726 on. He found the causes of this misunderstanding in the rapidly shifting intellectual currents of the seventeenth and eighteenth centuries. Wedel notes "the failure of posterity to appreciate the philosophical thesis of *Gulliver's Travels*" and goes on to explain this failure as the result of revolutionary changes in thought taking place in the seventeenth and eighteenth centuries. Pascal, La Rochefoucauld, Boileau, Montaigne, and Bayle, says Wedel, would have understood Swift, but their pessimism about human nature and their scepticism about human reason were now giving way to a new optimism toward human nature and reason. Rational, optimistic, sentimental theodicies—those of Hutcheson and Burnet are cited as examples—made an "avowed or tacit denial of the doctrine of original sin," thus "explaining away the evil from this best of all possible worlds." Readers of *Gulliver* in the eighteenth century and after, under the influence of the new view (Wedel suggests that by 1726 it was the dominant view and that " 'the dignity of human nature' was on everyone's lips"), could be expected to find the pessimism expressed in *Gulliver* uncongenial and repugnant, if they understood it at all. There will, of course, be exceptions, and Wedel points to John Wesley, who in 1757 quoted heavily from the fourth voyage in order to illustrate his *Doctrine of Original Sin*.

There had been hints of this view of *Gulliver* earlier. Courthope had called attention to Swift's pyrrhonism [58] and, as we saw in Chapter I, Thomas Tyler, an obscure scholar and habitué of the British Museum, had expressed something not unlike this in a letter to the *Academy* in 1883 [59]—but a twentieth-century movement in which this view is basic began with Wedel's interpretation.[60] Where Elder had seen the Houyhnhnms as a rational ideal toward which Swift, no less than Gulliver, was sympathetic, Wedel sees the Houyhnhnms as representing the impossible ideal of stoic self-sufficiency. The Yahoos, on the other hand, are pure animality, passion unrestrained by any touch of reason. "Designedly or not," writes Wedel, "we have in the last voyage Hobbes contrasted with Locke," meaning by this apparently that the Yahoos are men in Hobbes's state of nature, while the Houyhnhnms represent an overambitious ideal of reason which Wedel associates with Locke (an association which is perhaps not wholly proper in view of the sharp limits which Locke placed on the activities of reason). Wedel finds Swift to be "neither Hobbes nor Locke, just as Gulliver is neither Yahoo nor Houyhnhnm. . . . Gulliver, occupying a position between the two, part beast, part reason, is Swift's allegorical picture of the dual nature of man. He is not Houyhnhnm, *animal rationale*, nor is he Yahoo. He is *rationis capax*" (pp. 442–43). While Wedel's treatment of chronology, his handling of the "rationalism" of Locke, and his definition of such terms as "optimism" and "the classical and Christian tradition" were not as rigorous as could be hoped, his analysis was inspired and, within its limits, wholly accurate.

Rigorousness in definition and method was combined with the nineteenth-century view of Swift in Gordon McKenzie's "Swift: Reason and Some of Its Consequences" (1940).[61] Here we find a common practice among historians of ideas: the exhaustive analysis of a complex of meanings in a particular word or concept. "Reason," the word McKenzie chose to analyze, is a central one in Swift and in *Gulliver's Travels*. McKenzie finds that Swift gratuitously appropriates a meaning of the word from mystics and religious enthusiasts such as the Cambridge Platonists, availing himself tacitly of their supernatural, ideal world of vision, while at the same time using the word to mean clear, passionless thinking, thinking which is less intuitive and visionary than it is a kind of process, a means of inference. Swift, according to McKenzie, yearned for the harmony, unity, and quietude suggested in the first meaning of the word, but found himself in a real world full of dissent, disharmony and strife, where reason as a *process* permitted men to "argue with plausibility on both sides of the question." McKenzie sees this unresolvable conflict as the source of Swift's conservatism, his hostility to contemporary empiricism in science and philosophy, his opposition to all forms of dissent and all forms of speculation, his intolerance generally, his consequent bitterness and unhappiness, even his success as a satirist. "The savagery of his attack seems to function as the nervous balancing element to the impossibility of his ideal," and in *Gulliver* the very hopelessness of his ideal "provided him with a tremendous impetus to destroy." In *Gulliver* this ideal is taken to be embodied in the land of the Houyhnhnms, Swift's means of suggesting that "through reason the ordinary world could become utopia" (p. 102).

McKenzie's approach to Swift and to *Gulliver* testifies to the continuing viability of the nineteenth-century interpretation. There is the gloomy, ferocious satirist caught in hostile forces beyond his control, and the literary expression of his despair—*Gulliver's Travels*—solemnly offering an impossible ideal. While Wedel's view has strengthened among mid-twentieth-century Swift critics, the attractions of McKenzie's position, as we will see, are particularly irresistible to the non-specialist writing impressionistically of Swift and his work.

An interpretation close to Wedel's emerges from four

articles published since 1950: Kathleen Williams' two studies,
"Gulliver's Voyage to the Houyhnhnms" (1951) and "'Animal Rationis Capax,' A Study of Certain Aspects of Swift's Imagery" (1954),[62] Ernest Tuveson's "Swift: The Dean as Satirist" (1953),[63] and Samuel H. Monk's "The Pride of Lemuel Gulliver" (1955).[64] It would be too much to say that these critics are in perfect agreement on the meaning and effect of *Gulliver,* but they do represent a degree of unanimity rare in twentieth-century Swift criticism. Each of these studies embodies the best insights of the recent rhetorical studies of *Gulliver* and thus combines a sound critical approach with a firm grasp of Swift's relation to the intellectual currents of his time. These critics' common recognition of the limitations Swift placed on reason is a decisive development in current Swift criticism.

The first of Miss Williams' articles carefully reviews the problem of Swift's attitude toward the Houyhnhnms. The problem is made difficult by Swift's satiric artistry, a characteristic of which "is precisely his inability, or his refusal, to present us straightforwardly with a positive to aim at." While this habit "may be, at bottom, a psychological or spiritual weakness," Swift "turns it to satiric strength, and produces satire which is comfortless but is also disturbing and courageous" (p. 277). The Houyhnhnms reflect deistic and stoical self-sufficiency; they "are rational even in those things in which the wisest man's passions inevitably, and even perhaps rightly, rule him. . . ." (p. 281). Miss Williams concludes that "far from being a model of perfection, the Houyhnhnms are intended to show the inadequacy of the life of reason." Yet they are not to be taken as a model of imperfection either, for just as "Gulliver himself is now honest and kindly, now credulous and pompous, according to the momentary demands of the satire," so also the Houyhnhnms are complex and unpredictable, Swift being always quite ready "to sacrifice the consistency of the Houyhnhnms to their satiric function of innocent comment on unknown humanity" (p. 279).

Miss Williams relates Swift's disinclination for simplicity

and explicitness to his scepticism: his suspicion of all the vaunted products of human reason, simple and complex alike, left him with "little of which he could approve wholeheartedly." "It is his habit to look sceptically, not only at the evils of the world, but at those, including himself, who criticize such evils, and at those who present schemes for the betterment of mankind." Gulliver, for instance, "is quaintly indignant and surprised at the evils which still exist six months after the publication of his travels" (pp. 277–78).

Tuveson finds a new satiric dimension in the often emphasized distance between Houyhnhnm and human. "The culminating irony of *Gulliver* is that when we finally arrive in a utopia, we find it is the land of another species," and Swift's attack is not upon man but upon certain "illusory ideas"— stoicism, rationalism, benevolence, the inevitability of progress, the natural goodness or prefectibility of human nature. (Tuveson also cites other specific examples of the kinds of ideas Swift attacks in *Gulliver*, such as Shaftesbury's concept of the "innate moral sense" and other instances of the new, secular pelagianism in which the de-emphasis and even denial of original sin made redemption virtually superfluous; and the kind of departure from the Christian tradition represented by the ethical and metaphysical speculations of Bolingbroke [pp. 371–74].[65]) In aspiring to a Houyhnhnm-like existence Gulliver is pursuing an inhuman and impossible ideal. In Gulliver's impasse at the end of the book Tuveson finds "the bankruptcy of the 'natural' man"; we have reached "the limits of the human, . . . and are forced to seek guidance from beyond our own resources" (p. 375). Yet *Gulliver* is not a polemic, Tuveson reminds us, but "a supreme artistic image of human life in several societies, so constructed as to bring out the true characteristics of the human being and thus directly expose the fallaciousness of illusory ideas" (p. 375).

Williams' " 'Animal Rationis Capax' " discusses the theme of physicality in *Gulliver* and other works, both prose and verse, and shows that images of physicality such as the Yahoos, the Struldbruggs, and the Brobdingnagian maids

91

of honor are reminders of "how narrowly we are bounded by our bodies, by senses and passions, and by all the accidents of our physical presence in a material world." They are at the same time Swift's comment on man's "strange inability, shared with no other animal, to know his own capacities." The mathematics-ridden, otherworldly Laputans illustrate admirably the comedy of absentmindedness which results from ignoring the physical (pp. 196–97). Belief in the unimportance of the physical is thus what Tuveson might call another "illusory idea"—the other side of the coin of belief in the power of reason. Accordingly, Miss Williams sees Swift's satire as "a careful balancing of extremes, a realistic compromise." Shaftesbury and Mandeville, rationalism and enthusiasm, because "they oversimplified the complex and difficult reality of life," were hostile to this "perilous balance" in Swift (pp. 202–3).

Monk warns against taking the Yahoos as Swift's image of man or the Houyhnhnms as Swift's ideal of man. The Yahoos represent "the bestial element in man—the unenlightened, unregenerate, irrational element in human nature," a view close to Tuveson's characterization of the Yahoos as "the hypostatization of those irrational, wild drives toward evil which men inherit" (p. 372).[66] Monk joins Williams in seeing the Houyhnhnms as stoics modeled after Swift's description in *Thoughts on Various Subjects:* "The Stoical Scheme of supplying our Wants by lopping off our Desires, is like cutting off our Feet when we want Shoes" (HD, I, 244). The Houyhnhnms' success with eugenics and birth control is not so impressive once we know that they know no lust.

If the Houyhnhnms' stoicism is not a realizable human ideal, neither is their reason. Monk notes the Cartesianism of the Houyhnhnms' reason: as it "strikes you with immediate conviction," it is a "version of Descartes' rational intuition of clear and distinct ideas" (p. 67). Monk also supplies a succinct survey of all the ideas and tendencies opposed by Swift, adding to those cited by Williams and Tuveson, Swift's opposition to experimental and theoretical science [67] in its encouragement of secularism and its abolition of mysteries, the irresponsible moneyed wealth of the middle class, and the increasing power of centralized government (pp. 50–51).[68] As for Brobdingnagian society, Monk sees it as "a Swiftian utopia of common good sense and morality" (p. 59), just as Tuveson sees it as "not perfection, but the kind of relative goodness available to humanity" (p. 374). In settling on this relatively simple positive, Monk and Tuveson depart from Williams, but it is a departure that is built on the perception, common to all three critics, of the limits of reason as a key theme of *Gulliver.*[69]

HISTORY OF IDEAS: QUINTANA

The dean of twentieth-century Swift critics, Ricardo Quintana, is clearly enough an historian of ideas, but his contributions to the interpretation of *Gulliver* are so comprehensive as to call for separate treatment. Quintana is distinguished by a flexibility and independence of mind which have made possible a distinctive critical development, one which illuminates both Swift's works and Swift criticism. Quintana's work reflects some of the major trends in twentieth-century criticism of *Gulliver* —from history to rhetoric, from certainty to wariness, from solemn judgment and even condemnation to a readiness to laugh.

In *The Mind and Art of Jonathan Swift* (1936) Quintana placed Swift against the intellectual background of his time. He traced, in a separate chapter, what he considered to be Swift's "controlling ideas"—ideas already fully developed upon their first appearance in 1704 in *A Tale of a Tub*—and found that while Swift differed from the rising currents of benevolism, deism, and optimism, he was in essential agreement with the Enlightenment in (1) its negative philosophy of history, (2) its valuing of "reason," that is, the *consensus gentium,* the funded good sense of civilized intelligence, (3) its consequent opposition to intellectualism—which is primarily intellectual speculation or system building, and (4) its hatred of enthusiasm. Unlike Wedel, Quintana identifies

Swift's "ethical doctrine" with "the ethical doctrine of the seventeenth century," which he finds to be neo-stoical in its insistence that the passions be controlled by reason. The *saeva indignatio* of the satirist is directed at man's irrationality, a persistent characteristic of man in spite of his unique endowment of reason.

On the face of it Quintana's interpretation seems sound enough. The ideas he traces are clearly present in such a work as *A Tale of a Tub*. But in the far more complicated and subtle *Gulliver's Travels,* these ideas, while still part of its intellectual landscape, are refracted and often materially changed by Swift's irony. But in 1936, Quintana saw *Gulliver* as a relatively simple work in which the passionless life of the Lilliputians in the utopian sixth chapter of the first voyage, and the reasonable good sense of the Brobdingnagians, as well as the austere virtue of the "noble Houyhnhnms," were to be taken as embodying life according to nature, the intellectual life grounded upon "the law of the universality of reason"—to Quintana, a worthy and reasonable ideal. Thus, Quintana sees the comedy in the conclusions of the first three voyages, but he finds the total effect of the last voyage "anything but a humorous one" (p. 320). The Yahoos are found to be a more successful image than the Houyhnhnms, principally because they "are a perfect symbol for the communication of disgust." Though we understand the admirable Houyhnhnms, "we are not moved by them," because "ideal civilization as conceived by Swift is an emotionless thing" (pp. 320–21).

Quintana distinguishes the moods peculiar to each voyage, finding Part I "an ingenious fairy tale, delightful even when it stings;" Part II a sequel to Part I, but with the addition of "efficient, keen satire"; Part III an *"omnium gatherum"* with at least one chapter in which "a high level of satiric intensity" is achieved, but "frequently dull and, taken as a whole, markedly ineffective," and Part IV closest in spirit and execution to Part II, "but distinguished from it by a purpose altogether relentless and an execution which is ruthless" (p. 326). The idea of Part IV, moreover, is intensified, charged with emotions, and "thrust home in a manner that shocks the nerves before it arouses the mind." The reader's impression of the work as a whole becomes in effect "the impression left by 'A Voyage to the Houyhnhnms,' and this is evidence, not of artistic success, but a certain lack thereof" (p. 326). Furthermore, the theme of bestiality often leads Swift into "a sensationalism which diverts attention from the concurrent statement of the life of reason and comes perilously close to breaking down the perceptions and judgments enforced in this latter statement." In addition Quintana finds that the work suffers on purely historical grounds as a result of our inability to understand properly the term "pride" as it was used in 1726, so much has our concept of the word suffered "neutralization." He grants Parts I and II to be "almost perfect," but feels that "had Part III been omitted entirely and Part IV been toned down and brought into closer accord with the second voyage, *Gulliver's Travels* would have been a finer work of art." It is really for reasons of neatness and tightness of structure that Quintana in *The Mind and Art* rates *A Tale of a Tub* higher than *Gulliver* (pp. 326–27).

The decline in the historical and biographical methods in literary studies is reflected in Quintana's postwar studies of Swift and his satire. In *The Mind and Art*, when discussing the inferiority of *Gulliver* to *A Tale of a Tub*, Quintana invokes at one point the biographical explanation reminiscent of such nineteenth-century critics as Thackeray and Stephen. "Its tone," says Quintana, "sometimes becomes forced as external emotions break through and assume command. That is to say that Swift's personal disappointments, his wretchedness in Ireland, the Vanessa incident, and the bitterness which came from years of unflinching realistic observation of the world all find expression in the satire" (p. 302). It is as though he were consciously correcting this view when in 1948, in "Situational Satire: A Commentary on the Method of Swift," he begins a radically different approach to the art of Swift by stressing "the element of impersonality in literary art." [70] To regard "the work and the author as interchangeable" or to "take the work to be an act at the level of every-day behaviour" is to lose sight of "the impersonal element and the presence of anything in the nature of deliberate method and form." Thus "we often find it hard to come to terms with the lyric poem as poem, as a construct, with the result that much of our commentary on poetry turns out to be either description of our impressions or reconstructions—largely imaginary—of a precise moment in the poet's emotional history with which we have chosen to equate the poem." We find it even more difficult "to admit of any distinction between a satirist and his satiric composition—and this despite the fact that satire is much more obviously a form of rhetoric than is lyric poetry" (p. 130).

Quintana goes on to analyze the rhetorical devices which are characteristic of Swift's satire. He distinguishes "at least five . . . that strike us forcibly; drama by way of created characters; parody, or at any rate the imitation of a specific literary genre; allegory; the 'myth'; and 'discoveries, projects, and machines'" (p. 133). The first of these involves Swift's habitual use of a fictional character as "author" of his satires —Gulliver, Bickerstaff, the Drapier—and of a fully realized world—often fantastic—in which that character exists. In *Gulliver* the element of parody is "the faithful reproduction . . . of the style, tone, and matter-of-fact reporting found in the genuine travel books of the time," and for Swift, parody "is another means of creating and exploiting a situation having its own unmistakable thickness" (p. 133). Quintana refers to the "political allegory" in *Gulliver* but prefers to draw upon the *Tale* and works other than *Gulliver* to illustrate the two kinds of allegory he distinguishes in Swift. One of these is a sustained and clear correspondence between surface fable and underlying meaning—the three brothers and the division in Christendom, the spider-bee episode—the other, the momentary correspondences, hardly allegorical at all, which are the result of the nervous, enthusiastic wit of Swift's fictional "modern writers," as for instance the discussions "by way of allegory" in *The Mechanical Operation of the Spirit*, in which, as Quintana puts it, "almost any parallelism no matter how fantastic will serve."[71] Myths in Swift operate for the most part as expanded metaphors, but are "less in the nature of myths than anti-myths, being a kind of parody with a grim and earnest purpose." Quintana ventures the paradox that "the only myth embraced by Swift is the myth that there are no myths." In *Gulliver* Quintana points to the animal myth of the fourth book, a myth which also informs *A Modest Proposal.* A myth in the hands of a projector may blend into those characteristic features of the satires, the "discoveries, projects, and machines," an art or device "concocted in that madhouse which is the enthusiast's brain." Drawing freely upon all these, Swift sets up the *situations* of his satire. "Situational satire," an admittedly loose term, is what Quintana applies to Swift's approach as a whole, and it is as a whole that Swift's art must be apprehended. Quintana rightly warns against attempts to isolate one or another method—the parody, the allegory, or the dramatic construction—and regard it as "the gist of the matter." The dish offered to the gods is too various for that (pp. 133–35).

One hesitates to say whether the many purely literary and rhetorical studies of *Gulliver* and of Swift's satire generally which have appeared since 1948 are a response to Quintana's preliminary survey of this material in "Situational Satire," but it is clear that in that article Quintana suggested new problems of interpretation and new techniques of analysis which were to be of central importance in a host of subsequent studies. From the 1940's on, awareness of the work as a rhetorical construct became increasingly important in literary studies generally.

The Mind and Art was reprinted in 1953 with additional notes and bibliography, but without the revision which in a new preface Quintana recognized as necessary. The promise in the Preface of further material on Swift and his age, "but with a somewhat different tone and emphasis in keeping with certain shifts in perception," was realized in *Swift: An Introduction* (1955). Taking up *Gulliver* in this work, Quintana notes that while "it would be too much to say that there is now general agreement about its meaning and effect as satiric statement," our age does enjoy a better rapport with the eighteenth century than had any intervening period. "What used to be called Swift's pessimism strikes most of us today as merely common sense." Alongside some of our own satiric writings *Gulliver's Travels* might well "seem a comparatively cheerful book" (p. 143). Elsewhere in the chapter on *Gulliver* are several approving references to Arbuthnot's description of *Gulliver* as a "merry work," and there is indeed throughout Quintana's discussion a greater emphasis on the comedy of the work and frequent correction of what he saw as lugubriousness in his 1936 interpretation.

The rediscovery of humor is apparent in Quintana's changed attitude toward the Houyhnhnms. In 1936 Quintana defended the "humourlessness" of the Houyhnhnms on the score that eighteenth-century decorum necessitated such a—to us—repellent image. In Swift's day, Quintana pointed out, no such aversion was felt toward these "exemplars of the perfect life of reason." The priggishness of the Houhynhnms is no less repulsive than the solemn, inflexible morality of Swift's own *Project for the Advancement of Religion and Morals* (1709). Eddy, F. R. Leavis,[72] and others who feel an aversion to the Houyhnhnms, finding them dreary, priggish, and lifeless, merely reflect, Quintana explained, "the deep-rooted antipathy of a later age to the uniformitarianism of Swift's period" (*Mind and Art,* pp. 52–53). It would not be fair to say that a change in the temper of the age permitted Quintana to take a somewhat different view in 1955 from the one he took in 1936, but there is something of the postwar temper in Quintana's assertions in *Swift: An Introduction* that not merely "the Utopia of horses, filled with the sound of whinnying, hoofbeats, and the champing of oats," but the utopian institutions of the sixth chapter of the voyage to Lilliput, "are looking in two ways at once" and could have been devised only by "a confirmed Utopia-maker or one diabolically familiar with such a creature." Here "the satire directed at man's irrationality" may well "extend itself to his dreams of the good society." "There are moments," Quintana confesses, "when we have to ask ourselves whether our imaginary voyage is not becoming a parody of itself—whether, for instance, the Utopian elements are not slyly humorous" (pp. 159–60).

In passages of this sort Quintana shows an increased wariness of the shifting ironies of Swift's satire, a wariness and scepticism which are characteristic of *Swift: An Introduction*. While he does not say explicitly that the Houyhn-hnms are ridiculous and are meant to be, he clearly recognizes the possibility. Elsewhere he reveals a scepticism of the methods of the history of ideas when applied to literature, a scepticism which appears to be another form of this same wariness. "Today," he says, "we are fully aware that the total meaning of a literary work, be it poem, play, or novel, derives only in part from the theories, intellectual and moral, which are present in it" (pp. 152–53). It is, of course, the rhetoric of the author as it plays across the intellectual content of the work, which determines its meaning, and thus a *sine qua non* of any sound appraisal of *Gulliver*—as of any literary work—is rhetorical, that is, *literary* criticism.

With this *Swift: An Introduction* seems to be better supplied than *The Mind and Art*. At times the discussion suffers from what is perhaps an excess of wariness, as, for instance, when Quintana praises *Gulliver's* ability to hold our interest: "It keeps our interest at every point because we are never able to anticipate what is going to happen, and when it does happen we are not always sure what our response should be. The contradictory details and incongruities in the narrative, if we observe them, add to our perplexities" (p. 158). However, Quintana's critical discussion is notable for its *aperçus*. Besides his re-evaluation of the utopian elements, Quintana offers some rewarding insights into the three structural themes—"the account of actual travels, the imaginary voyage, and parody of the latter" (p. 159); an admirable defense of the esthetic function of the troublesome third voyage; [73] and a very perceptive and suggestive discussion of Gulliver as character, the "ironic refraction" which he supplies and the "comedy of exclusion" of which he is the victim (pp. 160–65). Quintana sees Gulliver as a character who, while suffering "a sudden conviction of guilt and displaying an extraordinary capacity for self-torture, . . . nevertheless remains a figure in a comedy." Quintana, apprehensive of the influence of contemporary existentialism, warns against taking Gulliver's story as "a drama of *Angst* and crisis" rather than as a comedy, "the merry work which Arbuthnot pronounced it" (p. 165).

Arbuthnot's phrase is a recurrent theme in Quintana's discussion. One might perhaps wish that Quintana had been more free with examples of the merriment itself, but perhaps out of a sound disinclination to explain jokes overmuch, he chooses to remain for the most part silent, preferring by means of shrewd and perceptive hints to help the reader discover the merriment for himself.

RHETORICAL STUDIES

We tend to associate the biographical approach to literature—elucidating the man in his work or interpreting the work in the life of its creator—with the nineteenth century, but (as we have seen even in Quintana's earlier work) the biographical strain was also very strong in the *Gulliver* criticism of the 1920's and 30's. Harold Williams, for instance, in his earlier edition of *Gulliver* (London, 1926), corrects nineteenth-century biographical extremists by asserting that "the despairing contempt of the human species which characterizes Part IV" is not to be taken as reflecting "the hastening of that subsidence into utter gloom which was Swift's last portion," but he nevertheless grants that "the bitter disillusions of a great, a proud, a lonely and intractable man are here concentrated within a few short chapters" (p. 484).

It was Émile Pons who had urged Eddy to overcome his difficulties with the Yahoos and the Houyhnhnms by discovering their source in the life of the author.[74] Eddy, it appears, responded readily to the suggestion, for in the Introduction to his Oxford Standard edition of *Gulliver* (1933) he observes that "in the cumulative disillusionment of Gulliver we have the spiritual biography of Swift," and "mirrored in the

gross complexions and offensive bodily odours of the Brobdingnagians [Swift] finds the ugly barriers to romance with
which he was daily becoming more familiar in the solitude of
the bed-chamber—the hospital of his failing body. Vanessa
was dead, and Stella was sinking into her final illness. Man,
as a biological animal, no longer delighted him, nor woman
neither." But the work is also capable of turning and regis-
tering itself on its creator: "The scars of Gulliver are registered on the body of Swift. The calamities of the traveller
are his own too, *nostra miseria,* and each voyage leaves the
author older and sadder than before" (p. vi).

To dispel the confusion of the literary work with the
biography of its creator, twentieth-century criticism of *Gulliver's Travels* needed first to distinguish the proper spheres
of biography and literary criticism.[75] While this task of clari-
fication fell to no one type of study, that formal and rhetorical criticism which concerned itself with Swift's fictional
window—Lemuel Gulliver—proved of special importance in
redefining the related yet distinct provinces of biography and
literary criticism.

An early and much neglected formalist study, John
Brooks Moore's "The Role of Gulliver" (1928),[76] was, like the
Wedel study of the philosophical background, out of step
with its time. Moore stressed the distinction between Swift
and Gulliver, analyzed Gulliver as a fictional character, and
examined his effect upon the reader. Moore notes two common errors with regard to Gulliver. One is that Gulliver is
Swift; the other, illustrated in a comment by Eddy, that
Gulliver is "the allegorical representative of man, as truly as
Christian is in *Pilgrim's Progress*" (*A Critical Study,* p. 100).
Moore denies unequivocally that Gulliver is Swift "in either
intellect or disposition." He is, Moore says, "a good sound
fellow enough, but slow to seize upon even an obvious new
idea;" and "though he may be the cause that wit sparkles
in other men, [he] is hardly witty in himself. . . . Only the
passion in readers for assuming the autobiographic can account for any confusion of Gulliver with Swift." Nor is
Gulliver a symbol of man, any more "than Parson Adams or

Squire Western." Gulliver's character—and here is Moore's central point—is carefully calculated "to infect others with [Swift's] own ardent misanthropy." Moore argues that if so sanguine and deliberate a person, so free of morbidity (examples of Gulliver's stolidity are frequent in the first three voyages) can become infected with misanthropy, then that misanthropy must be genuine and eminently warranted. Gulliver's disillusioning education, in which the early optimistic philanthropy gives way finally to violent misanthropy, is designed to discredit the former and, if not make the latter appear attractive, then at least make it appear intellectually inescapable. We are, says Moore, jolted into rejecting this trick only when (and if) we stop to think *after* the reading. Gulliver's "pilgrim's progress to misanthropolis . . . is real to us in the reading (if not in the afterthought) because Gulliver is in disposition and in intellect so credible, probable, recognizable, and trustworthy" (pp. 469–72, 480).

It is perhaps a question whether Swift's strategy, if it operates as Moore suggests, is as well chosen as Moore seems to think. It is also a question whether the alleged intention of propagating misanthropy does not lean rather heavily on biography—and not very reliable biography at that. Nonetheless, Moore's essay represents the modest beginning of a more rigorous, formalistic approach to *Gulliver,* an approach in which the work is regarded less as a key to Swift's character or as an expression of his spiritual malaise than as a work having a deliberate form designed to produce a certain effect. But since Moore's study was not in tune with the *Zeitgeist,* neither its method nor its strictures against the misapprehension of the character of Gulliver were much heeded in the ensuing decade. The occasional incisive descriptions of Gulliver as an independent literary figure occur not in studies devoted to Swift but in works such as Huntington Brown's *Rabelais in English Literature* (Cambridge, Mass., 1933), in which Gulliver's obtuseness is stressed: "Like Dr. Watson in *Sherlock Holmes,* Gulliver can understand the obvious or that which is carefully explained to him, but is deficient in perceiving subtleties. He is still more so in applying the moral lessons he learns to the conduct of his own life" (pp. 162–63). It was not until 1941 that a full-length analytical study was devoted to the character of Lemuel Gulliver.

This study, without doubt more important than any other single study in the rediscovery of Lemuel Gulliver, was "The Final Comedy of Lemuel Gulliver," by John F. Ross.[77] Ross repeats Moore's warnings against associating Gulliver with Swift; but he goes beyond Moore in forcefully distinguishing between the final misanthropy of Gulliver and the view of Swift, who "is above him in the realm of comic satire, still indignant at the Yahoo in man, but at the same time smiling at the absurdity of the view that can see *only* the Yahoo in man" (p. 196). To support this interpretation, Ross points to the many instances in the satire when Gulliver is the butt of Swift's comedy and to the ridiculous elements in the Houyhnhnms, who, according to Ross, are *meant* to be ridiculous. Ross explains that we are apt to be thrown off in the last voyage because its first nine chapters contain what he calls Juvenalian or corrosive satire, as distinguished from the "laughter-provoking" Horatian or comic satire which prevails elsewhere in the book. The change in satirical mode prevents our grasping "Swift's rounding of the whole of *Gulliver* in a superb return of comic satire" (p. 178) in the conclusion when Swift rises "to a more comprehensive view than he permits to Gulliver" and achieves a satiric comment "on the insufficiency of the corrosive attitude," which, along with "the Gulliverian discontent" (the aping of horses and other maladjustments) is "inadequate and absurd" (p. 196).

The Henry James revival in the forties and the consequent critical concern with the "controlling consciousness" doubtless contributed to the increasing attention shown to *Gulliver* as a formal structure and to Gulliver the character as fictional window. After Ross's study several critics who drew upon his suggestions were consciously Jamesian in their approach. In "What Gulliver Knew" (1943), Joseph Horrell described the fourth voyage as "an ultimate in sustained fictional irony to be compared with one of another kind, James's

Turn of the Screw" (p. 500).[78] Whether Gulliver has a cousin in the enigmatic governess is perhaps best left an open question, and it is an overstatement to call the fourth voyage, with its various and shifting ironies, a *sustained* irony; but Horrell does add further evidence to convict Gulliver of occasional, if not chronic, absurdity. He notes, for instance, the absurd inconsistency between Gulliver's early statement to the Houyhnhnm master that horses in England "have not the least tincture of reason" and his later remarks regarding his pet English horses: "My Horses understand me tolerably well; I converse with them at least four Hours every Day" (IV, xi; HD, XI, 274). Horrell's interpretation of the culmination of Gulliver's education widens still further the gulf between Swift and Gulliver: the four voyages lead Gulliver to a "fateful unbalance of emotion and intellect," in which intellect "weighs and even disputes the report of the senses" and is "the exclusive arbiter of his restricted knowledge of the world." It is only Gulliver's intellect which tells him his wife smells—not his nose (pp. 503–4).

Samuel Kliger, in "The Unity of *Gulliver's Travels*" (1945),[79] has some hard words for critics who resort to history of ideas, psychiatry, and sociology in interpreting *Gulliver* and urges rather that critical commentary on the work —which he insists on calling "a novel"—be "aimed at a consistent analysis of the novel itself with a view to discovering the implicative relations between ideas raised in different parts of the novel in different ways." While Kliger's ostensible subject was the work as a self-contained whole, his most valuable observations were of some of its parts. Kliger is good, though ponderous, on what he calls "the return motif," that is, Gulliver's peculiar difficulties of adjustment upon his several returns home. "The balance and contrast"—a cant phrase to which Kliger is unfortunately given—"in the management of the return motif draws the reader's attention to the fact that Gulliver, in every instance of his return, is reacting excessively in a way which belies his own nature and the situation itself." Gulliver's "excessive behavior is symbolic of a contrast which Swift is trying to enforce between

Contrast

an impossible and a possible situation, between the ideal and the actual circumstances which govern." As an afterthought Kliger defends the scatology as a device for exposing man in his "egotistical pride," a reminder of "the physical basis upon which the human ego rests" (p. 415)—and thus, he might well have added, a reminder of "the actual circumstances which govern." Kliger concludes that Gulliver is not a misanthrope, for "Gulliver has experienced perfection among the wise and kindly horses, but he is no perfectionist when he judges his fellow men. Consequently he does not rail, as the misanthrope does, on the imperfections of men" (pp. 401–5). Surely this is not our Gulliver!

Kliger's discussion of anti-perfectionism in *Gulliver* is far better. After permitting himself a glance at Swift's correspondence and another at Mandeville, Kliger rightly asserts that "Swift, like Mandeville, gave over perfection to a millennial kingdom." Anti-perfectionism, Kliger finds, is shown in the Houyhnhnms, who represent "Christian asceticism," a view "which defined virtue as a triumph of sheer reason over the passions, a self-conquest." "Christian asceticism" is apparently a misnomer for neo-stoicism, a confusion which appears again when Kliger asserts that "Reason . . . cannot cope with the problem of evil, traditional Christian ethics notwithstanding." But Kliger is quite sound in seeing the Houyhnhnms as Swift's subtly absurd image of the futility of the perfectionist attitude (pp. 405, 414).

While Kliger leaves a good bit of *Gulliver* undiscovered and often misrepresents what he does find, his study marks a stage in the formal analysis of the work. Kliger, like Horrell, has a strong inclination—reflected no doubt in Kliger's application of the term "novel"—to regard *Gulliver* as the kind of deliberately and carefully wrought artistic structure we associate with the novels and tales of James. Later studies continued to apply—devastatingly sometimes—standards derived from the Jamesian novel.

Edward Stone, in "Swift and the Horses: Misanthropy or Comedy?" (1949),[80] suggested that to "determine what Swift was really saying," we need to study (1) the intent of the author; (2) the significance of the beast-fable tradition, and Swift's use of it; (3) the characterization of Gulliver; and (4) what has been recorded concerning the reception of the supposedly offensive Part IV by its first readers." In those passages in the correspondence which have often been cited to reveal Swift's intention, Stone finds a "pseudo-pontifical pose" traceable also in *Gulliver*. He suggests that the beast-fable in *Gulliver* is related to the theriophily of writers such as Montaigne in the *Apology for Raymond Sebond,* a tradition taken up in an admirable study by George Boas, *The Happy Beast* (Baltimore, 1933). Stone points out that the essence of theriophily in this tradition was paradox, and expressions of theriophily were, in the words of Boas, "certainly not written for other than conversational purposes" with the motive "simply to wound man's pride, reduce his arrogance, a moral like that of most satirists and no more to be taken as founded upon a serious zoology than *Gulliver's Travels*." [81]

On the character of Gulliver, Stone refers to Kliger approvingly and emphasizes Gulliver's comic habit of over-reacting to his experiences, his gullibility, and his persistent discontent, which leads to his wandering and final *Weltschmerz*. Stone compares Gulliver's final state of mind to Don Quixote's, suggesting further that Gulliver, like Quixote, is an object of pity as well as laughter.

In treating the contemporary reception of Part IV, Stone is limited by scanty evidence. However, what evidence there is in letters and *jeux d'esprit* points to anything but a lugubriously philosophical or solemnly moral response. The ironic and playfully approving tone of those contemporary comments which Stone cites indicates that Arbuthnot was not alone in his approbation of *Gulliver's* merriment. Stone makes no claim that his conclusions on this matter are definitive, but he rightly points to "the strong possibility that the reputation of Part IV has undergone an unfortunate deterioration," and suggests that a truly thorough study of eighteenth-century reactions to *Gulliver* would be well worth undertaking (p. 376).

Gulliver's Travels

Gulliver's resemblance to likable, often pitiable, humorous characters such as Sir Roger de Coverley and Uncle Toby was argued at length by Harold Kelling in *"Gulliver's Travels:* A Comedy of Humours" (1925).[82] Gulliver, Kelling asserted, like all of Swift's personae except the narrator of *A Tale of a Tub,* is not a personification of folly, but essentially a sincere and admirable character with "credible eccentricities and aberrations from common sense." Gulliver's humor is a combination of gullibility and dogmatism; he is "basically a naive, dogmatic humourist who is much concerned with public welfare." But he is a humorist among humorists. In each of his voyages he encounters a people of a certain humor, each humor being a form of pride. The Lilliputians have pride of size; the Brobdingnagians, pride of strength or "physical accomplishment"; the Laputans, pride of systems and projects, that is, intellectual pride; and the Houyhnhnms, moral pride (pp. 365–71). In the fourth voyage, Gulliver's gullibility makes him a prey to the "distorting humour" of the Houyhnhnms—"an abnormal emphasis on moral perfection, resulting from the instinctive inclination to good," and thus Gulliver is Swift's "means of producing an indirect, ironic effect. The writer does not state his private conclusions but allows the reader to come to his own, guided by common sense. . . ." (p. 364).

The critical failure over the fourth voyage is, Kelling says, the result of mistaking "Gulliver's humour for Swift's bad humour." Kelling finds Gulliver to be a purveyor of corrosive satire—which is a result of Gulliver's dogmatic humor—but the reader's perception of and allowance for Gulliver's distortions make the work as a whole not corrosive satire at all, but an extremely mild form of comedy. How mild and toothless this comedy is, is revealed in Kelling's discussion of the Yahoo passion for shiny stones, which Kelling regards as "so obviously an abstraction drawn by a madman (Gulliver, not Swift), that the reader should be impelled to fill out the abstraction with the saving qualities of civilized man (and might even laugh at the Yahoos)" (p. 373). We are here at the farthest extreme from nineteenth-century views—and deep in another kind of error. Kelling's comment on the work as a whole reflects a theme altogether new: "*Gulliver's Travels* is in the tradition of great comedy, offering hope for man's situation;" and "Even Gulliver sees hope at the end of his book; he has become somewhat reconciled to things as they are—to death, even to vices in society" (p. 374). Gulliver becomes a consistent and lovable booby, but at the cost of an unconscionable amount of satirical bite.

All previous attempts at Jamesian analysis of *Gulliver* pale before Robert C. Elliott's intrepid study, "Gulliver as Literary Artist" (1952).[83] Elliott, in what seems at times a tour de force reminiscent in its breathtaking logic of *A Modest Proposal*, probes the work relentlessly in the light of its "fictive premise," namely, "that Gulliver, a retired sea captain, writes his memoirs." Once this premise is accepted—and it seems on the face of it both innocuous and inescapable—"we immediately encounter complex problems involving Swift's formal control of his materials, the development of Gulliver's character, and the final 'meaning' of the entire work" (p. 49). The rigor of Elliott's analysis is already suggested in his careful distinction between Gulliver-character and Gulliver-author. The former is, of course, the young Gulliver, particularly the pre-Houyhnhnm Gulliver, an *ingénu* with whom we are often amused. Gulliver-author, as we know, is a confirmed misanthrope, yet with a reticence worthy of the best of James's "compositional centres" he holds back "his mature point of view" in the early voyages. Indeed, for the early voyages Gulliver-author projects himself "as a character as he in fact was in time past" and even creates "the illusion of the immediacy of the younger Gulliver's experience," all this in spite of the fact that "at the time of writing he must have been extremely contemptuous of what he had been as a young man" (pp. 51, 53).

As Elliott gauges the distance between Gulliver-author and Gulliver-character, he poses some curious problems. For instance, from what we know of the attitude of Gulliver-author, he ought to agree wholeheartedly with the Brobdingnagian king's judgment on that "most pernicious Race of little

odious Vermin," yet Gulliver at this point urges that "great
Allowance should be given to a King who lives wholly se-
cluded from the rest of the World" and even ascribes the
king's outburst to "a certain Narrowness of Thinking; from
which we and the politer Countries of *Europe* are wholly
exempted" (II, vi, vii; HD, XI, 116–17). To which of the
two Gullivers is this irony to be ascribed? Elliott answers by
pointing out that "it is inconceivable that he [Gulliver-
author] would praise so smugly (note the present tense) the
'politer Countries of *Europe*.' Thus the passage must . . . be
read on two levels: literally for the naive Gulliver; as conscious irony on the part of Gulliver-author" (pp. 54–55).
Again we find ourselves here at a considerable remove from
the nineteenth-century critics of *Gulliver*. Swift as author
and even Swift as ironist have been refined out of existence.
The "artistic failure" of the work, Elliott suggests, takes place
in the last voyage when the distinction between Gulliver-
author and Gulliver-character is obliterated and "the man
who suffers and the mind which creates" become as one, an
"artistic failure" in which Elliott finds "a reflection of Gulliver's greater moral failure" (pp. 62–63).

In fixing responsibility for ironies near or after the point
of "artistic failure," Elliott is more willing to permit Swift a
positive role as ironist. He even concedes, as he had done in
an earlier footnote, that "for purposes of interpretation there
is no significant distinction between Swift and Gulliver-
author," a concession which in the footnote had been made
rather gingerly and with an apprehensive glance at "the old
trap which has vitiated so much criticism of Swift's work:
the identification of Swift and Gulliver." But there are, as
Elliott points out, some very real—indeed tremendous—differences between his approach and "the old trap" (pp. 62,
52 n.).

If Gulliver-author were the ironist in the comments on
the Brobdingnagian king's "Narrowness of Thinking," one
would expect Gulliver-author to be the ironist in the fourth
voyage when he describes European warfare and praises the
"Valour" of the English: "And, to set forth the Valour of my

own dear Countrymen, I assured him, that I had seen them blow up a Hundred Enemies at once in a Siege . . . and beheld the dead Bodies drop down in Pieces from the Clouds, to the great Diversion of all the Spectators" (IV, v; HD, XI, 231). But here Elliott says:

> It is much less satisfactory now to have recourse to the double point of view to interpret statements like these, for Gulliver-voyager should by this time (if we assume development in his personality) have approached so closely to Gulliver-author that he would be incapable of such moral obtuseness. Yet if we do not read these statements as those of the *ingénu*, then we must assume that Gulliver *as character* has become an ironist; that is, that as the events being described approach more and more closely in chronological time to the actual time of the writing, Gulliver-character and Gulliver-author are tending to merge, to have the same characteristics; and that Gulliver in speaking to the Houyhnhnm is, on occasion, speaking ironically. This interpretation has a certain attractiveness in that it tends to give consistency to the characterization of Gulliver; but for all that it simply will not do, if for no other reason than that the Houyhnhnm, before whom Gulliver was desperately concerned to speak nothing but the truth, would not understand irony ("the Thing which is not"). Clearly Gulliver as character holds, simultaneously, two completely incompatible attitudes toward human experience. Psychologically, this is of course perfectly feasible, and a case might be made out for the view that in this section of the work Gulliver is in the last throes of his struggle to cling to what has been for him the real world. But the case would be pretty strained; Swift was not writing a psychological novel; and he does not exploit artistically any such psychological split in Gulliver's character. In any logical sense, then, we must conclude that Gulliver is here not a "consistent" character. (p. 58)

Not here, in truth, nor hardly anywhere. For this and other reasons—the inappropriateness of applying the critical principles of Percy Lubbock to a novel *manqué* ought to be sufficiently obvious—the Jamesian approach seems singularly ill-advised when applied to *Gulliver*. Elliott, whose aim in part was the resolution of "certain formal inconsistencies" (p. 52 n.), surprisingly found only a few which resisted resolution. Each of these is adjudged an artistic blunder, a slip of the artist's hand. Since, as we know, Gulliver-author is, for all practical purposes, Swift himself, the responsibility for artistic blundering falls to Swift. Elliott in this article appears finally to stand with the Quintana of *Mind and Art*, W. B. C. Watkins,[84] and others who choose to regard the work as a flawed masterpiece and its author as an artist lacking sufficient control over his materials.

For clarity, thoroughness, and soundness of judgment, Martin Price's *Swift's Rhetorical Art: A Study in Structure and Meaning* (New Haven, 1953), is the best full-length presentation of the various rhetorical devices in the important works. As the subtitle indicates, however, Price is more interested in structure and meaning than in Swift's rhetorical strategies.

Gulliver is taken up along with *A Tale of a Tub* in a chapter entitled "The Symbolic Works." While the narrator of the *Tale*—Price calls him the Tale Teller—is garrulous and bold, "the victim of his own wit, which escapes his control and carries him along, a helpless rider, in a direction he did not intend," Gulliver "is spare in comment, literal-minded, stolidly dedicated to factual reporting." Gulliver's blindness becomes evident when "the scenes he describes demand a moral judgment he has no capacity to make." Price carefully gauges the degree to which Gulliver can be regarded as a fictional character: since Gulliver changes in the last part of the book, he "comes closer to being a true fictional character than any of Swift's other ironic masks" (pp. 86–87), a judgment which marks off Price from the somewhat less restrained approach of Elliott in "Gulliver as Literary Artist." [85]

In plotting the rhetorical situation in *Gulliver*, Price includes an essential object often neglected by critics—the reader. Irvin Ehrenpreis, in a general essay on Swift's satire, had called Gulliver "the reader." [86] Price emends this designation perceptively, finding that *Gulliver* is "recounted by an author who is the counterpart neither of Swift nor of the intelligent reader." There is all the world in the qualifying adjective *intelligent,* for there is a sense, doubtless also what Ehrenpreis had in mind, in which Gulliver *is* "the reader," that is, the naive reader voyaging through the *Travels* for the first time. No reader is exempt—all suffer the "bite" until they grow wary. Something of this gambit seems to be suggested by Price in his discussion of the ironic mask as used in the *Tale* and in *Gulliver:* "The common dupe Swift invents, *like his counterpart in the reader,* is not clear-sighted in selfishness; he is neither a rebel nor a Machiavel. A man of middling virtue, he would recoil from an accurate recognition of the ends he is promoting, and Swift, of course, never allows him that recognition *but demands it instead of the reader*" (p. 87, italics mine). Where Elliott distinguished two Gullivers, we ought here apparently to distinguish two readers: reader₁ is a *naïf,* a dupe; reader₂ is reader₁ grown older and wiser since his first (or hundredth) reading, and is now trying it again, but on his guard against Swift's "bite"; that is, he is ready and able to give the "recognition," bestow the judgment, which Swift demands.

Exploring the particular susceptibilities of Gulliver in his "drama of incomprehension," Price finds that "the tradition of travel books provided Swift with a useful type, the voyager whose judgment is easily corrupted either by his pleasure in the strange or by his complacent condescension toward it" (p. 95). In the first voyage Gulliver fails to see the pettiness of the Lilliputians. In Brobdingnag, when his pride in European man prompts the panegyric which the king in turn probes so acutely and crushes so mercilessly, Gulliver accounts for the king's judgment as best he can. In the third voyage Gulliver dismisses as " 'visionary' those few political projectors . . . who have a rational program" (pp. 96–97). But in the fourth voyage the scales fall from Gulliver's eyes.

Price describes the change which Gulliver experiences in the fourth voyage as "largely an emotional conversion. Having resisted all the lessons which have confronted him in the first three voyages, he is now led into a dilemma." The dilemma is a false one: Gulliver must either accept his human-ness, which to him equals Yahoo-ness, or become like the Houyhnhnms. Faced with one undesirable impossibility and one desirable one, Gulliver opts for the latter. In his struggle to dissociate himself from the loathsome Yahoos and identify himself with the Houyhnhnms, a struggle between what are in a sense mere appearances, "his clothes become his sole defense." Shortly the secret of his clothes is revealed, and his recourse is "to establish himself as at least a rational Yahoo." That he is incapable of doing so is primarily the result, Price explains, of the unreality of his choice, in which "extremes are presented as necessary alternatives, and the mean is ignored." He has taken the symbols, which are really "aspects of man," and regarded them as though "they were solid realities." Soon it is clear that "he is no longer interested in saving appearances"; that he has, indeed, "given up the defense of his fellow men and hopes only to cast his lot with the Houyhnhnms." Having taken symbols to be realities, "he has little difficulty reducing reality to the symbolic patterns." To illustrate this confusion of symbol and reality, Price cites Gulliver's statement on war: "a *Soldier* is a *Yahoo* hired to kill in cold Blood as many of his own Species, who have never offended him, as possibly he can." Price finds this to be the characteristic Gulliverian distortion, and he offers a daring and original interpretation. "This [Gulliver's oversimplification] divorces the soldier from patriotism or duty and the means of killing from the end; one need not commend war to recognize it as something more than this." This same type of distortion through oversimplification Price finds present also in Gulliver's ludicrous list of differences of opinion over which Yahoos will fight: "whether *Flesh* be *Bread*, or *Bread* be *Flesh*: Whether the Juice of a certain *Berry* be *Blood* or *Wine*: Whether *Whistling* be a Vice or a Virtue: Whether it be better to *kiss* a Post, or throw it into the Fire: What is the best Colour for a *Coat*, whether *Black, White, Red,* or *Grey*; and whether it should be *long* or *short, narrow* or *wide, dirty* or *clean*; with many more" (IV, v; HD, XI, 230–31; Price, pp. 98–99). Thus Gulliver's conversion in the fourth voyage turns him into an enthusiast of ideology. Anguished in a false dilemma, repeatedly embracing the uncreating word, he is the embodiment of all the vices Swift saw in system-building.

Price agrees essentially with Ross regarding the comic conclusion, in which Gulliver suffers "from a kind of inverted pride, a hatred of all humankind for the qualities which he himself shares"; Gulliver here exhibits and castigates pride at the same time. "Gulliver, who began with a pride in man that found him above criticism, ends with a pride in reason that finds man insupportable. Even as he warns men of the vice of pride, he entreats 'those who have any Tincture of this absurd Vice, that they will not presume to appear in my Sight.'"

On the objects of Gulliver's *idée fixe*, the purely rational Houyhnhnms, Price differs from the "tendency in recent critics to find the Houyhnhnms inherently ridiculous." Price grants that "Swift's rational horses are clearly no model for man," but "it seems as much beside the point to deny the appeal of their life as to follow Gulliver in succumbing to it." While "it is important to see Gulliver's folly in taking the Houyhnhnms as a model for man, . . . there is a danger of multiplying ironies." The simple, cold life of the Houyhnhnms, Price seems to hint, is the typical heaven or Garden of Eden found in Shaw or Milton, and these are, paradoxically, notoriously forbidding places. Furthermore, "If we consider the Houyhnhnm life ludicrous in itself, we are likely to fall into the Mandevillian celebration of a corrupt world for its richness and complexity," a way of saying, apparently, that Swift was not, nor should we be, overthankful for the feast of fools (p. 102 n.).[87]

Price's argument does not come to grips with the Houyhnhnms' irrepressible absurdities, which distressed even those critics who wished to see Houyhnhnmland as a utopia. When Eddy, discussing his disappointment with the Houyhnhnms, asks, "Does not a horse lose some of his dignity when riding in a carriage?" (*A Critical Study*, p. 189), his perplexity might well be our revelation. Nor can any candid reader mistake the effect of, if not the intention in, the Houyhnhnm widow's excuses for her tardiness (IV, ix; HD, XI, 258–59). Price is unique in his argument for the *neutrality* of the Houyhnhnm symbol. The usual tendency among critics who resist the ridiculousness of the Houyhnhnm is to bathe the Houyhnhnm in *lachrimae rerum,* which convinces us of the critics' wistful yearning for a better society, or at least a more tractable human being, rather than of the Houyhnhnm's freedom from absurdity.

William Bragg Ewald's *The Masks of Swift* (Oxford, 1954) appeared too early to take account of Price's work but late enough to offer some comment on Elliott's "Gulliver as Literary Artist." Ewald recognizes that Elliott's reading, in which Gulliver himself at times becomes an ironist, "tends to make him a consistent character and gives the book a well-defined point of view, in Henry James's sense." However, Ewald is less inclined to impose such Jamesian standards on the work, and finds it "more likely that Swift saw [that] Gulliver could be useful in two primary capacities: as a naive voyager and as a disillusioned misanthrope." The inconsistencies between these two Gullivers, the unlikelihood, for instance, that Gulliver-misanthrope would—or even could—describe Lilliput and Brobdingnag as he does or make the affectionate references to his family found in the first three voyages, are probably best explained, as Ewald suggests, as the result of Swift's "free use of the mask," unrestricted by "a novelist's primary regard for the absolute integrity of the fictitious character itself" (p. 148). That Gulliver is an incorrigibly inconsistent fictional character is evident in his several lapses into the purest naiveté—even pre-misanthropic naiveté—as late as the last chapter of the book, where, for instance, he discusses the feasibility of English subjugation of the lands he visited, surely not a proper concern for the Gulliver now dedicated to wisdom and goodness.

Ewald is not always as judicious and penetrating as he is in his short discussion of Elliott. Elsewhere he frequently contradicts himself and labors the obvious. For instance, after stressing throughout the book the sharp distinctions and contrasts between Swift and his masks, in his final paragraph he praises the masks for reflecting "facets of the character of the complex man who was [Swift]" (p. 189). Ewald's recognition that Gulliver is not to be straitened into a consistent character is curiously contradicted when he elsewhere says, "Swift's greatest masterpieces are written by 'authors' who are clearly conceived and, for the most part, consistently maintained individuals" (p. 184), and that Swift's irony depends upon "fully rounded character" (p. 186). As for laboring the obvious, Ewald spends pages in demonstrating that Gulliver is a liar before making the salient point of the matter—that Gulliver is in the tradition of lying travellers found in Lucian, Rabelais, and others. Other character traits of Gulliver—his heroism, his attachment to the sea, his ingenuity, his leadership qualities, and so forth—are analyzed exhaustively and shown to contribute to the vividness of the narrative and to the "subtle burlesque on writers of travel literature." More successful is the discussion of Gulliver's bungling use of Latin quotations, each of which contributes materially to the comedy (p. 138).

Ponderous solemnity characterizes not only Ewald's style but also his interpretation. We are told that the separation of children and parents in Lilliput "suggests more the reality that parents do not treat their own children rationally than that not having them rear their own children will solve the problem"; and "when Gulliver says that the Brobdingnagians have not many books and the Houyhnhnms none at all, Swift probably means that Europeans would be wise to have fewer and better books." Ewald is especially solemn on the Houyhnhnms, who, he notes, "have been condemned as unsympathetic, inhuman, cold creatures, who are unintelligent because they read nothing and have no comprehension of the intricacies of human warfare." This condemnation is in error, Ewald feels, and must be corrected by recognizing that they are Swift's norm, "a source of strength, not confusion" and the fitting vehicle for Swift's "permanent" values: "the belief, for example, that fraud, war, and madness are bad and that truthfulness, reason, and humility are good"

(p. 188). Thus Ewald approves Gulliver's "honor" in kissing the Houyhnhnm's hoof, "For this noble creature, unlike the monarchs in the first three voyages, truly deserves Gulliver's respect" (p. 155). Ewald grants that subsequently Gulliver's respect for the Houyhnhnms is carried too far, and Gulliver "at the end of Voyage IV is somewhat ridiculous in his failure —being among men—to return at once to imperfect human ways and to accept with resignation the inescapable and humbling fact that he is like other human beings whom he so violently rejects" (p. 156). Thus Ewald agrees with Price and others who find Gulliver to a considerable degree an object of comedy, and especially so at the close, but not the Houyhnhnms, who remain a symbol of a worthy, albeit unattainable, ideal. For Ewald the Houyhnhnms apparently are not the neutral symbol they were for Price, though it must be said that Ewald by no means regards them as fit objects for human emulation.

Recently Robert C. Elliott has been heard from again on *Gulliver*, and this discussion, in his *The Power of Satire* (Princeton, 1960), differs markedly from his earlier, novelistic treatment of the work. Employing the same keenness but now more tactfully, and influenced now by Northrop Frye and Erich Auerbach instead of T. S. Eliot and Percy Lubbock, he delivers what is probably our finest *literary* criticism of *Gulliver's Travels*. Throughout his discussion Elliott concentrates on the literary values of the work, clarifying the tone, noting the position of the definable positives, analyzing the rich inconsistency and unpredictability of the satiric masks. No critic has so perceptively and convincingly demonstrated that the masks in *Gulliver* are multiple: sometimes a mere attitude, not a personality at all, will serve as mask. At times characters within the story—the Brobdingnagian king, for instance, and of course Gulliver himself —become satirists, fictional ones, to be sure, under the control of that other, ironical satirist, Swift (pp. 184–222).

Elliott's discussion, because it approaches the work as art and not as polemic or sermon, is free of that heavy burden of didacticism which weighs down so many earnest analyses of *Gulliver*. Recently a group of these studies, by overstating the conclusions of Wedel, Kathleen Williams, Monk, and others, have argued that the Houyhnhnms are deists, thus reducing the fourth voyage to a kind of High-Church polemic. In arguments like those offered by Irvin Ehrenpreis (*Personality of Swift*, pp. 99–109), Calhoun Winton, and Martin Kallich,[88] the emphasis placed on what these critics take to be Swift's didactic intention has throttled the comedy, the literary fun, the merriment and complexity of the work, in the same way that overly didactic discussions of the *Tale* have obscured its comedy.

There can no longer be any question that *Gulliver's Travels* is congruous with Christian values of an Augustinian cast. Even the most severe opponents of the new deistic theory of the Houyhnhnms—Quintana, Sherburn, and R. S. Crane[89]—will hardly contend, as did virtually all nineteenth-century critics, that the tone and *Tendenz* of the work are out of harmony with Swift's professed Christian beliefs. But it is quite another thing to claim, as Ehrenpreis, Winton, and Kallich do, that there are distinctly Christian positives in the work. Kathleen Williams is much closer to the truth when she says that Swift's characteristic habit is "his inability, or his refusal, to present us straightforwardly with a positive to aim at." If *Gulliver* has a presiding attitude or philosophy, it is one metaphysically prior to Swift's Christianity and is perhaps best identified, as Miss Williams has shown (*Jonathan Swift and the Age of Compromise*, pp. 60–62 *passim*), with pyrrhonism. But this is not to suggest —and Miss Williams nowhere does—that the work is a pyrrhonist tract or has any design to propagate pyrrhonism or subvert anti-pyrrhonists.

In the argument that Swift is satirizing deism in the Houyhnhnms we have an example of one of the vagaries of intentionalism. R. S. Crane rightly accuses Winton and Kallich "of so 'reading' the [fourth] Voyage as to make it fit [their] presupposition about its author's intentions" (p. 428). In a complex and subtle satire such as *Gulliver*, in which irony is the dominant mode, whatever there is of definable intention must be intuited. Our reading of the work would be comfortable and restful if the thread of a single intention could guide us through its labyrinth. But the labyrinth is too cunningly contrived, and no single and unbroken thread is there to lead us on. The intention, for which we instinctively grope, is various and needs constantly to be rediscovered and redefined. When we feel we have located the intention, it is the irony, the hyperbole, the absurdity, the distortion, the incongruity, in short, the literary and artistic value which has become clear. The intention remains something else; the attempt to discover it has been a means to quite other ends.

Ehrenpreis' interpretation is an illuminating example of the pitfalls of didacticism. Ehrenpreis asserts that *Gulliver* is held together by Swift's morality: "Its true coherence," he says, "rests on the moral pattern, the chain of values which the author advocates" (*Personality of Swift*, p. 116). From such a critical base the heavy hand of didacticism will stretch to all corners of the work. As Quintana, noting a characteristic oversimplification of intention, puts it, "Are we really to take it that the comic-satiric import of the 'Voyage to the Houyhnhnms' resides in a grave message to the effect, as [Ehrenpreis] would have it, 'that anyone who believes in the adequacy of reason without Christianity must see himself as a Houyhnhnm and the rest of mankind as Yahoos'? When Gulliver faints at the smell of humanity, are we to understand that his error lies in forgetting to add Christianity to reason?" (p. 355). Again, in Ehrenpreis' treatment of Gulliver's asking his Houyhnhnm master's forgiveness "if I did not expose those Parts, that Nature taught us to conceal. He said . . . he could not understand why Nature should teach us to conceal what Nature had given" (IV, iii; HD, XI, 220–21): "Here," explains Ehrenpreis, "Gulliver's error resides in his logic rather than his modesty. It was not nature that taught us to conceal our genitalia; it was a supernatural moral law" (p. 100). That Swift would take such a view is gratuitous; that it presides here is beyond demonstration, though its subversion of the comedy ought to be sufficiently obvious.

Quintana's current stress on the priority of the comedy over the allegory, along with his insistence that a "grave message" would be inimical to the comedy, marks him off from Sherburn and Crane among the opponents of the deist theory of the Houyhnhnms. Sherburn and Crane, indeed, through their preponderantly intentionalist emphasis, have a grave message of their own to impose on *Gulliver*. Sherburn, resisting what Ross and others have called the final comedy, prefers to see there "Swift's fundamental horror of the gulf between the actual and the ideal." [90] Sherburn argues that the Houyhnhnms could not have been an "obnoxious" symbol for Swift, pointing out that for his image of perfection Swift chose his favorite animal, the horse, whose "control, composure, affection, and intelligence . . . Swift obviously admired and here consistently portrayed" ("Errors Concerning the Houyhnhnms," [1958], p. 93). Sherburn grants that Swift treats this image "with unrealistic playfulness," but this playfulness is at best a kind of sugar-coating extraneous to the essentially serious purpose, which he has elsewhere described as "preaching against intellectual arrogance, against pretentiousness, against the dominance, whether political or intellectual, of the many for the selfish interests of the few," as well as "preaching in favor of established and tried codes of thought and action as opposed to new and untried methods." [91] The playfulness of Swift's reference to Houyhnhnms in a letter to Ford—"I would have . . . you know that I hate Yahoos of both Sexes, and that Stella and Madame de Villette are onely tolerable at best, for want of Houyhnhnms" (*Letters to Ford,* p. 100)—does not deter Sherburn from concluding that "there can, then, be no doubt that, for Swift as well as for Gulliver, the Houyhnhnms were a *ne plus ultra*" ("Errors Concerning Houyhnhnms," pp. 93–94). Sherburn likens Gulliver's vision of perfection to St. Paul's blinding on the road to Damascus; Crane, with similar effect, associates Gulliver's final difficulties with the dazzling effect of the sun on one permitted to emerge from Plato's cave ("Rationale of the Fourth Voyage," pp. 306–7; see note 84).

This view of the fourth voyage is, of course, a persistent one. We have seen it flourish in the nineteenth century, continue strong in such critics as Eddy, Kliger, Case, and the early Quintana, and then undergo modification (primarily through an admission of greater ironic diffraction) in Price and Ewald. In Charles Peake's "Swift and the Passions" (1960) [92] we have the interpretation stated with a kind of classic purity. Peake has defended this interpretation as that of the common reader: "No common reader doubts," he asserted,

> that the Houyhnhnms are presented for his admiration as noble though inhuman creatures worthily called 'the Perfection of Nature'; that the account of Gulliver's happiness among them is intended as a picture of the blessings of a simple and rational life; or that Gulliver, despite disappointments and difficulties of adjustment, is supposed by the author to have become a wiser and better man as a result of the teaching and example of the Houyhnhnms. And Swift's satire was directed to the ordinary man, the common reader, not to learned and ingenious critics (p. 177).

In an argument echoed by Crane (*PQ*, XL, 329), Peake regards dissenters from Houyhnhnm perfection as critical parvenus. "Swift was far too good and conscientious a satirist to bury a vital part of his message so deep that over two hundred years should pass before it was disinterred" (p. 177), a statement which also reflects the didacticist's incorrigible habit of thinking of literature as a vehicle for carrying messages. Picking up Faulkner's story that Swift claimed to have written "to the Vulgar, more than to the Learned," Peake asserts that there need to be "very good reasons for supposing that he concealed his satirical point not only from the Vulgar but also from the Learned for more than two centuries" (p. 180).

But the work described by Peake is surely not the work that Arbuthnot could have described as "merry," nor is it the work that could have elicited the several scriblerian *jeux d'esprit*,[93] nor is it the work that could have delighted the Princess of Wales and her court, as Gay delightedly reports. Indeed, one will search in vain through the correspondence of Swift and his friends (uncommon readers all) for any hint of Peake's lugubrious if not lachrymose response to the work. The ironic tone of all those responses to *Gulliver* is unmistakable. It is at the same time in harmony with the mock pontification of the letter to Sympson, which, unless one regards it as mere extraneous playfulness, is a very real part of the work, a final comment on the Gulliver-Houyhn-hnm fable, and an invaluable illumination of Swift's singularly complex intentions in the last voyage.

The solemn view of the Houyhnhnms was not born in the nineteenth century. There were common readers enough in the eighteenth century to establish it solidly from the very first. It has doubtless always been, as Peake rightly claims, the majority's view. The nineteenth century did, however, add its own emphases to the already dominant tradition, and the spectacle of Swift vexing *that* part of the world carries its own peculiar enjoyment. But the nineteenth century had an Abdiel in Thomas Tyler, whose departure from the common view ought at the very least to dispel the notion, entertained by both Crane and Peake, that the "new" attitude toward the Houyhnhnms is a unique, latter-day product of *nouveau* criticism.

The "new" attitude has led to the twentieth century's own peculiar overstatement, the left-wing didacticism of the deist theory of the Houyhnhnms, which has in turn given rise to lively skirmishes between left and right. Crane has called for a candid, uncommitted reading of *Gulliver,* a reading which would be difficult if not impossible for our present-day array of Swift specialists. However, without inquiring too closely into the candor or commitments of A. E. Dyson, we might well have in his "Swift: The Metamorphosis of Irony" (1958) [94] something as close to what Crane has in mind as this world can afford. In it Dyson suggests, not unequivocally, that Swift, when his irony is most complex and memorable, leaps beyond moral and didactic purpose, and the irony then seems, "in undergoing its metamorphosis, to bring us nearer to Swift's inner vision of man and the universe.

It ceases to be a functional technique serving a moral purpose, and becomes the embodiment of an attitude to life" (pp. 53–54). Dyson's reading of *Gulliver* which then follows shows every sign of being the most candid account of a reader's encounter with Swift since Leavis' "The Irony of Swift," but with what different results! It is the sanest and yet most exciting release from the tyranny of didacticism in all of Swift criticism. Dyson's suggestion, which, as he says, "most commentators upon *Gulliver* seem oddly afraid of," is that Swift,

> writing for gentlemen, intended to give pleasure by what he wrote. When Gulliver says of the Yahoos (his readers), "I wrote for their amendment, and not their approbation," there is a general readiness to accept this at its face value, and to credit Swift with a similar sternness. Sooner or later most writers about *Gulliver* hit upon the word "exuberance," and then pause doubtfully, wondering whether, if Swift is so moral and misanthropic as we think, such a word can have any place in describing him. Yet "exuberant" he certainly is, even in Book IV of *Gulliver*. The "vive la bagatelle," the flamboyant virtuosity of *A Tale of a Tub* is less central, but it is still to be detected, in the zest with which Gulliver describes bad lawyers, for example, and in the fantastic turns and contortions of the irony. Clearly, Swift enjoyed his control of irony; enjoyed its flexibility, its complex destructiveness, his own easy mastery of it. The irony is not *only* a battle, but a game: a civilized game, at that, since irony is by its very nature civilized, presupposing both intelligence, and at least some type of moral awareness. The "war" is a battle of wits: and if one confesses (as the present writer does) to finding *Gulliver* immensely enjoyable, need one think that Swift would really, irony apart, have been surprised or annoyed by such a reaction? (p. 66)

The oppressive didacticisms of right and left could find here a wholesome antidote.

V

swift the man

The partisanship which characterized studies of Swift in the late nineteenth century also marked the early twentieth-century studies. Wanting the care and depth of scholarship of a Forster, Craik, or Lecky, early twentieth-century students of Swift offered appreciations and depreciations whose warmth came from feeling rather than fact. Thus the favorable biography by Sophie Shilleto Smith which appeared in 1910 pointedly sets out to rehabilitate Swift, and includes passages of indignation directed against Swift's detractors, principally Ainger,[1] Thackeray, and Hay. Mrs. Smith is in turn chided for sentimentality by Paul Elmer More in a review—later reprinted as a Shelburne Essay—which took exception to her Swift "as the great and clean and typical humanitarian." More is prompted to confess, indeed, that he prefers Thackeray for accuracy.[2]

The same almost polemical spirit infuses Charles Whibley's eloquent and powerful defense of Swift in a Leslie Stephen Lecture delivered at Cambridge University in 1917, a lecture in which Stephen himself appears as one of Whibley's "opponents."[3] Whibley, primarily intent on removing from Swift the onus of misanthropy and cynicism, pointed to Swift's many strong and lasting friendships, his preference for being "a friend to men" rather than "a Friend to Man." "We know well enough whither universal philanthropy leads us," Whibley observed, noting that Robespierre and Joseph Le Bon are apt examples of Friends of Man (pp. 10–11). For

125

Whibley, as for Craik in the previous century, Swift's efforts on behalf of the Irish and his interest in individuals are sufficient to belie charges of cynicism. "The heart torn by *saeva indignatio*," Whibley argues, "was no cynic's heart" (p. 24). But Whibley's partisanship carries him too far, leading him to such a misrepresentation as his reference to Swift as "a born idealist," moved constantly by "the pure and lofty idealism that burned within him" (p. 26).

Smith's and Whibley's refurbishings of Swift are attempted on the old ground of Victorian values, by which only a lofty or humanitarian Swift could be admirable, or even forgivable. But for Swift to be seen as lofty or humanitarian, a great deal needed to be de-emphasized or suppressed, and the resulting attenuated image of Swift proved to be unsatisfying and finally unconvincing.

THE POPULAR IMAGE

A far stronger and more influential image—still today the popular image—is found in a group of essentially hostile critics influenced by a strain of romantic subjectivism and by the distinctively modern vitalism associated with Shaw, Bergson, D. H. Lawrence, and the early Aldous Huxley. Choosing to regard Swift's attacks on civilized society (in *Gulliver,* for instance) as attacks on the status quo, they saw in those attacks something of their own iconoclasm. "As the greatest of doubters and iconoclasts," wrote Ernest Boyd in the midst of the jazz age, "Swift is supreme, and it is in their flight from his merciless irony, his superb irreverence, and his magnificent contempt for the incurable imbecility of the human race that the orthodox have done everything possible to frustrate his influence."[4] But the iconoclasts of the jazz age realized that Swift's spirit in these attacks was by no means their own, that Swift was not, as some of them put it, "on the side of life." Aldous Huxley's essay in *Do What You Will* (1929)[5] illustrates the strategies and the values of this twentieth-century Swiftophobia. Huxley, on the basis of his reading of *A Lady's Dressing Room* and *Gulliver's Travels,* charges Swift with an

intense "hatred of bowels"—in effect a profound disaffection
from life and the vital processes—"which is the essence of
his misanthropy and which underlies the whole of his work"
(p. 105). Thus "Swift's prodigious powers were marshalled
on the side of death, not life," and while "every man has a
right to look at the world as he chooses," judged by the results in personal character and temperament, "the Swiftian
world-view is obviously bad" (p. 109).

Much the same kind of devaluation of Swift is found in
Herbert Read's *The Sense of Glory* (Cambridge U., 1929) [6]
where Swift's "negative" and "disconsolate" philosophy is
traced to La Rochefoucauld, who shares with Swift a too-
sophisticated suspicion of all simple and natural goodness.
This oversophistication breeds a "vulgarity of sentiment
hardly consistent with the right kind of superiority" and results in Swift's constant habits of deviousness and indirection.
"The error of Swift's philosophy," Read explains, "lies in the
uniformity and perfection of its pessimism" (p. 211). Though
"Swift's style cannot be sufficiently praised for its vigour,
clarity, and economy," his art is limited to sardonic invective,
being denied the eloquence of ideas, that is, "the creative
energy of life itself" (p. 212).

F. R. Leavis in "The Irony of Swift" (1934) [7] promises
to resist the biographical "irrelevancies" of Thackeray but
arrives ultimately at some biographical judgments of his own
which strongly reflect a growing attraction to Lawrentian
vitalism. Finding Swift's irony to be purely negative, something designed "to intimidate and to demoralize" (p. 75),
a means of mere self-assertion having no higher aim, Leavis
denies that Swift's achievement as a writer has anything "of
moral grandeur or human centrality." *Saeva indignatio*, says
Leavis, "is an indulgence that solicits us all, and the use of
readers and critics for the projection of nobly suffering selves
is familiar." Swift was instead "curiously unaware—the re-
verse of clairvoyant," and Leavis concludes that "we shall
not find Swift remarkable for intelligence if we think of
Blake" (pp. 86–87).

G. Wilson Knight (1939) [8] also finds negativism to be

127

the distinguishing characteristic of Swift's irony, noting that "any consistent satirist should sooner or later put his positive cards on the table, as Lawrence tried to do." For want of positives, "Swift has none of any *emotional* power. . . . His Hellenic sympathies are all castrated before fit for use. . . . Erotic emotions are either ignored or impregnated with disgust. He seems to endure a stoppage where there should be a flow" (p. 129). Swift's disinclination to hazard a positive vision or panacea is particularly provoking to these critics, a shortcoming they found especially unforgivable in an intellect of Swift's peculiar power and skill. "Swift has no sense of a possible music-cosmic intuition," Knight regrets, pointing to the "Beethoven incident" in *Point Counterpoint* to illustrate what he misses in Swift, a judgment congruous with Leavis' assertion that Swift is not Blake. Ernest Boyd, writing sympathetically in 1925, noted that Swift would have been a less disturbing figure if he had simply advocated some dogma, like vegetarianism or anarchy, which time could now prove futile, leaving Swift a humorous and picturesque character (p. 591).

The adverse judgments delivered by pragmatic and proto-vitalist critics are perhaps precisely what one should expect, given their particular biases. That their perpetuation of a cynical, negative, and misanthropic Swift—misanthropic in Timon's manner, that is—had and still has pervasive influence is indicated by its recurrence in less likely places—in, for instance, such a sturdy academic as Basil Willey;[9] in the oracle of twentieth-century neoclassicism and conservatism, T. S. Eliot;[10] and in intuitive biographers like Shane Leslie,[11] Rossi and Hone,[12] and J. Middleton Murry.[13]

Willey, who refers with apparent approval to Leavis and Huxley, argues that the negativism and the tendency to expose and destroy are necessary characteristics of the satirical temper. The satirist, he points out, must above all refuse to understand and explain. Because Cervantes, Fielding, and Dickens had a sympathetic understanding of their subjects, they produced something other than satire. To understand would be inimical to the satirist, for it would

128

require him to forgive. "Instead [Swift] barricades himself within his ivory tower of reason, and there 'enjoys' the bitter satisfaction of knowing himself the only wise being in an insane or bestial world" (pp. 107–8). This is the Swift who, according to T. S. Eliot, "hated the very smell of the human animal" and registered his feelings in a "work of cynicism and loathing, *Gulliver's Travels*" (*Selected Essays,* pp. 166–67); and whom Shane Leslie in *The Skull of Swift* found wanting a soul, Leslie here in some respects anticipating the "egotist" theory of Rossi and Hone in which Swift is granted but one overriding motive, a radical and all-consuming conceit which separates him from all normal human relationships.

None of the twentieth-century biographies seems to have escaped the influence of this popular image. The proud, embittered misanthrope destined for tragedy and blackness is again and again the image against which the biographers struggle. What variation there is, is in the "keys" by which the image is "explained." In the best of the biographies, Carl Van Doren's *Swift* (New York, 1930), he is a type of Lear: mistaking his friends, misjudging and misapplying his powers, he moves with bitterness toward the final tragedy, when the conjured spirit finally escapes, but "only with fearful convulsions of its heavy carcass" (p. 257), the violence here suggesting, one suspects, that the spirit is damned as well as conjured. The biographers, themselves perhaps conjured by the melancholy and melodramatic potential of those final scenes, establish their black moods early and eschew, as did Forster, Craik, Stephen, and Collins, the Swift of "*vive la bagatelle,*" the Swift who actually laughed—if only inwardly—with a few friends in a corner. Thus Rossi and Hone are horror-struck that the Yahoos "were made a society-joke by Swift's friends and contemporaries" (p. 411, n. 36), and Van Doren chooses to give even the *Verses on His Own Death* a solemn interpretation in which the "cynicism" and "intensity" are stressed along with Swift's tendency in these lines to be inaccurate about his own character (p. 254).

Most of the twentieth-century lives of Swift are the

work of "professional" biographers who are content to retell and reinterpret the facts and legends without pretense to original scholarship. Doubtless the persistence of the stock figure can be attributed in part to the dearth of scholarly biographies.[14] Though studies of special biographical problems, as we shall see, have not been wanting, no biography of Swift comparable in scope to Edgar Johnson's life of Dickens or James L. Clifford's study of Mrs. Thrale has yet appeared in this century. Pons's study of the early years, *Swift: les années de jeunesse et le 'Conte du tonneau'* (Strasbourg, 1925), was scholarly and ambitious, but was never followed by the further volumes which were to have completed the story. But perhaps the most grievous shortcoming among Swift's twentieth-century biographers is their resolve to remain innocent of the very active literary criticism of Swift's works. Thus recent biographers such as Evelyn Hardy and J. Middleton Murry, who had adequate correctives available to them, followed Rossi and Hone, Van Doren, and other predecessors in identifying Swift with Gulliver and in finding only sacrilege in *A Tale of a Tub*. A biographer who could see that it is Strephon, the starry-eyed beau of *A Lady's Dressing Room,* and not necessarily Swift, who is distressed by Celia's natural functions, might well deliver us from the tyranny of Huxley's "hatred of bowels."

If it is true that Swift as hater of bowels, as nay-sayer to life, is primarily a formulation of vitalists, then a succinct and categorical judgment of Swift by Bernard Shaw, that patriarch of vitalists, ought to be a classic statement of the vitalist point of view. Shaw does not disappoint us. In the Postscript to the World's Classics edition of *Back to Methuselah* Shaw pontificates revealingly:

> The history of modern thought now teaches us that when we are forced to give up the creeds by their childishness and their conflicts with science we must either embrace Creative Evolution or fall into the bottomless pit of an utterly discouraging pessimism. . . . This happened in dateless antiquity to Ecclesiastes the preacher and in our own era to Shakespear and Swift. . . . Had Swift seen men as creatures evolving

toward godhead, he would not have been discouraged into the absurdity of describing them as irredeemable Yahoos enslaved by a government of horses ruling them by sheer moral superiority.[15]

Ranging easily over the history of modern culture, Shaw notes that "Goethe rescued us from this horror"—that is, of despair and pessimism—with the " 'Eternal Feminine that draws us forward and upward,' which was the first modern manifesto of the mysterious force in creative evolution" (p. 261). The propagators of the popular image have not always seen Swift in historical perspective with such stark clarity. If they had, perhaps they would have recognized, not without some real basis, that "the hater of bowels" was really the nemesis of the Eternal Feminine.

The comments of Huxley, Knight, Leavis, and Shaw reveal nothing so much as a profound lack of sympathy with Swift, a radical uncongeniality of philosophy and temperament. Although their essentially hostile reactions have yielded and sustained what is undeniably the reigning image, one feels nonetheless that the twentieth century, because of a marked rapport with Swift evident in some quarters, is capable also of submitting a highly creditable minority report. Quintana said in 1940 that Swift "is generally better understood today—as a man, as a public character, as an artist—than perhaps at any time since the eighteenth century," [16] and Swift scholarship since 1940 has provided an even better basis for an understanding of Swift. But Swift *scholarship* remains a mere minority report. While partisanship for Swift need not be a prerequisite for understanding him, doubtless what understanding the twentieth century has achieved must be discovered outside the fabricators of the stock image.

The bumptious optimism which underlay the Shavian demand for a transvaluation of all values and the Shavian antipathy to Swift was by 1946, the time of Shaw's statement, being strongly challenged. One such challenge, an early one, is revealed in a letter of Yeats to Olivia Shakespeare. Writing in 1922 of the violence of the Black and Tans, who "flogged young men and then tied them to their lorries by the heels," Yeats asked a question as significant for Swift criticism as it was for literature generally. "I wonder," he wrote, "will literature be much changed by that most momentous of events, the return of evil." [17] It is perhaps a nice question whether evil returned or was simply rediscovered, but in either case a growing sense of the reality of evil beginning in, let us say, 1914, did have considerable effect on literature and criticism. Faith in the pliability—much less the perfectibility—of human nature was maintained with increasing difficulty in the face of this "return of evil," and Swift's was among the various kinds of astringent conservatism—Burke's, Dr. Johnson's, John Adams', Lancelot Andrewes' also come quickly to mind—which figured in twentieth-century attempts to negotiate with the freshly realized potential for evil in human nature.

It was, of course, something more than mere toryism which attracted Yeats to the "half-symbolic image" of Swift which he confessed had a special hold upon his imagination,[18] but the effect of Swift as a political figure upon Yeats is not to be minimized. Swift was part of that quadrumvirate which Yeats credited with bringing the Renaissance to Ireland. In Yeats's poem *The Seven Sages,* the sixth sage brings the quadrumvirate together:

> Whether they knew it or not,
> Goldsmith and Burke, Swift and the Bishop of Cloyne
> All hated Whiggery; but what is Whiggery?
> A levelling, rancorous, rational sort of mind
> That never looked out of the eye of a saint
> Or out of a drunkard's eye.[19]

While Yeats's lines do not make Swift either a drunkard or a saint, the suggestion of breadth (if not greatness) of soul is refreshing after the narrow, rigid, and melodramatic image of popular myth. This hatred of Whiggery, as Jacques Barzun [20] has suggested, "is what over the years has made Swift so many self-righteous enemies" (p. xvii). To be sure, Yeats is not untouched by the darker side of Swift. Parnell, he says,

drew "bitter wisdom" from "Swift's dark grove" (p. 276),
and it is Swift's epitaph—the greatest in history, Yeats calls
it in several places [21]—which Yeats both translates (*Collected Poems*, p. 241) and reflects, perhaps with significant
inversion, in his own:

> Cast a cold eye
> On life, on death.
> Horseman, pass by! (*Collected Poems*, p. 344).

There is no doubt that for Yeats Swift never ceased to represent something positive, something worthy of contemplation.

Yeats's most extensive use of the Swift image is in his
play *Words upon the Window-Pane* (1930),[22] which was
presented by the Abbey Players in both Dublin and New
York. In this play Swift is a restless if not a conjured spirit
who insists on intruding on a twentieth-century Dublin
séance, to the discomfort of the medium and her circle. One
member of the circle, however, a Cambridge student who is
sceptical of spiritualism's hocus pocus, will evidently profit
from the experience. We are led to believe that his doctoral
dissertation on Swift will be the better for this "contact" with
the unlaid ghost. But Yeats's primary purpose in the play and
in the accompanying essay was to reach "the Cellars and
Garrets" of Dublin, where the uncertain and unstable powers
of groups dedicated to "general improvement" stood in need
of the steadying, sobering, resolute image of the Drapier-
Dean and of the aristocratic, civilizing values of eighteenth-
century Protestant Ireland.

Like so much of what Yeats exploited in his poetry, his
image of Swift remains more private than public. An image
is there, however, engaging, powerful, sharply distinct from
the popular one. Future biographers and others intent on
assaying Swift's character will ignore it at their peril. But it
is incomplete and, as Yeats himself declares, half-symbolic.
To fill in its various shadows the twentieth-century student
must sift the host of studies dealing with particular aspects
of Swift the man.

THOUGHT AND RELIGION

On the subject of Swift's ideas, twentieth-century critics and scholars have pulled in all directions. G. Wilson Knight, in the already cited essay published in 1939, misses a fair share of the ironies in *Gulliver* and in the *Tale* and says that "no defence of Swift's fundamental religious orthodoxy can stand the test of such writings. He is a sceptical humanist who again and again tilts at Christian belief" (p. 125). Knight cites the geometrical wafer, the war of the Big-Endians and Little-Endians, and the Struldbruggs' red spot on the forehead as jests against the sacraments, revealing "Swift's slight sympathy for the mystical and ritualistic." Final proof for Knight of Swift's irreligion is that "the Houyhnhnms have no religion" (p. 125). F. M. Darnall (1942),[23] on the other hand, sees optimistic commitment. He refers to Swift's "positive ethical ideas far in advance of the eighteenth century," ideas which embody his belief in man's "infinite possibilities for good." Among Swift's "reformatory suggestions," which he covered with satire "all too deeply perhaps," (pp. 54–55) are educational systems very like our own. "For now, indeed, the educational systems of England and America are quite in line with his recommendations intimated two hundred years ago" (p. 59). Louis Kronenberger (1942)[24] accuses Swift of being a religious bigot, but one devoid of religious feeling, for his was "a madman's logic" and "a madman's shrewdness." "No one in history has argued more brilliantly and unanswerably from false and grotesque premises" (p. 48). Louis A. Landa anticipated in 1946 some of the recent criticism of *Gulliver* when he suggested that Part IV is "in its implications Christian apologetics, though of course in non-theological terms."[25]

In correcting misconceptions and in building a reliable account of Swift's ideas—one hesitates to apply the words "thought" or "philosophy" here—Continental scholars have played an important role. Pons's *Swift* (1925) remains valuable for its wealth of background material, though when relating this material to Swift and his works one needs to be wary. Pons explores such matters as the intellectual climate at Trinity College during Swift's stay there, Swift's reading at Moor Park, and the main philosophical currents of Swift's time. Pons's grasp of Swift's attitude toward his material is sometimes dubious, as for example when he takes the clothes philosophy of the *Tale* too seriously and too literally, as though it were Carlyle's and not the mere trapping it is for Swift. Pons offers what must surely be the most brilliant and exhaustive survey of the metaphysical exploitation of clothes in philosophy and literature from the Old Testament to the Renaissance. Reflected in Pons, as in the early studies of *Gulliver*'s sources, is the faith that the meaning of a work can be discovered in its backgrounds, in the thought of its time as a process emerging from the past. When Swift and his works were considered as mere products of literary and philosophic traditions, or when Swift was taken to be merely representative of the thought and values of his time, the real Swift, the anachronistic critic of the contemporary scene, escaped the toils of this otherwise worthy method.

In the mid-thirties Swift received a sudden burst of attention from Continental scholars, seven weighty monographs appearing within a few years, all except one the product of German scholarship.[26] Of these seven studies, three addressed themselves primarily to the elucidation of Swift's ideas. Camille Looten, a Roman Catholic canon, devoted himself in *La Pensée religieuse de Swift et ses antinomies* (1935) to demonstrating what he considered to be Swift's essentially irreligious nature, his total lack of "le sentiment intérieur de Dieu." For Looten, Swift's disinclination to intellectualize religious belief was a failure of spirituality and an index of Swift's disbelief in the existence of God and in the mysteries.[27] Since only one-sixth of Swift's library was devoted to theology, Looten thought it no wonder that Swift fell under the baneful influence of such figures as La Rochefoucauld, Samuel Butler, and Montaigne. Pyrrhonism, if it can be applied to Swift, is for Looten the pyrrhonism of Rochester and the *libertins,* not that of Pascal or Dryden. Swift's works, while they were written against the enemies of Anglicanism, in fact did Anglicanism no credit, as "la pauvre arme du ridicule" was an ill-chosen weapon, and "les énormités" of the satires proved offensive to truly religious sensibilities Swift entered the Church, then, purely as a hypocrite and opportunist, or, as Herbert Read had put it earlier, "with the calculating purpose of a career-ist" devoid of "the talents appropriate to his calling" (p. 209).

Less strident in his indictment of Swift's deficiencies as a clergyman, Hans Reimers in *Jonathan Swift: Gedanken und Schriften über Religion und Kirche* (1935) found a similar dualism between Swift's activities in the Church and a scep-tical rationalism which stood in the way of genuine belief. Reimers, echoing many nineteenth-century critics, argued that Swift, the political moralist, had no real faith in the doctrines of the Church and supported it only as a necessary social institution, a preserver of public morality. In this, Swift illustrates what Reimers calls the growing utilitarian ethics of the time.

Max Armin Korn in *Die Weltanschauung Jonathan Swifts* (1935) applied the historical method systematically and perceptively and, guided by a definite conception of the personality of Swift, produced a truly valuable exposition of Swift's ideas. Taking up Swift's *"religionsphilosophische Weltbild,"* Swift's ideas on church and state, on the ideal and the real, on past and present, Korn produced a more solid and credible Swift than had appeared since Craik's biography, a Swift in which the anti-intellectualism, the eth-ical seriousness, the pessimism and scepticism, the antago-nism to enthusiasm and metaphysics, somehow co-existed in a not uneasy relationship. An important ingredient in the achievement of this unity is the element of compromise, which Korn, unlike many other interpreters, regarded as ap-propriate to Swift's character.[28] Thus out of Swift's acute awareness of the gulf separating the ideal and the real, comes his commitment to a life of action. Swift is of his time in his

rationalism and his opposition to enthusiasm, in his preference for common sense over metaphysical speculation, as
well as in his reticence—even furtiveness—regarding religion. Religion was a matter which the eighteenth-century
gentleman kept, for the most part, to himself.

Korn's sensitive application of the historical method enabled him to anticipate some of the conclusions regarding
Swift's ideas offered by Quintana in *The Mind and Art of
Jonathan Swift* (1936), the first major work in English to
apply the historical method to Swift. By the thirties the historical method of scholarship had established itself every-
where. In intellectual history the work of such scholars as
R. F. Jones on the quarrel between the ancients and moderns,[29] A. O. Lovejoy on deism, classicism, and primitivism,[30]
and R. S. Crane on the idea of progress was particularly impressive.[31] Louis Bredvold had shown in *The Intellectual
Milieu of John Dryden* (Ann Arbor, 1934) that the historical
approach could illumine an individual figure and correct
long-standing misconceptions. Quintana, working in this tradition, related the mind of Swift to the *Zeitgeist* of the late
seventeenth century as it had been defined by historical
scholarship, especially in Lovejoy's "Parallel of Deism and
Classicism" (1932). The portrait of Swift that emerges from
Quintana's study suggests both the virtues and the hazards
of the historical method: the portrait is fully drawn, but only
at the cost of overemphasizing the representative character
of Swift's genius, especially Swift's reasonableness in an age
of reason. But despite its flaws, the book was a welcome
antidote, for it gave to English readers virtually the only
weighty and influential opposition to the twentieth-century
Swiftophobes and those who less wittingly perpetuated the
image of the sneering and snarling misanthrope.

In Quintana's analysis the *Zeitgeist*, of which Swift was
both a manifestation and a product, was at the same time the
locus and limit of his ideas. Quintana emphasized that Swift
was not original but representative, that his ideas reflected
the distinctive characteristics of the Enlightenment—its "uniformitarianism" (that is, its belief in the uniformity of nature

137

and reason), its rationalism, its consequent hatred of enthusiasm, its equalitarianism, and its anti-intellectualism (p. 51). The "uniformity of nature and reason" Quintana applied rather gingerly to Swift and failed to define the phrase clearly or explain its implications fully. As used by Lovejoy, "uniformitarianism" involves the belief that reason is identical in all men, in all times and places; consequently the life of reason admits of no diversity. Thus the mark of truth is its universality of appeal; a sure sign of error, the taint of differentness, peculiarity, limitation to a particular time or place. As Lovejoy rightly pointed out, under this view Christianity was but a "local custom" of the European peoples, and thus suspect. Neither this view nor the various shifts to meet it on its own terms—progressive revelation, figurism, or "reasonable" Christianity [32]—were at all congenial to Swift, a fact which Quintana unduly slights. If a uniformitarian, Swift could not admit the various restraints and limits which he saw fit to place upon reason, nor could he have entertained the greater part of his political principles, which hardly favored democracy or universal suffrage, nor could he have "laughed with a few friends in a corner," or shown his other marked partialities for particular men as against Mankind.

That Swift had considerable respect for reason as an intellectual standard for thought and conduct, no one will deny; but there are at least two areas—love of life and propagation of the species—besides the not inconsiderable space occupied by the Christian mysteries, where we know Swift ruled reason out of bounds. Neither does the enlarged scope of reason which Quintana ascribes to Swift leave much place for the imagination. Indeed, Quintana asserts that Swift, an "extremist" here, did in fact "shrivel up the imagination" (p. 64), a curious judgment on one whose imagination was prodigious by any standards, and in whom overt statements approving imagination, or what was in effect its equivalent, invention, are not wanting.[33] It would be far safer to say that Swift insisted on the subjection of imagination to reason, which in this case meant an intelligible order or form. Unbridled imagination resulted in the formless chaos of the works and techniques of composition parodied in *A Tale of a Tub*, a work where all the elements of an unbridled imagination are present, with the subtle addition of Swift's control over the whole by means of his evaluation of it. It is the audacity of Swift's imagination, what Quintana saw as "sensationalism" in *Gulliver*, which is one of Swift's distinguishing characteristics. This audacity *plus* the evaluation of it gives Swift his peculiar position as satiric artist.

While Quintana's *Swift: An Introduction* (1955) reasserts the representative rather than the original character of Swift's genius, it corrects several of the overstatements of 1936. There is, for instance, an avoidance of the insistence in *Mind and Art* that Swift's was "a perfectly ordered system of thought" (p. 147), uniformitarian in character. The abstract reason of the Enlightenment which Quintana in 1936 found Swift sharing with his time, becomes in *Swift: An Introduction* something approximating the *consensus gentium,* common sense, the funded experience of mankind, an entity which clearly admits of some diversity and thus offers a far more likely foundation for Swift's traditionalism and conservatism. Reason in 1955 became simply avoidance of extremes. Thus Anglicanism was "reasonable" for Swift because it was a *via media,* "the middle way between Roman Catholicism and Puritan Dissent" (p. 33). "Swift's relentless moral rigorism," which in 1936 came perilously close to deism and stoicism, is identified now as "essentially traditional and Christian," though Quintana rightly adds that "it was not as a rule expressed in the language of theology" (p. 33).

Among the recent more serious students of Swift, Quintana has been the least inclined to grant him anything more than a barely nominal Christianity. It is true that he has often sought to correct those earlier critics—Churton Collins, Herbert Read, and others—who disparaged the sincerity of Swift's attachment to the Church and to Christian belief. Yet Quintana himself nowhere succeeds in making Swift's religious beliefs meaningful or credible. Perhaps this is the result of Quintana's early commitment to a Swift representative of his age. There are times indeed when Quintana seems intent

139

on isolating Swift from the more lively and enduring elements of Christian doctrine—the belief in original sin, for instance—by simply associating such elements with a period of history (and consequently a habit of mind) lying outside Swift's own. Quintana speaks in *Swift: An Introduction* of an historical change which brought later satirists, those of the nineteenth century and after, "a sense of guilt and of implication in some vast cosmic evil" (p. 39), as though Swift and Molière, Ben Jonson and Dryden, living under another *Zeitgeist,* were somehow immune to guilt and implication in cosmic evil. Swift's obvious fideism, which has received careful attention from several critics, is evidently simply distasteful to Quintana, as a footnote on the matter in *Mind and Art* reveals: "This bifurcation of reason and faith seems to the present writer, who speaks merely as a historian and from a purely historical point of view, to be the central weakness in Swift's religious system" (p. 151 n.).

Swift's fideism has been given most complete attention by Louis A. Landa, first in his "Swift, the Mysteries and Deism" (1945),[34] and again three years later in his introduction to the Sermons in the Shakespeare Head edition (HD, IX, 97–132). In the former study he calls attention to Swift's statement to Delaney that "the grand points of Christianity ought to be taken as infallible revelations" (*Corresp.,* IV, 289), a statement which "may well serve as a key to much of his religious thinking" ("Mysteries and Deism," p. 256). In his well-known attacks Swift chose to avoid arguments proper to Christian apologetics, using instead his familiar weapons of ridicule and invective. Indeed, Swift's disinclination to puzzle over nice points of theology doubtless encouraged a great deal of subsequent misunderstanding and misinterpretation of his religious position, as we have seen in the case of Looten.

Landa found in Swift's neglected sermons (eleven authenticated ones survive) a comprehensive statement of Swift's religious beliefs, with his attitude toward the role of reason and faith in the acceptance of the mysteries succinctly outlined in *On the Trinity.* Using *On the Trinity* as evidence,

Landa demonstrated that Swift's hostility to the deists was based in part on his recognition that their pervasive rationalism endangered the mysteries by simply denying them. In opposing the deists, Swift used two arguments in *On the Trinity* which have had some currency in twentieth-century Christian existentialism and in the neo-orthodoxy of Niebuhr and Tillich. Mysteries, argued Swift, are inescapable; even in the natural world we are surrounded with mysteries which we have no choice but to accept without understanding them. "How little do those who quarrel with Mysteries, know of the commonest Actions of Nature? The Growth of an Animal, of a Plant, or of the smallest Seed, is a Mystery to the wisest among Men" (HD, IX, 164). This argument by analogy was a common one in Swift's day and was given its most famous expression in Bishop Butler's *Analogy of Religion* (1736). Corresponding to the mysteries in the world of nature are the divine mysteries, such as the Trinity, reincarnation, and the like, which, as they are beyond the comprehension of human reason, require acceptance on faith alone, and thus they, according to Swift, "try our Faith and Obedience, and encrease our Dependence upon God" (HD, IX, 165). Landa insisted that this is not "a thorough-going scepticism" or a total rejection of human reason, but rather a "rescuing of faith from the malign charge that it is opposed to reason." For Swift, Landa argued, faith was "highly reasonable" and may be acquired "without giving up our senses or contradicting our reason" ("Mysteries and Deism," p. 251). There is, in other words, no humbling of reason, no surge of emotionalism, no passionate mysticism in this act of faith. It remains austere.

Not uncongenial with Landa's interpretation of Swift's religious beliefs were several earlier, rather more conjectural views. Rossi and Hone, whose "egotist" theory of Swift's personality led their interpretative biography into many absurdities, somehow managed in their estimate of Swift's religious character to avoid the far-fetched. Taking advantage of Swift's characteristic reticence on these matters, they suggested the not altogether unlikely influence of Calvin [35] in

Swift's awareness of the remoteness, omnipotence, and unintelligibility of God. Such a Calvinistic, unloving Jahveh is not far to seek in Swift's writings. Both "the mysterious incomprehensible One God" of *On the Trinity* (HD, IX, 168) and the Jove of *The Day of Judgment* are examples. "The measure of religious consciousness is, roughly expressed, the distance man feels between himself and God. And Swift felt the distance," Rossi and Hone asserted. "He thought of God as infinitely distant from him; veiled and remote, yet present in a potential way through Grace" (p. 109). Bertram Newman, whose biography, *Jonathan Swift* (London, 1937), is one of the better twentieth-century efforts, agreed with Rossi and Hone in this interpretation and went on to explore the psychology of this belief more fully. Newman pointed to a pertinent and revealing utterance in *Thoughts on Religion:* "Miserable mortals! can we contribute to the *honour and Glory of God?* I could wish that expression were struck out of our Prayer-books" (HD, IX, 263). Newman also related this attitude to Swift's sense, "as keen as Pascal's, of the impotence of the human intellect to 'search out the Almighty to perfection'; of the narrow bounds set to human knowledge; of the precariousness of Man's lot on earth" (p. 211).

All of this suggests a great deal about Swift's religious sensibility, the definition of which is a task for which the twentieth century is not unsuited. Swift, it appears, might well preach—in the pulpit and out—the text of Kierkegaard's country parson: "As against God we are always in the wrong." [36] Despair has often enough been an element in the popular image of Swift. Perhaps twentieth-century scholars, especially those made aware of a non-optimistic side of Christianity by Kierkegaard, Niebuhr, Tillich, Auden, Thomas Mann, and others, are now coming to a just apprehension of that despair. Nichol Smith, for instance, in a much neglected essay, "Jonathan Swift: Some Observations" (1935),[37] corrected a common misconception of Swift's remark in a letter to Ford in 1736: "I have long given up all hopes of Church or Christianity" (*Letters to Ford*, p. 169). Smith suggested, "The man who despairs of Christianity is probably a Christian," a view which may well seem parodoxical to those critics, Quintana for instance, who found it difficult to dissociate Christianity from optimism.[38] Landa, striking the same note as did Smith, explored in a perceptive critique the Christian base of the voyage to the Houyhnhnms and noted that Swift "would have held an optimistic divine to be a contradiction in terms; . . . his own pessimism is quite consonant with the pessimism at the heart of Christianity."[39]

The names Calvin, Pascal, Tertullian, John Wesley, have been increasingly associated with Swift in recent criticism, and these associations along with Landa's careful analysis of Swift's fideism would seem to place him quite firmly in the Augustinian tradition. There has never, of course, been much danger of associating him with any form of Thomism. The chief danger has always lain in misjudging his "scepticism" and "rationalism," making him variously deistic, stoical, anti-Christian, utopian, perfectionistic, or merely cynical. While venturing to call Swift an Augustinian and associating him with so diverse a group as that named above may be helpful, studies analyzing differences between Swift and kindred sensibilities would be of greater value. A study of Swift and Dr. Johnson or of Swift and Dryden might well illuminate the often puzzling antagonisms felt for Swift by Johnson or for Dryden by Swift.[40]

Although overt connections between Pascal and Swift are not to be found—unless one traces a connection through Arbuthnot's *Know Yourself* (1734) to the *Entretien de Pascal avec Saci* (1728)[41]—a provocative and thoughtful but not wholly reliable comparative study of the two figures has been offered by Pons (1951).[42] After arguing for Swift's direct acquaintance with the works of Pascal on the basis of similar thoughts and ideas, Pons declares the similarities are of the surface only. On a deeper level their essential differences become evident. Thus Pons finds that Pascal contemplating the starry heavens shows an imaginative strength in his sense of cosmic reality and order which is totally alien to Swift. Pascal finds reason inadequate because it is too leaden, too dull, too inclined to mislead and make drowsy; thus he supplements reason with intuition and faith. On the other hand, Swift, according to Pons, finds himself at an impasse when for the demented reason of the Lagadoans he substitutes what Pons considers to be the spiritless, impoverished, barren, and paltry good sense of the Houyhnhnms. Pascal takes off on intellectually limitless flights, searching for God and moral perfection; Swift's intellectual quests check themselves at their very outset and reveal his profound denial of his need for joy. While some of Pons's contrasts between Swift and Pascal are sound enough, others suggest, perhaps because of Pons's evident disenchantment with Swift, the heavy hand giving us false weight.

Ernest Tuveson in *Millennium and Utopia: A Study of the Background of the Idea of Progress* (Berkeley, 1949) analyzed the several kinds of optimism and perfectionism at work in the seventeenth and eighteenth centuries. Tuveson in this study built upon and amplified the earlier work of R. S. Crane ("Anglican Apologetics"). Tuveson's subsequent study, "Swift and the World-Makers" (1950),[43] concentrated on Swift's hostile relationship to a particular form of progressivism found in the rationalizing divines and physico-theologians such as Thomas Burnet. (Burnet's *Sacred Theory of the Earth* [1684–90], an effort to strengthen Scripture by bringing philosophy over to its side, offered a "Christian geology" in which the flood and the creation were explained naturalistically.) Swift, argued Tuveson in his summary, was "reacting against 'modernism,'" whose elements appeared in the controversy between religion and science in the 1690's, and among whose characteristics Tuveson cites "the faith in teleological progress and a kind of 'progressive' religion; the testing of revelation and authority in general by reason and scientific concepts rather than vice versa; the supremacy of materialistic physical law"; and "the tendency to replace the Christian humanist conception of man's nature with one which tended inevitably to deny original sin, spiritual salvation, and the place of 'mystery' in religion" (p. 74).

For those who might find incongruity in a Christian divine who is also a satirist, James Brown in "Swift as Moralist" (1954) [44] offers common ground for these allegedly antipodal occupations. However, the opposition Brown sees between "Christian" and "satirist" is factitious, and more than anything else the article reveals the need to rescue such terms as "Christian" and "satirist" from too narrow or too unconsidered an application. Perhaps the chief value in Brown's article lies in his comparison of Bishop Butler's religious and ethical position, which is discussed at length, and that of Swift.

The twentieth-century rediscovery of Swift as moralist has led to at least one weighty attack on the grounds and expectations of Swift's ethics. Walter J. Ong, S.J., in "Swift on the Mind: The Myth of Asepsis" (1954),[45] turns Swift into a moral perfectionist who mistakenly thought evil could be isolated and sterilized out of existence, a kind of Savonarola. Father Ong, taking Swift's personae for Swift (he regards as Swift's own the description of the mind in *The Mechanical Operation of the Spirit*: "A Crowd of little Animals" who determine thought according to their bites), associates Swift with the materialistic and mechanistic views of Hobbes. "In his concern with psychological operations," Ong argues, "Swift tends frequently to conceive of them in a mechanistic or geometrical fashion—a fashion at once gross and vigorous. He favors immediate reduction of complex issues in terms of position or local motion. Swift was moving in the current of mechanistic thought so strong in his day" (p. 216). Most critics, however, even hostile ones, appear to be sufficiently aware of how firmly Swift stood against the currents of materialism and mechanism, subtly parodying them in such works as *The Mechanical Operation* and *A Tale of a Tub*. One is tempted to see in Father Ong's misinterpretation something of Thomistic objection to Augustinianism.

A full and convincing account of Swift's ideas remains a desideratum of current Swift scholarship. Landa's careful scrutiny of sermons and other evidence corrected long-standing errors and began a movement in a new and exciting direction. Students of Swift's ideas would do well not to expect a carefully ordered system, keeping in mind Swift's statement in *Thoughts on Various Subjects:* "If a Man would register all his Opinions upon Love, Politicks, Religion, Learning, and the like; beginning from his Youth, and so go on to old Age: What a Bundle of Inconsistencies and Contradictions would appear at last?" (HD, I, 244) A willingness to admit contradictions and inconsistencies—not to be confused with what nineteenth-century critics called Swift's paradoxes—is what makes D. Nichol Smith's modest "Jonathan Swift: Some Observations" (1935) still the best twentieth-century insight into Swift the man. Smith carries the basically pessimistic and misanthropic Swift as close to optimism and purposiveness as can be done with any safety. For Smith, the Dean of St. Patrick's is unequivocally Christian, committed to the Anglican Church simply because it was, as Swift had asserted in the "Apology" to the *Tale,* "the most perfect, of all others, in discipline and doctrine"—a relative perfection, Smith explains, in that "to him there was no perfect church any more than anything in this world could be perfect; but it was the best of any he knew" (p. 36).

No small virtue of Nichol Smith's essay is his disinclination to idealize Swift, a tendency which can be as disastrous to a likely portrait as the ranting of the Swiftophobes. Certain prejudices of Swift do not deserve the dignity of such terms as "thought" or "ideas": his hostility to pure as against applied mathematics is one such prejudice. Anyone who has floundered in vector analysis or calculus will know Swift's feeling exactly. It is not a feeling which deserves praise or even sympathy. The same is true of Swift's impatience with pure science or pure research, which he somehow associated with vain speculations in philosophy. The twentieth century has the advantage of hindsight; few today will regret that Swift's values did not control, for instance, pure medical research during the past two hundred years. It is true, as Smith points out, that it is the "corruptions" of science which Swift attacks, and that in Swift's day the *Philosophical Transactions* of the Royal Society showed "a large proportion of chaff to wheat" (p. 40), but one fears nonetheless that Swift viewed the corruptions of science—as he did the corruptions of learning—rather narrowly.

Another unfortunate idealization of Swift is the tendency to make his ethics overpure, to see him burning constantly with righteous indignation. The truth is that his indignation was at times all too unrighteous. His animus toward his Uncle Godwin, for instance, from whom he received his education, cannot be described as anything but the grossest ingratitude.[46] The indignation directed at Lord Berkeley and Arthur Bushe in *The Discovery* was compounded of hurt pride, jealousy, and wilful self-deceit. Nor should any claim for righteousness be made for *The Windsor Prophecy* or *The Problem.* At other times the indignation was hardly more than a satiric fiction, that is, an artifice for the sake of the satire. Such a mood lies behind the burlesques of medicine and law in the fourth voyage of *Gulliver,* and it is also apparent in *A Panegyric on Dean Swift,* a libel on himself which Swift sent by an unknown hand to a Whig printer, who duly published it. The danger in idealizing Swift is that Swift becomes merely priggish if not inhuman, Houyhnhnm-like; the human Swift, full of pride, anger, and their consequent frailties, is lost from view. Too often the short biographical sketch—or even the full-length biography—has taken its tone and theme from the epitaph, which as a rule has been made to bear more weight than is reasonably warranted. It should be remembered that the epitaph was written by Swift in 1740, when he was seventy-three, two years before he was declared *non compos mentis;* that it is a conventional statement and is no more apt to be a reliable index of character than other statements of a like order; and that when a satirist refers to his "*saeva indignatio,*" he is most likely trying to raise his ethos so as to improve the effect of his satire.[47] When Swift is solemn and grave, especially about himself, one ought to be on his guard.[48]

SATIRE

Although generalizations on the distinctive quality of Swift's satire might seem hopeless, thankless, and empty, the achievements of critics here have often been happy and revealing. Coleridge's witty definition, though its accuracy has sometimes been challenged,[49] intuitively gauged the tone and effect of Swift's satiric art. "Swift," wrote Coleridge in *Table Talk*, "was *anima Rabelaisii habitans in sicco*,—the soul of Rabelais dwelling in a dry place." [50] Whibley, attempting to place Swift's characteristic manner, reminded his audience of Castiglione's definition of irony— ". . . when with a grave and dry speech and in sporting a man speaketh pleasantly that he hath not in his mind"—adding that in the irony of Swift "the word and the spirit are opposed to the sense" and a "heightened effect is produced by overstating the other side of the case. There is no artifice of literature more instantly effective for those who appreciate it. There is none more fertile in misunderstanding. In England especially it is used at the writer's peril" (p. 34).[51] There have been biographical, historical, formalistic, utilitarian, and moralistic estimates of Swift's satiric technique, ranging in their emphases from the author's intention—both conscious and unconscious—to the effect on the reader.

The marks of biographical influence are upon Herbert Read's judgment that Swift's satire is essentially sardonic. Glancing over a series of definitions of such terms as *irony, sarcasm*, and *satire*, found in Fowler's *Dictionary of Modern English Usage*, Read hits upon *sardonic* as an appropriate definition of Swift's quality. Fowler had found the motive of the sardonic to be "self-relief," its province "absurdity," its method "pessimism," and its audience "the self." Applying this to Swift, Read argues that the "sardonic pages of *Gulliver*" are "the release of a mind from the strain of an intense emotion," an emotion which Read traces to conflicts involving Stella and Vanessa (pp. 206–7).

Quintana's historicism has often colored the place and character he has given to Swift's art. Thus in *Swift: An Introduction* he places Swift "alongside of Samuel Butler, Pope, Goldsmith, Fielding, Jane Austen, for it is in such writers that the age of comic vision spoke most clearly. . . . Theirs was not a vision of progress but of man's habitual involvement in ridiculous circumstances." The disappearance of this *vis comica* is also explained historically: "But such a comic mode as this—hard-tempered, alive with energy, working often through grotesque representations—did not fare well in the presence of the new romantic spirit, the rise of which spelt the end of so much that had been characteristic of the Enlightenment." When men under the later, "romantic" vision came to appear less ridiculous than "unfortunate and frustrated," the *"vis comica"* had turned into something else, tainted with "a sense of guilt and of implication in some vast cosmic evil" (pp. 38–39).

Many critics engaged in defining the peculiar character of Swift the satirist as artist reject the biographical and historical approaches in favor of the utilitarian one. This approach stresses the moral fervor and earnestness of the author, his zeal to enlighten an audience or to disabuse it of prejudices and false notions. A discussion of Swift by William Lyon Phelps [52] in 1927 illustrates an elementary kind of moralistic criticism. Thinking doubtless of Thorne Smith and the satirists of the twenties, Phelps asked why Swift was so much greater than these. His answer is neat: "Our present contemporary satirists ridicule virtue; Swift ridiculed vice" (pp. 97–98). Herbert Davis in *The Satire of Swift* (New York, 1947) also sees Swift ultimately as an unmasker, rather joylessly jolting complacencies, including those of hopeful reformers like Gulliver and even himself. Similarly, the unmasking role is central in "Jonathan Swift, the Disenchanter" (1946),[53] in which Ruby Redinger finds that when Swift rises above mere particularities in his stripping away of illusions from the ugly truths of human existence, he achieves the universality of great art. (Conspicuous failures are such works as the *Bickerstaff Papers,* too particular in their attack to achieve what Miss Redinger calls "transcendent irony.") Quintana's recurrent description in *Mind and Art* of Swift's effect on the reader—"It is not as you think—look!" (p. 51) —is yet another attempt to convey the effect of unmasking so often associated with the satires. The social and ethical value of satire and ridicule as background for Swift's satires is discussed at length in *Jonathan Swift and the Anatomy of Satire* (Cambridge, Mass., 1953), by John M. Bullitt, whose detailed analysis and isolation of satiric devices unfortunately tends to obscure the larger effects of entire works. Bullitt, relying heavily on Bergson's theory of comedy, points out that situations become comic in Swift when we perceive a character relinquishing rational or intelligent control of his behavior in favor of mechanical and irrational modes of control (or, more appropriately, non-control) (pp. 1–37).

The growing interest in the technical strategies of the satirist that has marked twentieth-century Swift criticism has led to the full-length rhetorical studies of Bullitt, Price, and Ewald, with more modest anticipations in Quintana's "Situational Satire" (1948) and Ehrenpreis' "Swift and Satire" (1952).[54] An early remark by Mark Van Doren indicates the peculiar emphasis of this basically formalistic criticism: speaking of *Gulliver* in 1926, Van Doren argued that in such works Swift "has devised a series of traps into which the running mind must fall." [55] F. R. Leavis in his close reading of the "Digression on Madness" in his "The Irony of Swift" (1934) candidly demonstrates his own entanglement in such a trap (pp. 78–84). For Jacques Barzun (note 20), Swift's satire is yet more deadly than a trap. He warns against "its flexible turns and lunges against all objects within reach, from a centre which is itself ever shifting" (p. xii). From another perspective F. W. Bateson describes Swift's strategy with remarkable accuracy and insight. "Swift's technique," wrote Bateson in *English Poetry: A Critical Introduction* (London, 1950), "is to insinuate himself into the enemy ranks disguised as a friend, and once he is there to spread all the alarm and despondency he can" (p. 179). The notion that Swift the satirist stalks, traps, trips, dupes, and embarrasses the reader has encouraged the wariness of recent Swift criticism and has doubtless influenced reinterpretations of *Gulliver* and the *Tale*.

POLITICS

By the end of the nineteenth century the Jeffrey-inspired myth of Swift's political apostasy had been strongly challenged. Twentieth-century criticism has more fully and carefully explored Swift's political principles and has demonstrated conclusively that politically and ecclesiastically, while human and thus often self-regarding, Swift was by no means an unprincipled opportunist. The standard analysis of Swift's change from Whig to Tory is R. W. Babcock's study published in 1932, "Swift's Conversion to the Tory Party." [56] Studies of Swift's political and economic views include Louis Landa's "Swift's Economic Views and Mercantilism" (1943),[57] and "Swift and Charity" (1945).[58] The former corrects the common misconception that Swift and the Tories were hostile to trade; the latter article demonstrates the highly practical and traditional character of Swift's charity. In this study Landa draws upon *On Mutual Subjection* and *On the Poor Man's Contentment* —both sermons—for Swift's theory, while illustrating his practice by means of entries in Swift's account books, his plan to supply beggars with badges, and his activities in the charity-school movement. Irvin Ehrenpreis in "Swift on Liberty" (1952) [59] quotes copiously and somewhat indiscriminately from the works and correspondence in arguing that Swift's failure in his political and ecclesiastical careers was the result of his loyalty to a "declining landed aristocracy and rejection of middle-class merchants and financiers." "A vision turned early, firmly, nobly, and mistakenly to the past ruined his career" (p. 146). An easily misunderstood matter which Ehrenpreis discusses revealingly is Swift's stand on freedom of conscience and freedom of the press. Swift habitually upheld the former, arguing all too irreproachably that everyone was free to think his own thoughts. However, overt expression of ideas harmful to the Established Church and state were not to be tolerated. Liberty of the press, consequently, did not extend so far as to include publication of material subversive of the established order. Ehrenpreis points out that under Walpole Swift stood firmly for liberty of the press, although he had recommended otherwise to Bolingbroke during the Queen Anne ministry.

Swift's halting progress in the Church was first given detailed and scholarly treatment by Sir Charles Firth in "Dean

Swift and Ecclesiastical Preferment" (1926),[60] a study which is now superseded by a great achievement of twentieth-century Swift scholarship, Louis Landa's *Swift and the Church of Ireland* (Oxford, 1954).[61] This study corrects two major misconceptions: one, the old story propagated by Swift himself that his failure to secure the Deanery of Derry in 1700 was the result of the corruption of Arthur Bushe, Berkeley's secretary; the other, also encouraged by Swift, that after initial difficulties Swift was able to subdue the cathedral chapter to his will. Landa's careful research shows that Swift was never seriously considered for the Deanery of Derry, and that a strong Whiggish faction in the cathedral chapter, a faction accountable for the most part to Archbishop King, never ceased to harass Swift in his management of cathedral business. Landa also marshals evidence of the abject and ruinous state of the Irish Church, ample cause for Swift's pessimism in such statements as "I have long given up all hopes of Church or Christianity" (*Letters to Ford,* p. 169).

LOVES

While Swift's alleged apostasies in religion and politics have been firmly set aside by recent scholarship, Swift the apostate of love remains a persistent figure. Love's votaries have never found much to please them in Swift's conduct with women, and this situation is not apt to change materially.

All of the early biographers from Orrery (1751) through Scott (1814) credited the alleged marriage to Stella, though they found little enough to praise in Swift's conduct, which, whatever the reality of the marriage, doubtless pleased Juno no more than it did Venus. Nineteenth-century biographers were divided on the question of the marriage, with Scott and Craik holding that a ceremony had taken place, and Monck Mason, Forster, Stephen, and Collins variously unconvinced or neutral. Most twentieth-century scholars have been sceptical regarding the marriage. Weighing heavily against it is the absence of any records, a negligence one would hardly expect of St. George Ashe, the Bishop of Clogher, who allegedly performed the ceremony. Those who hold that a marriage took place do so wholly on the basis of hearsay evidence. One suspects that some who have credited the marriage, especially the early propagators of the story, were prompted by a desire to improve Swift's reputation and thought that a married Swift is somehow less Love's apostate—or Juno's offender—than an unmarried one.

A commendably objective survey of the available facts and of eighteenth- and nineteenth-century opinion is J. H. Bernard's "The Relations between Swift and Stella" (1908),[62] in Volume XII of the Temple Scott *Prose Works*. Bernard is to be credited with bringing to light the earliest extant gossip on Swift's relationships with Stella and Vanessa: a letter dated July 23, 1723, from John Evans, Bishop of Meath and an old enemy of Swift's, to William Wake, the Archbishop of Canterbury. The gossip of the letter includes much that later students, in spite of inadequate evidence, have been too readily inclined to credit: that Stella was a natural daughter of Sir William Temple, that Swift and Stella were man and wife, and that Vanessa was moved to disinherit Swift when she was informed of the marriage on her deathbed. Bernard stands, somewhat gingerly, with those who credit the marriage.

Maxwell Gold in *Swift's Marriage to Stella* (Cambridge, Mass., 1937) claims new evidence in the form of annotations to a copy of Orrery's *Remarks* in the Harvard Library, but Gold's own view that a ceremony took place remains as conjectural as earlier opinion. Gold is among the few twentieth-century critics who have dealt at length with the problem,[63] most students preferring to avoid this rather opaque area of Swift's private life. Curt treatment has been the rule. Whibley objects to those "who, with something of the eavesdropper's impertinence, would pierce the mystery of his loves" (p. 45), while Carl Van Doren declares boldly, "Call Stella his wife or be pedantic" (p. 149). Quintana in *Mind and Art* dismisses the marriage claims with a few strokes: "Both Swift and Stella lived with superb pride by the code of rational conduct. If they broke this code to participate in a secret ceremony that had no significance, the explanation must be sought not in the realm of reason but of nonsense" (p. 233), a view maintained also in Quintana's *Swift: An Introduction* (pp. 11, 19).

Herbert Davis' Alexander Lectures of 1942, delivered at the University of Toronto and published as *Stella: A Gentlewoman of the Eighteenth Century* (New York, 1942), cover thoroughly what can be known of Stella and her place in Swift's life on the basis of the existing documents. Davis' urbane scholarship presents a credible Stella in a credible and not unsatisfying relationship with Swift uncomplicated by consanguinity,[64] insanity,[65] or sexual anesthesia.[66]

The closely related and no less clouded matter of Swift's relationship with Vanessa has received considerable attention from twentieth-century scholars. Here too the most credible studies have kept close to the existing documents and have avoided bold intuitions such as H. L. Mencken's, "She was indubitably his mistress, whether they sinned or simply burned," [67] or Rossi and Hone's on Vanessa's desperation, in which they see "the terrible sexual dependence of the woman on her lover" (p. 247). Of particular value is A. Martin Freeman's *Vanessa and Her Correspondence with Jonathan Swift* (London, 1921), which prints all the relevant documents and includes an introduction in which Freeman reviews the whole matter and the available correspondence. George Yost, Jr., in "Well-Filled Silences: The Case of Swift and Vanessa" (1953),[68] surveys the wealth of conjecture which has filled the gaps and reticences of the Swift-Vanessa relationship. Critics, disappointed that the correspondence with Vanessa does not read quite like the letters which passed between Flaubert and Louise Colet, have often tried to remedy matters by taking the frequent references to coffee to mean sexual intercourse. Thus Sybil Le Brocquy in *Cadenus: A Reassessment in the Light of New Evidence of the Relationships between Swift, Stella, and Vanessa* (Dublin, 1962) offers some broad hints about the coffee (pp. 89, 94) and then conjectures that Vanessa had a child by Swift,

Bryan M'Loghlin, whom Stella subsequently cared for and named in her will (pp. 111 ff.).

NEUROSES*

Psychoanalytic literature is replete with efforts to draw Swift out of the shadows—only to immerse him in other, darker ones. Swift, like Sophocles, contributed a term—"Gulliver fantasies"—to psychoanalytic jargon, but Swift has been repaid with attentions which Sophocles, ever fortunate, has been spared. Once the psychoanalysts achieved "the recognition that dreams invented by writers will often yield to analysis in the same way as genuine ones," [69] the reduction of a complex work of literary art such as *Gulliver's Travels* to the same status as the haphazard free associations of the patient on the couch was assured. The pychoanalytic approach—essentially a matter of viewing Swift's writings as symptoms—is itself symptomatic of the survival in this century of the Victorian view of the works as self-revelation, the chief difference being that the self which Swift reveals is not the malicious desecrator of the "human form divine" but the helpless victim of assorted neurotic disturbances.

Freudianism first touched Swift in 1926 when Sandor Ferenczi read his paper on "Gulliver Phantasies" [70] before the New York Society for Clinical Psychiatry. In this study Ferenczi is concerned primarily with illustrating the technical characteristics of what he calls "Gulliver phantasies," and he does so by treating *Gulliver* itself as a neurotic fantasy. Thus Gulliver in Lilliput is a wish-fulfilling dream which compensates for genital inadequacy (p. 292), while Gulliver in Brobdingnag is a manifestation of the anxiety of one who, because of weakness and insecurity, "resists sexual intercourse by making excuses" (p. 295). Gulliver as Lilliputian fire department is a fantasy of intercourse; his unpopularity,

---

* A revised version of this section appeared in the *Western Humanities Review* for Autumn 1962 under the title "Swift and Psychoanalytic Criticism."

155

in spite of his success, suggests neurotic guilt feelings. The review of troops marching through Gulliver's legs "sounds exactly like the reassurance-phantasy or dream of an impotent man" (p. 292).

By way of explaining these neurotic symptoms, Ferenczi argued that sons who grow up without fathers are seldom normal, and "from the psychoanalytic standpoint one would describe [Swift's] neurotic sexual behavior as an inhibition of normal potency with a lack of courage in relation to women of good character and perhaps with a lasting aggressive tendency towards women of a lower type. This insight into Swift's life surely justifies us who come after him in treating the phantasies in *Gulliver's Travels* exactly as we do the free associations of neurotic patients in analysis, especially when interpreting their dreams" (p. 299). Henceforth the method is applied without further ceremony.

It was Adolf Heidenhain in *Ueber den Menschenhass: Eine pathographische Untersuchung über Jonathan Swift* (Stuttgart, 1934) who, by calling Swift's scatology coprophilia and relating it to anal fixation, enabled Swiftophobia to become scientific. This stress on coprophilia as a neurotic symptom in Swift is the primary substance of all subsequent Freudian studies. It is really a revival of a nineteenth-century tradition in which the scatology had produced a prolonged and anguished gnashing of teeth. Although the new Swiftophobia is systematized and fortified with a method, a sacred literature, and an evangelistic program, the same indignation over Swift's "soiled pages"—and frustrated and frustrating life—which stirred the hearts of staid Victorians, now burns as warm as ever in such Freudian critics as Dr. Benjamin Karpman, Miss Evelyn Hardy, and Dr. Phyllis Greenacre. In fairness to Heidenhain it must be pointed out that his study is free of the animus toward Swift which marks other Freudian studies.

Dr. Karpman, chief psychotherapist at St. Elizabeth's Hospital, Washington, D.C., referring to W. Cooke Taylor's 1840 edition of *Gulliver*, uses Taylor's puzzled concern over the scatology as a springboard for his own discussion. Taylor, rephrasing a passage in Dr. Johnson's "Life of Swift," had wondered "by what depravity of intellect [Swift] acquired a taste for loathsome and filthy ideas, from which every other mind shrinks with disgust." [71] Dr. Karpman's answer in "Neurotic Traits of Jonathan Swift as Revealed by *Gulliver's Travels*" (1942) is that "the entire narrative may be viewed as a neurotic phantasy with coprophilia as its main content" and with "numerous other related neurotic characteristics," including psychosexual infantilism, emotional immaturity, anal erotism, zoophilia, sodomy, exhibitionism, voyeurism, paraphilia, sado-masochism, guilt feelings, mysophilia, mysophobia, and compensatory potency reactions (pp. 30, 40).[72] Amid wringing of hands and shaking of head over Swift's "smearing his pages with . . . excrements" (p. 42) and "highly objectionable descriptions" (p. 41), we are told that the urination passages "express omnipotence and exhibitionism" (p. 166), the Voyage to Brobdingnag is "a confession of impotence" (p. 181), and the account of the female Yahoo's attack on Gulliver is "reversed voyeurism," though in the latter "an element of narcissistic gratification is probably involved" as well as "the author's unconscious fear of women" (p. 180). Even the "intestine Disquiets" in Lilliputian politics (I, iv; HD, XI, 32), are not without significance for Dr. Karpman, as, we are told, "it is indeed intestine disquiets which afford the anal-erotic the greatest anticipations of pleasure" (p. 166). A particularly strong indication of Swift's neurosis, however, is "the fact that not once in the narrative do we find an account of actual coitus" (p. 169), an omission twentieth-century readers would find rather singular, and sufficient to place any book under suspicion.

The most extensive Freudian study of Swift thus far is Dr. Phyllis Greenacre's *Swift and Carroll: A Psychoanalytic Study of Two Lives* (New York, 1955), in which Swift and Dodgson are taken up separately and then compared. Dr. Greenacre, writing thirteen years after Dr. Karpman, agrees substantially with her predecessor but is not content to restrict herself to the more overt signs of coprophilia. While "intestine disquiets" represented perhaps the outer limits of

Karpman's reach, Dr. Greenacre, availing herself of more esoteric tools, can find coprophilia in even less likely places. Thus she points out that "the proper names in *Gulliver's Travels* are heavy with repeated consonants and duplicated syllables overburdened by consonants, e.g., Glubbdubdrib, Luggnagg, Traldragdubh, Glumdalclitch, Clumegnig. These words suggest an onomatopoeic derivation from the sound of drippings and droppings, possibly originating in the overly intense preoccupation with toilet functions, which seemed for the child Jonathan to engulf and then to color his important infantile philosophies" (p. 102).

To Dr. Greenacre, Gulliver's misadventure with the monkey in Brobdingnag "appears clearly to be a homosexual fellatio fantasy, the reverberation of which appeared in Swift's own life in his sickness from 'too much stone fruit' at a time when he was first drawn to Sir William Temple" (p. 113). In *Gulliver* "active and passive voyeurism is ubiquitous" (p. 95), as are masturbation fantasies, exhibitionism, and other anal- and oral-erotic manifestations. Dr. Greenacre's tour de force, however, is her discovery of masturbation in Gulliver's references to his apprenticeship to "good Master *Bates*" (I, i; HD, XI, 3–4), a view she maintains resolutely even in the face of evidence that the word was not current in Swift's day.

Dr. Greenacre goes more deeply into the biography than previous psychoanalytic investigators, dwelling especially on the early years. Of the nurse who kidnapped the young Jonathan, Dr. Greenacre appears to know more than any previous biographer, finding that "however devoted to her little charge, [she] was in some way overly conscientious and harsh in her early toilet training, and left this stamp of the nursery morals of the chamber pot forever on his character" (p. 107). Dr. Greenacre stresses the recurrent failure of Swift, the posthumous child, to find satisfying parental attachments. Sir William Temple in her account becomes a father substitute who fails Swift after inspiring him with sharply ambivalent feelings. Dr. Greenacre cannot resist the picture of a despondent Swift, unloved and rebuffed at Moor

Park, withdrawing frequently to Mother Ludwell's Cave, "where he found inspiration and calm" (p. 30). Should any still wonder at Swift's donning the cassock of the Anglican priesthood, Dr. Greenacre's suggestion of "a hidden tendency" toward transvestism might quiet doubts and make all plain (p. 109).

Other works besides *Gulliver* have furnished the psychoanalysts with evidence. I. F. Grant Duff (1937) [73] found the *Meditation on a Broomstick* to be a castration fantasy (p. 251); Dr. Greenacre saw in it "a strong preoccupation with sexual inversion" (p. 37), while Evelyn Hardy, whose *The Conjured Spirit: A Study in the Relationship of Swift, Stella, and Vanessa* (London, 1949) is a Freudian biography, devoted several of her pages to Boyleian platitudinizing in which the broomstick becomes a simile for Swift himself (pp. 77–80, 246). For Grant Duff *A Modest Proposal* is, as might be expected, a cannibalistic fantasy "reflecting Swift's fear of talion punishment for his own cannibalistic wishes as an infant" (p. 250).

Freudianism has also been an ingredient in studies of a more critical and literary character. William Barrett in "Writers and Madness (1947) [74] ranges widely once he takes up Swift, asserting that in *Gulliver* Swift's madness "unconsciously carried him, an unquestioning Christian, for the moment outside Christianity: the rational and tranquil Houyhnhnms do not need a Messiah's blood and an historically revealed religion in order to be saved, while the Yahoos could not possibly be saved by any savior," while in the prayers for Stella, "sublimating, he gropes, touches, fondles her in God. What happened beyond this we do not know" (p. 10). After casting about for some connection between Swift and the twentieth century, Barrett, sounding much like the modern in *A Tale of a Tub*, begins to descry [in Swift] the shadows and depths of a *psychic type*, the writer—which has emerged, to be sure, spectacularly only in the two following centuries. This psychic type or bent of mind, Barrett avers, "must result primarily from some special strength or strain in the oedipal relation" (pp. 12–13). D. S. Savage,[75] writing three years later in *Western Review,* makes much of "unconscious incestuous longing" in Swift, without which the relation with Stella and later with Vanessa "cannot be understood" (p. 32). Swift's "failure to reflect himself into the incestuous situation and creatively to transfigure it" resulted in a retrogression to "Innocence" and consequent "emasculation" explainable in terms supplied by Blake's *Marriage of Heaven and Hell* and the romantic revival, where "recovery of the symbol for English poetry" and "conscious reunion of Energy and Reason" were attempted (p. 35).

Other more critical and scholarly Freudians have attempted to correct the excesses and superficialities of the earlier studies. Thus Donald R. Roberts,[76] writing in *Literature and Psychology* in 1956, asserts that the studies of Ferenczi, Grant Duff, and Karpman "all suffer from inadequate preparation and a tendency to hypothetical conclusions" (p. 8). In his own more sober interpretation, Roberts, however, is no less clairvoyant on Swift's nurse than was Greenacre, finding the same severity toward her little charge but now also supplementing her exactions "with caresses of a faintly lascivious character" (p. 10). Roberts finally falls into the old habit of identifying Gulliver with Swift—a confusion of persona and author to which the Freudians appear particularly liable—taking Gulliver's praise of Houyhnhnm eugenics and planned parenthood to be Swift's own cherished belief, and Gulliver's fright at the overzealous female Yahoo to be Swift's own fright at sexuality [77] (pp. 16–17).

Yet tactful application of Freudian theory to authentic (as distinct from fanciful) Swift biography is by no means impossible. Witness, for instance, the recent work of Irvin Ehrenpreis, whose sensibly speculative account of Swift's relations with women is frequently Freudian in substance and method, yet keeps the known facts in view. In "The Pattern of Swift's Women" (1955) [78] Ehrenpreis suggests that Swift's attitude toward women was formed in his somewhat singular childhood, in which the prenatal loss of his father and later abduction by his nurse left him with some confusion regarding the source of paternal and maternal affection. In later roles with women Swift became a surrogate parent, thus yielding for himself "a double pleasure: first, he could provide his beloved with that guidance and warmth which he himself had missed; . . . second, he could make up to himself for the inadequacy of his childhood," and thus "[reach] back into the 1670's and in an odd but vivid way treat the other person as a deputy for his younger self" (p. 713). Ehrenpreis' willingness to see allusions to Stella in Gulliver's "little nurse," Glumdalclitch, is less apt to inspire confidence and, indeed, seems a return to the phantasmagoria of the most uncritical Freudians. Whenever art is reduced to wish-fulfillment—Ehrenpreis calls Gulliver's interlude with Glumdalclitch a "reverie" (p. 715)—we get a mishmash that is neither biography nor criticism, but an exercise indulged for its own sake.

Oddly enough, the most forceful attack on such mistreatment of Swift comes from the *enfant terrible* of the current Freudian shock troops, Norman O. Brown. In his apocalyptic, evangelistic, scholarly, and lively *Life Against Death: The Psychoanalytical Meaning of History* (Middletown, Conn., 1959) Brown devotes an entire chapter, "The Excremental Vision," to Swift, in which he sharply chides the Freudians from Ferenczi to Greenacre for their obtuse misreadings of Swift and for their failure "to appreciate his insight into the universal neurosis of mankind." Swift, argues Brown, is a proto-Freudian: "If we are willing to listen to Swift we will find startling anticipations of Freudian theorems about anality, about sublimation, and about the universal neurosis of mankind" (pp. 185–86). The willingness to listen requires first of all that psychoanalytic critics set aside their compulsion "to explain away Swift's literary achievements as mere epiphenomena on his individual neurosis." Only then can psychoanalysis become "a method not for explaining away but for explicating Swift" (pp. 185–86). In his explications Brown is more careful than other Freudians to distinguish Swift from his fictional characters. These include Gulliver, of course, but especially Strephon and Cassinus, the starry-eyed beaus in *The Lady's Dressing Room* and *Cassinus and Peter,* whose prudery Swift is challenging, not encouraging. The universal neurosis of mankind, according to Brown, is simply this sterile decency which sublimates all that is unpleasant and then denies its existence, a denial whose implications Swift understood as well as Freud.

Brown leaves Swift's "neuroses" an open question, suggesting that, whatever they were, they probably intensified but did not vitiate his vision. At the same time Swift's anticipations of Freud do not prompt Brown to turn Swift into a special oracle. It is evident from Brown's discussion that what Swift shared with Freud can also be found in St. Augustine. One is tempted to see in Brown a most welcome domestication of psychoanalytic criticism, its *rapprochement,* as it were, with the history of ideas. After the Ferenczi-Greenacre tradition that seems a real gain.

MEDICAL HISTORY

Since the time of Wilde's *The Closing Years of Dean Swift's Life* (1849), advances in medical knowledge along with competent investigation have clarified Swift's medical history. The nausea, dizziness, and deafness which troubled Swift from the age of forty-two were diagnosed in 1881 [79] as Labyrinthine Vertigo, or Ménière's Syndrome, a disorder of the inner ear first described by Ménière in the *Gazette médicale de Paris* in 1861. A competent and complete discussion of Swift's medical history is available in T. G. Wilson's "Swift's Deafness and His Last Illness" (1939).[80] Wilson takes up Swift's shingles and gout and is otherwise thorough to a fault, pursuing even the "ossified thyroid cartilages," stolen at the exhumation in 1835, and "last heard of in New York" (p. 303). A more recent discussion by the eminent neurologist Sir Walter Russell Brain,[81] delivered on the occasion of his being made Honorary Fellow in the Royal College of Physicians in Ireland in 1952, investigates the final illness more minutely and arrives at quite definite conclusions. Sir Walter finds that the painfully swollen eye of 1742, often called the "crisis" of Swift's illness, "was an infective intracranial complication of his orbital cellulitis, leading to severe and lasting motor aphasia" (p. 340). "It is rather surprising," Sir Walter asserts, "that there should have been so much discussion about Swift's sanity, since he showed no symptoms suggesting mental deterioration until he was over seventy years of age. By this time he was almost completely deaf, his eyesight was impaired, and he refused to wear spectacles." As for the behavior which then necessitated the declaration of *non compos mentis,* Sir Walter declares, "In all this there is nothing more than can be readily explained as the effect of blindness, deafness, and cerebral arteriosclerosis upon a man of Swift's temperament, amounting by 1742 to involutional melancholia" (p. 339). Thus twentieth-century medical studies have simply amplified Wilde's assertion in 1849 that insanity was nowhere a part of Swift's medical history.

A summary assessment of Swift's place in twentieth-century letters requires an initial recognition that the status of his major works as classics ensures him a place on the scene in any period, regardless what its intellectual temper or prevailing literary fashion. Perhaps it is the enigmatic character of his works which yields him such status. Let it suffice that convention demands the ascription of genius in such cases. Each age will then define itself in its apprehension of the genius. Our age, by objecting less than the Victorians to Swift's "brutality," outspokenness, and pessimism, defines itself as tough-minded, sophisticated, and disillusioned. If, as Paul Elmer More suggested, Swift was no proper custodian of the higher illusions of society, he may yet preside over our private illusions, both high and low, exposing the most fatuous of them and reminding us constantly that they *are,* all of them, illusions. Like the twentieth century since World War I, Swift ventured few hostages to fortune.

If a characteristic of the Romantic and Victorian audience was a willingness to respond readily to the emotions found on the surface of literature—indeed, Wordsworth promised to make simple feeling easily accessible there—then Swift's reception in the nineteenth century is wholly accountable. The surface of Swift's works calls for a response, but always a violent one, hostile in Thackeray and Jeffrey, sympathetic in Hazlitt. Taught indirection by James and Eliot, twentieth-century readers of Swift look for what is artfully complicated, peer beneath the surface of Swift's satires, and offer a new estimate. No longer a Timon-like misanthrope or a raging madman, Swift is now a careful craftsman, a wit, an ironist.

The current interest in the art or craft of Swift's works, the anatomy of his masks, his rhetorical strategies, has encouraged rather than discouraged a new engagement with his substance, an engagement not limited to the surface. Analytical criticism has pierced that surface and has discovered a lost, if not a new, world. Once inside that world one might agree with Quintana in *Swift: An Introduction* that "our ultimate judgement of Swift may properly be more a moral than an artistic one" (p. 52), so long as adequate artistic judgments (without which that world remains inaccessible) have not been shirked. In any case, moral judgments, mature and premature, have seldom been resisted by critics of Swift, as this study abundantly shows. An index of Swift's genius is perhaps the authenticity of the moral judgments he inspires. The wildest of these will still have some relation to that discoverable world beneath the surface, may even be uncomfortably, unknowingly, within it.

notes

ABBREVIATIONS

CE	*College English*
Corresp.	*The Correspondence of Jonathan Swift, D.D.*, ed. F. Elrington Ball, London, 1910–14.
ELH	*ELH, a Journal of English Literary History*
HD	*The Prose Works of Jonathan Swift*, ed. Herbert Davis, Oxford, 1939– .
HLQ	*Huntington Library Quarterly*
JEGP	*Journal of English and Germanic Philology*
JHI	*Journal of the History of Ideas*
MLN	*Modern Language Notes*
MLQ	*Modern Language Quarterly*
MLR	*Modern Language Review*
MP	*Modern Philology*
N&Q	*Notes and Queries*
NYHTB	*New York Herald Tribune Books*
PMLA	*Publications of the Modern Language Association of America*
PQ	*Philological Quarterly*
RES	*Review of English Studies*
RLC	*Revue de littérature comparée*
SAQ	*South Atlantic Quarterly*
SP	*Studies in Philology*
SR	*Sewanee Review*
SRL	*Saturday Review of Literature*
TLS	*London Times Literary Supplement*
UTQ	*University of Toronto Quarterly*
VQR	*Virginia Quarterly Review*
YR	*Yale Review*

I
NINETEENTH-CENTURY VIEWS

Wherever possible, full citation will be given in the text. Works other than books will be given full bibliographical citation in the initial footnote. Subsequent references, limited wherever possible to citation of pages, will appear in the text.

[1] Edward Dowden, *Academy*, XXII (September 30, 1882), 233–34.

[2] Émile Pons, *Swift: les années de jeunesse et le 'Conte du tonneau,'* Strasbourg, 1925, pp. 62–70.

[3] Donald M. Berwick, *The Reputation of Jonathan Swift, 1781–1882*, Philadelphia, 1941, pp. 51–52.

[4] Francis Jeffrey, review of Scott, *Edinburgh Review* XXVII (September 1816), 1–58. I quote from Jeffrey, *Contributions to the Edinburgh Review*, London, 1844, I, 158–226.

[5] W. M. Thackeray, "Swift," in his *English Humourists of the Eighteenth Century*, London, 1853. I quote from the Grey Walls Press edition, London, 1949, pp. 13–45.

[6] Hippolyte Adolphe Taine. "Jonathan Swift: son génie et ses oeuvres," *Revue des deux mondes*, xxviiiᵉ Année (August 15, 1858), 869–940. Reprinted in *Histoire de la littérature anglaise*, Paris, 1863–64. English translation by H. Van Laun, 1871. I quote from the New York edition of 1896.

[7] James Russell Lowell, review of Forster, *Nation*, XXII (April 13, 1876), 248–50; (April 20, 1876), 265–67. I quote from this essay reprinted as "Swift," in Lowell, *The Function of the Poet and Other Essays*, Boston, 1920, pp. 173–99. The review was unsigned at its first appearance.

[8] For an exhaustive discussion of nineteenth-century Swift criticism, see Berwick, *op. cit.*, which is the definitive work. Other valuable surveys are Pons, *Swift*, pp. 6–105, and Merrel D. Clubb, "The Criticism of Gulliver's 'Voyage to the Houyhnhnms,' 1726–1914," *Stanford Studies in Language and Literature*, ed. Hardin Craig, Stanford University, Calif., 1941, pp. 203–32. My immense debt to these three studies will be apparent.

[9] Samuel T. Coleridge, "On Wit and Humour," Lecture IX, *Miscellaneous Criticism*, ed. T. M. Raysor, Cambridge, Mass., 1936, p. 114.

[10] T. B. Macaulay, review of *The History of the War of Succession in Spain*, by Lord Mahon, *Edinburgh Review* (January 1833). I quote from the Albany edn. of Macaulay's *Works*, London, 1908, VIII, 307.

[11] John Forster, *The Life of Jonathan Swift*, Vol. I (no more published), London, 1875, p. 151.

[12] John Hill Burton, *A History of the Reign of Queen Anne*, Edinburgh, 1880, III, 280.

[13] Edmund Gosse, *History of Eighteenth Century Literature*, London, 1889. I quote from the New York edn., 1911, pp. 161–62.

[14] Augustine Birrell, *Essays about Men, Women, and Books*, London, 1894. I quote from the New York edn., 1909, pp. 2–3.

[15] W. E. H. Lecky, "Biographical Introduction," *The Prose Works of Jonathan Swift, D.D.*, ed. Temple Scott, London, 1897, I, xl, a revision of "Swift," *The Leaders of Public Opinion in Ireland*, London, 1861, pp. 1–60.

[16] John Churton Collins, *Jonathan Swift: A Biographical and Critical Study*, London, 1893, pp. 230, 259–60. This work is an extension of two articles which appeared in the *Quarterly Review* CLVI (1882).

[17] First to apply the word in this way to Swift was Scott, *The Works of Jonathan Swift*, Edinburgh, 1814, II, 10.

[18] *Spectator*, LXXI (August 19, 1893), 247.

[19] *British Quarterly Review*, LXIII (1876), 161.

[20] Bulwer-Lytton, *Dramas and Poems*, Boston, n.d., p. 324.

[21] George Gilfillan, "Thackeray," *A Third Gallery of Literary Portraits*, Edinburgh, 1854, p. 264.

[22] George Gilfillan, "Satire and Satirists," *Scottish Review* (January 1856). I quote from *A Gallery of Literary Portraits*, London, 1909, p. 237.

[23] David Masson, "Dean Swift," *British Quarterly Review*, XX (1854), 528–60; reprinted in *Essays Biographical and Critical*, Cambridge, 1856, pp. 140–77. I quote from *The Three Devils*, London, 1874, pp. 285–89.

[24] Patricius Walker, Esq. (William Allingham), "Moor Park and Swift," *Fraser's Magazine*, LXXVI (1867), 653.

[25] Charles Mills Gayley, "A Madman of Letters," *Dial*, III (December 1882), 165.

[26] John Mitford, "Life of Swift," *Poetical Works of Jonathan Swift*, 3 vols., London, 1833. I quote from the New York edn., 1871, I, lxxxii.

[27] This phrase occurs frequently in nineteenth-century discussions of the fourth voyage. I quote from *Chambers' Cyclopedia of English Literature*, Edinburgh, 1844, I, 575.

[28] William Hazlitt, "On Swift, Young, Gray, Collins, Etc.," *Lectures on the English Poets*, London, 1818. I quote from *Works*, ed. A. R. Waller and Arnold Glover, London, 1902, V, 110–11.

[29] Leslie Stephen, *Swift*, London, 1882, p. 183.

[30] Henry Craik, *The Life of Jonathan Swift*, London, 1882, p. 393.

[31] Thomas Tyler, *Academy*, XXIV (August 18, 1883), 113–14.

[32] Anna B. Jameson, *The Loves of the Poets*, London, 1829, II, 240.

[33] Henry T. Tuckerman, "Swift," *The Southern Literary Messenger*, XV (March 1849), 145–46.

[34] Thomas De Quincey, rev. of Schlosser's *Literary History of the Eighteenth Century*, *Tait's Edinburgh Magazine*, XIV (September–October 1847), 575–83, 690–96. I quote from De Quincey, *Collected Writings*, ed. David Masson, London, 1897, XI, 14.

[35] George Saintsbury, *Short History of English Literature*, London, 1898, p. 530.

[36] *A Tale of a Tub* is evidently the work Lowell has in mind.

[37] Lowell, "Pope," *My Study Windows*, Boston and New York, 1871, pp. 385–483. I quote from Lowell, *Literary Essays*, Cambridge, Mass., 1899, pp. 18–19. Once convinced that Swift was unprincipled, Lowell does what no other critic—not even Thackeray—had the temerity to do: he insinuates that Swift was a Jacobite, pointing out that for one who prided himself on a Cavalier grandfather, "it would not be hard . . . to become first a Tory and then a conniver at the restoration of the Stuarts," and "a man of Swift's way of thinking would hardly have balked at the scruple of creed." (*The Function of the Poet*, p. 193.)

[38] Edmund Gosse, *A Short History of Modern English Literature,* London, 1897. I quote from the New York edn., 1906, p. 222.

[39] Leslie Stephen, *History of English Thought in the Eighteenth Century,* London, 1876. I quote from the New York edn., 1881, II, 372.

[40] Craik describes Swift's conception of religion as that of "a politician much more than of a divine" (p. 162). Collins' statements, pp. 13–14 and pp. 243–46, are inconsistent, though the latter, which compares Swift to Fielding's Thwackum and declares Swift's interest in religion to be primarily in its function as a "coercive moral agency," appears to be the considered judgment. Moriarty finds Swift as churchman to be "like a soldier at his post" (a description which echoes Swift's own in "Thoughts on Religion"), but whose religion was hardly more than a compound of ignorance and prejudice. (*Dean Swift and His Writings,* London, 1893, pp. 63–64.)

[41] Thomas Beddoes, *Hygeia, or Essays Moral and Medical,* Bristol, 1803, III, 188–89.

[42] Nathan Drake, *Essays Biographical, Critical, and Historical, Illustrative of the Tatler, Spectator, and Guardian,* London, 1805, III, 168.

[43] Sir Walter Scott, ed., *Works of Jonathan Swift, D.D.,* 2nd edn., Edinburgh, 1824, I, 241.

[44] W. R. Wilde, *The Closing Years of Dean Swift's Life,* Dublin, 1849, p. 111.

[45] Jeffrey, I, 204.

[46] Monck Mason, *The History and Antiquities of the Cathedral Church of St. Patrick,* Dublin, 1820. Mason discusses Swift on pp. 225–444. Berwick demonstrates conclusively that Mason's work had little effect on the nineteenth-century image of Swift. (*The Reputation of Swift,* pp. 59–62.)

[47] Wilde, for instance, is less rigorous on the subject of Stella's parentage than he is on Swift's: "That Stella was the daughter of Sir William Temple appears more than probable; but that Swift was his son, and consequently her half brother, remains to be proved." (*The Closing Years,* p. 108.)

[48] In 1835, a group of phrenologists happening to be by at the time some repairs were being made to the floor of St. Patrick's Cathedral, the Rev. Henry Dawson, Dean, "with his usual liberality and anxiety for the advancement of science," permitted the removal of Swift's skull for purposes of phrenological analysis. Another skull, which they took to be Stella's (see H. J. Lawlor, "The Graves of Swift and Stella," *English Historical Review,* XXXIII [1918], 89–93), was also removed. After due observation and measurement, Swift's skull was declared to indicate, among other things, "large amativeness and small wit." *Phrenological Journal and Miscellany,* IX (1836), 466–71, 603–8.

II
TEXTUAL CRITICISM

[1] Stanley Lane-Poole, "Notes for a Bibliography of Swift," *The Bibliographer,* VI (1884), 160–71.

[2] W. Spencer Jackson, "Bibliography of Swift's Works," *The Prose Works of Jonathan Swift, D.D.,* ed. Temple Scott, London, 1908, XII, 109–241.

³ John Hayward, *A Catalogue of Printed Books and Manuscripts by Jonathan Swift, D.D.*, Cambridge, 1945. Autrey Nell Wiley, *Jonathan Swift, 1667–1745, An Exhibition of Printed Books at the University of Texas*, Austin, 1945. See also *The Rothschild Library*, Cambridge, 1954, II, 543–643.

⁴ Lucius L. Hubbard, *Contributions Towards a Bibliography of Gulliver's Travels*, Chicago, 1922.

⁵ Harold Williams, "The Motte Editions of *Gulliver's Travels*," *The Library*, 4th ser., VI (1925), 229–63. Williams, ed., *Gulliver's Travels*, London, 1926. Williams, "*Gulliver's Travels:* Further Notes," *The Library*, 4th ser., IX (1928), 187–96.

⁶ An exchange of letters between Swift and Tooke contains adequate external evidence of Swift's authorship of the *Tale*. Swift to Tooke, 29 June 1710; Tooke to Swift, 10 July 1710; *Correspondence*, ed. F. Elrington Ball, London, 1910, I, 183–86. Printed by Guthkelch and Smith, *A Tale of a Tub*, London, 1920, pp. 333–34.

⁷ In two instances he follows Hawkesworth, preferring "Hobbes's" (HD, I, 24, line 25) to "Hob's" (5th edn.) and "Hobs's" (edd. 1–4). Davis' other reading from Hawkesworth, "Guild" (HD, I, 94, line 1) for "Field" (edd. 3–5 and Guthkelch-Smith), remains dubious even after his learned suggestion that "yield" (edd. 1–2) is a misprint for "yeld" or "yild," early forms of "guild." Davis' reversion (HD, I, 63, line 32) to the reading of the first edition ("stay for a second") in preference to edd. 2–5 and Guthkelch-Smith ("stay not for a second") deprives the passage of its proper meaning. Nichol Smith in his second edition has chosen to follow Davis in this deletion of "not."

⁸ J. C. Maxwell, "The Text of *A Tale of a Tub*," *English Studies*, XXXVI (1955), 64–66, argues for a freer emendation of the copy-text than is evident in Guthkelch-Smith or Davis.

⁹ *Gulliver's Travels*, Volume VIII, *Prose Works*, ed. Temple Scott, London, 1899.

¹⁰ An exception, however, is G. A. Aitken, whose Temple Classics edition of *Gulliver* (London, 1896) was the first to print the passage on Lindalino's four towers, the allegorical representation of the Wood controversy which apparently both Motte and Faulkner regarded as too treasonable to publish.

¹¹ W. Cooke Taylor, ed., *Gulliver's Travels*, London, 1840.

¹² Williams is of the opinion that some of the corrections show signs of an intent to revise. "The Motte Editions," *The Library*, 4th ser., VI (1925), 257.

¹³ John Hayward, ed., "*Gulliver's Travels*" *and Selected Writings in Prose and Verse*, London, 1934, p. 2. Other texts using the 1735 edition are the Everyman's, ed. H. Williams, London, 1940; the Rinehart, ed. John F. Ross, New York, 1948; the Cresset Library *Selected Prose Writings*, ed. J. Hayward, London, 1949; the Collins Classics *Gulliver's Travels*, ed. Peter Quennell, London, 1952; the Modern Library, ed. R. Quintana, New York, 1958; the Riverside, ed. Louis A. Landa, Boston, 1960.

¹⁴ Arthur E. Case, *Four Essays on "Gulliver's Travels,"* Princeton, 1945, p. 49. Reissued, Gloucester, Mass., 1958.

[15] *MLN*, LXII (1947), 206–8.

[16] *JEGP*, XLVI (1947), 322–24.

[17] Carl Van Doren, ed., the Viking Portable *Swift*, New York, 1948, p. 202.

[18] Williams, *RES*, XXIII (1947), 367–69; Herbert Davis, "The Canon of Swift," *English Institute Annual, 1942*, New York, 1943, p. 131.

[19] Williams, *The Text of "Gulliver's Travels,"* Cambridge, 1952, p. 86.

[20] Todd, *The Library*, 5th ser., VIII (1953), 280–82; Williams, *ibid.*, pp. 283–84; Todd, *ibid.*, IX (1954), 135–36; Williams, *ibid.*, p. 270.

[21] *TLS*, December 19, 1952, p. 844; *TLS*, January 9, 1953, p. 25.

[22] Irvin Ehrenpreis, review of Williams' *The Text of "Gulliver's Travels,"* *PQ*, XXXII (1953), 299. Ehrenpreis follows the textual principles of W. W. Greg. See Greg's "Rationale of Copy-Text," *Studies in Bibliography*, III (1950–51), 19–36, and Ehrenpreis' recent application of the same principles in his edition of *An Enquiry into the Behavior of the Queen's Last Ministry*, Indiana University Publications, Humanities Series No. 36, Bloomington, 1956, where he uses a first draft (A) in Swift's own hand as copy-text, correcting for changes in sense from a later ms. (B) in the hand of an amanuensis. In the Shakespeare Head edition, Davis and Ehrenpreis, the co-editors, followed the principles set forth in its first volume and offered an almost pure text of the *Enquiry* based on the fair copy (B) (HD, VIII, xxxi–xl, 131–80, 215–31).

[23] Herbert Davis, ed., *The Drapier's Letters*, Oxford, 1935, pp. lxviii, lxxv.

[24] Davis subsequently extended this view to include all four of the 1735 volumes: ". . . I am inclined to believe that there is nothing in those first four volumes which he had not written." Davis is more inclined to question material in Faulkner's later volumes, including Vols. V and VI, which appeared in 1738. By 1769 Faulkner's edition had grown to twenty volumes. (Davis, "The Canon of Swift," p. 125.)

[25] In 1941, however, Davis places the "Advertisement to the Reader," from Faulkner's edition, less ambiguously in an appendix.

[26] See Harold Williams, ed., *Journal to Stella*, Oxford, 1948, I, 1 n. 1.

[27] Craik, *Life*, p. 530.

[28] The original plan to devote volumes IV and V of the Shakespeare Head edition to the *Journal to Stella* has been abandoned.

[29] Émile Pons, "Du nouveau sur le 'Journal à Stella,'" *Études anglaises*, I (1937), 210–29.

[30] *Essays on the Eighteenth Century Presented to David Nichol Smith*, ed. J. R. Sutherland and F. P. Wilson, Oxford, 1945, pp. 33–48.

[31] Irvin Ehrenpreis, "Swift's 'Little Language' in the *Journal to Stella*," *SP*, XLV (1948), 80–88; reprinted in Ehrenpreis, *The Personality of Jonathan Swift*, London, 1958, pp. 50–58.

[32] Roland M. Smith, "Swift's Little Language and Nonsense Names," *JEGP*, LIII (1954), 178–84. The latter part of this article is devoted to "derivations" of names in *Gulliver*.

[33] "The Canon of Swift," *English Institute Annual*, and "The Conciseness of Swift," *Essays Presented to D. N. Smith*, pp. 15–32. The latter reprinted in *Eighteenth-Century English Literature: Modern Essays in Criticism*, ed. James L. Clifford, New York, 1959, pp. 84–101.

[34] Paul Fussell, Jr., disagrees with Davis on the weight and character of the internal evidence: "Speaker and Style in *A Letter of Advice to a Young Poet* (1721) and the Problem of Attribution," *RES*, n.s. X (1959), 63–67.

[35] H. Teerink, *The History of John Bull*, Amsterdam, 1925. Answered by Émile Pons, *Revue anglo-américaine*, IV (1927), 354–56; Thomas F. Mayo, *PMLA*, XLV (1930), 274–82; Lester M. Beattie, *John Arbuthnot, Mathematician and Satirist*, Cambridge, Mass., 1935, pp. 36–58. See *Journal to Stella*, ed. Williams, II, 532 and note.

[36] Reported in *The Library*, 4th ser., XVI (1935), 61–90, 343–44. See also Williams' Introduction, *Four Last Years*, HD, VII, ix–xxviii. Other manuscript discoveries include Swift's Preface to Sir William Temple's *Works*, by Shane Leslie (*TLS*, July 24, 1930, p. 611); the poem, "Apollo to the Dean," in Swift's hand; and, by James L. Clifford, some manuscript hints for Intelligencer papers and Maxims Examined.

[37] Davis, "Verses on the Death of Dr. Swift," *The Book-Collectors' Quarterly*, II (1931), 57–73.

[38] Sidney L. Gulick, Jr., "Jonathan Swift's 'The Day of Judgment,'" *PMLA*, XLVIII (1933), 850–55.

[39] The text in the *Monthly Review* is evidently derived from the *St. James Chronicle*.

[40] Irvin Ehrenpreis, "Swift's First Poem," *MLR*, XLIX (1954), 210–11.

[41] See the handy Muses Library edition: *The Collected Poems of Jonathan Swift*, ed. Joseph Horrell, 2 vols., London and Cambridge, Mass., 1958.

III
A TALE OF A TUB

[1] A. C. Guthkelch, "Swift's 'Tale of a Tub,'" *MLR*, VIII (1913), 301–13; (1913), 454–63; IX (1914), 100; X (1915), 181–87.

[2] *The Protestant Advocate* for May, 1814 printed a letter signed "Indagator" which asserted that Swift's source for the allegory of the will and the inheritance was a sermon delivered in London in 1686 by John Sharp, later Archbishop of York. Churton Collins amplified this view in *Jonathan Swift: A Biographical and Critical Study*, London, 1893, p. 47. Guthkelch and Smith in their edition of the *Tale*, Oxford, 1920, pp. xxix–xxxiv, point to the slight resemblance between the allegories of the sermon and *Tale* and assert that Sharp is no more likely a source than earlier examples of the same allegory, such as the allegory in Dryden's *Religio Laici*, ll. 388–97.

[3] René Macé, in his edition of *Les Trois justaucorps*, Dublin, 1721, had asserted that work to be a source for the allegory of the three contending religions in the *Tale*. Voltaire took the same stand in *Lettres philosophiques*, ed. Gustave Lanson, Paris, 1909, II, 136.

[4] *A Tale of a Tub*, ed. A. C. Guthkelch and D. Nichol Smith, Oxford, 1920, p. 4. References to the *Tale*, the *Battle*, and the *Mechanical Operation* will be to this edition. The pagination of the second edition, 1958, differs only slightly.

[5] Hermann Hofmann, in *Swifts "Tale of a Tub*," Leipzig, 1911, argues that the first three sections of allegory (II, IV, VI) are anti-papist and

anti-Jacobite and were composed at Trinity College in 1687–88, while the remainder reflects Swift's pessimism and hostility to dissenters, attitudes encouraged by his experiences in Kilroot and his stay in England in 1702–4, during which time this second part of the *Tale*, Hofmann conjectures, was composed. Hofmann's argument minimizes the role of Moor Park in the redaction of the *Tale*.

⁶ See introductory note to the *Battle* in *The Prose Works of Jonathan Swift, D.D.*, ed. Temple Scott, London, 1897, I, 156; and George Aitken, "Swift," *Cambridge History of English Literature*, Cambridge, 1912, IX, 113, where Aitken asserts, "The controversy has now lost its interest."

⁷ R. F. Jones, "The Background of the *Battle of the Books*," Washington University Studies, VII, Humanistic Series, II (1920), 99–162. Abridged in *The Seventeenth Century: Studies in the History of English Thought and Literature from Bacon to Pope*, Stanford University, California, 1951, pp. 10–40. See also *Ancients and Moderns: A Study in the Background of the "Battle of the Books,"* Washington University Studies, new series, Language and Literature, VI, St. Louis, 1936. Philip Pinkus has recently argued that Jones oversimplified Swift's place in the controversy, and that Swift was not a partisan ancient, but one who took careful note of ridiculous excess on both sides of the argument. "Swift and the Ancients-Moderns Controversy," *UTQ*, XXIX (1959), 46–58.

⁸ Clarence M. Webster, "Swift and Some Earlier Satirists of Puritan Enthusiasm," *PMLA*, XLVIII (1933), 1141–53. Webster's "The Satiric Background of the Attack on the Puritans in *A Tale of a Tub*," *PMLA*, L (1935), 210–23, is an annotated bibliography of the earlier satires.

⁹ W. A. Eddy, Introduction to *A Tale of a Tub*, in *Gulliver's Travels, A Tale of a Tub, Battle of the Books, etc.*, Oxford Standard edition, New York, 1933, p. iii. When it appears, this introduction (pp. i–xv) stands between pp. 358 and 359.

¹⁰ J. Middleton Murry, *Jonathan Swift: A Critical Biography*, New York, 1955, p. 94.

¹¹ Paul Elmer More, "Dean Swift," *Nation*, CI (August 5, 1915), 171–73, reprinted in *Shelburne Essays*, Tenth Series (*With the Wits*), Boston, 1919, pp. 101–21. I quote from the latter.

¹² Émile Pons, *Swift: les années de jeunesse et le 'Conte du tonneau,'* Strasbourg, 1925.

¹³ F. R. Leavis, "The Irony of Swift," *Scrutiny*, II (1934), 364–78; reprinted in Leavis' *Determinations*, London, 1934, pp. 78–108. I quote from the same essay in his *The Common Pursuit*, London, 1952, pp. 73–87.

¹⁴ See F. R. Leavis, "Literary Criticism and Philosophy: A Reply," *Scrutiny*, VI (June 1937), 59–70; "Tragedy and the 'Medium': A Note on Mr. Santayana's 'Tragic Philosophy,'" *Scrutiny*, XII (1944), 249–60.

¹⁵ Mario Rossi and Joseph Hone, *Swift, or the Egotist*, New York, 1934.

¹⁶ D. Nichol Smith, "Jonathan Swift: Some Observations," *Essays by Divers Hands: Transactions of the Royal Society of Literature*, XIV (1935), 29–48.

¹⁷ George Sherburn, "Methods in Books about Swift," *SP*, XXXV (1938), 650.

¹⁸ Herbert Davis, "Recent Studies of Swift," *UTQ*, VII (1938), 273–88.

[19] The kind of form one can expect in satire, including such a work as the *Tale*, is clarified admirably and simply in Northrop Frye's *Anatomy of Criticism*, Princeton, 1957, especially the paragraph pp. 233–34.

[20] Philip Pinkus, "*A Tale of a Tub* and the Rosy Cross," *JEGP*, LIX (1960), 669–79.

[21] Louis I. Bredvold discusses the latter misapprehension in "The Gloom of the Tory Satirists," *Pope and His Contemporaries*, ed. James L. Clifford and Louis Landa, Oxford, 1949, p. 4.

[22] Robert C. Elliott, "Swift's *Tale of a Tub*: An Essay in Problems of Structure," *PMLA*, LXVI (1951), 441–55.

[23] Harold D. Kelling, "Reason in Madness: *A Tale of a Tub*," *PMLA*, LXIX (1954), 198–222.

[24] James L. Clifford, "Swift's *Mechanical Operation of the Spirit*," *Pope and His Contemporaries*, pp. 135–46, argues for the unity of the three works.

[25] Ricardo Quintana, "Situational Satire: A Commentary on the Method of Swift," *UTQ*, XVII (1948), 130–36.

[26] On this matter Miss Williams' acute observation clears the air admirably: "Of all Swift's mouthpieces, the 'supposed author' of *A Tale of a Tub* is one of the least tangible. Gulliver, though changeable, is generally, except for particular uses, solid enough at a given moment, and the full extent and the precise nature of the satiric treatment he is to receive is only gradually revealed. But the author of the *Tale* is from beginning to end a fantastic creature, a mere bundle of unrelated qualities. Though it is useful to speak of him so, it is not really possible to regard him as a person." *Jonathan Swift and the Age of Compromise*, p. 132.

[27] Desiderius Erasmus, *The Praise of Folly*, trans. Hoyt Hudson, Princeton, 1941, p. 49. See also Hudson's Introduction, p. xxx. Hudson mentions Swift only in passing, but students of Swift's satire will find his discussion of the Lucianic tradition, of learned parody, and of the mock panegyric extremely helpful. See also Henry Knight Miller, "The Paradoxical Encomium with Special Reference to Its Vogue in England, 1600–1800," *MP*, LIII (1956), 145–78, especially 168, for a discussion of the *Tale*'s relationship to the tradition of paradoxical encomia.

[28] When Paulson turns from Gnosticism and controlling images to a comparison of *The Praise of Folly* and the *Tale*, he illuminates Swift's Erasmian "blame by praise" most admirably. *Theme and Structure*, pp. 249–53.

[29] Such a willingness weakens two recent, otherwise excellent "background" studies, Phillip Harth's *Swift and Anglican Rationalism: The Religious Background of "A Tale of a Tub,"* Chicago, 1961, and Elias Chiasson's "Swift's Clothes Philosophy in the *Tale* and Hooker's Concept of Law," *SP*, XIX (1962), 64–82.

Also more valuable for background than for critical insight is Irvin Ehrenpreis' discussion of the *Tale* in his *Mr. Swift and His Contemporaries* (London, 1962), Volume I of his three-volume biography (still in progress), *Swift: The Man, His Works, and the Age*. Ehrenpreis, evidently unsympathetic toward the emphasis on the *ingénu* or persona in recent criticism of the *Tale*, prefers to see Swift himself in that role, wielding irony as one would in conversation. The result is a kind of Ptolemaic criticism full of epicycles and, not surprisingly, frequent wonder at the *Tale's* sacrilege and nastiness. See especially pp. 210–15.

[30] Edward Rosenheim, Jr., devotes the greater part of his recent *Swift and the Satirist's Art* (Chicago, 1963) to the *Tale* and is particularly rewarding on its parody of Roger L'Estrange (pp. 60–66, 83–88).

IV
GULLIVER'S TRAVELS

[1] Knowles, *N&Q*, 4th ser., I (March 7, 1868), 223.

[2] Th. Borkowsky, "Quellen zu Swifts *Gulliver*," *Anglia*, XV (1893), 345–89.

[3] Orrery, *Remarks*, London, 1752, p. 145.

[4] John Colin Dunlop, *The History of Fiction*, London, 1814. I refer to the revision of Dunlop by Henry Wilson, Bohn's Standard Library, London, 1888, II, 525–36.

[5] Erwin Hönncher, "Quellen zu Dean Swifts *Gulliver's Travels*," *Anglia*, X (1888), 297–427. After analyzing parallel passages and ideas common to both, Hönncher concludes that a marked dissimilarity of mind and temperament gave each satire a distinctive structure and development. While *Gulliver* does not, in Hönncher's opinion, show the immediate influence of *L'Histoire comique*, analogous situations may have been the result of Swift's familiarity with Cyrano's work. Hönncher is also disinclined to ascribe immediate influence on Swift to Bishop Godwin's *Voyage of Domingo Gonsales to the Moon* (1638), a source first suggested by Scott, a text of which Hönncher prints (pp. 428–52) along with "Bemerkungen zu Godwins *Voyage of Domingo Gonsales to the Moon*" (pp. 452–56).

[6] G. Ravenscroft Dennis, ed., *Gulliver's Travels*, Vol. VIII, *The Prose Works of Jonathan Swift, D.D.*, ed. Temple Scott, London, 1899, xxiii–xxiv. Paul Thierkopf, *Swifts Gulliver und seine französischen Vorgänger*, Magdeburg, 1899. Max Poll, *The Sources of Gulliver's Travels*, University of Cincinnati Bulletin No. 24, Publications of the University, ser. 2, Vol. III, Cincinnati, 1904. Pietro Toldo, "Les Voyages merveilleux de Cyrano de Bergerac et de Swift et leurs rapports avec l'oeuvre de Rabelais," *Revue des études rabelaisiennes*, IV (1906), 295–334; V (1907), 24–44. For *Gulliver's* alleged relation to the *Arabian Nights* see also Martha P. Conant, *The Oriental Tale in England in the Eighteenth Century*, New York, 1908, pp. 259, 262. However, Sheila Shaw, by demonstrating that the *Arabian Nights* was known in eighteenth-century England only in an abbreviated form, casts strong doubt on its being a source for *Gulliver*. See her "Early English Editions of the *Arabian Nights*: Their Value to Eighteenth Century Literary Scholarship," *Muslim World*, XLIX (1959), 232–38.

[7] Princeton, 1923. Peter Smith, who reissued Case's *Four Essays* (Gloucester, Mass., 1958) has also reissued Eddy (Gloucester, Mass., 1963).

[8] On the extraordinary voyage in France see Geoffroy Atkinson, *The Extraordinary Voyage in French Literature before 1700*, New York, 1920;

The Extraordinary Voyage in French Literature from 1700 to 1720, Paris, 1922. A helpful checklist and discussion of the imaginary voyage is Philip B. Gove, *The Imaginary Voyage in Prose Fiction,* New York, 1941.

[9] Aline Mackenzie Taylor, "Cyrano de Bergerac and Gulliver's Voyage to Brobdingnag," *Tulane Studies in English,* Vol. V, New Orleans, 1955, 83–102, explores this thoroughly.

[10] J. Churton Collins, *Jonathan Swift: A Biographical and Critical Study,* London, 1893, p. 205.

[11] E. N. S. Thompson, "Tom Brown and Eighteenth Century Satirists," *MLN,* XXXII (1917), 90–94.

[12] Eddy, in a happy conjecture, identifies the "three little volumes of Lucian in French," which Swift mentions purchasing in the *Journal to Stella* (January 6, 1710–11), as d'Ablancourt's translation.

[13] References to *Gulliver* will indicate voyage and chapter, followed by citation in Herbert Davis' edn. of 1941. The revised edition of 1959 has a differential of 16 in its pagination (p. 1 in 1941 is p. 17 in 1959). All copies of 1959 which I have seen transpose pp. 215 and 283.

[14] Harry C. Morris, "The *Dialogues of Hylas and Philonous* as a source in *Gulliver's Travels*," *MLN,* LXX (1955), 175–77, doubts Swift's use of *Theory of Vision* and argues that Swift's images of size differentia probably have their source in Berkeley's *Dialogues.* Edward Wasiolek, "Relativity in *Gulliver's Travels*," *PQ,* XXXVII (1958), 110–16, argues ingeniously that Berkeley's relativism enabled Swift in *Gulliver* to distinguish merely human, pride-sprung values from those divine and unchanging. Helmut Papajewski, "Swift und Berkeley," *Anglia,* LXXVIII (1959), 29–55, minimizes Berkeley's possible influence.

[15] Pons, *RLC,* IV (1924), 149–54.

[16] Eddy had identified Swift's French Lucian as d'Ablancourt in an earlier article, "A Source for *Gulliver's Travels*," *MLN,* XXXVI (1921), 419–22.

[17] Secord, *JEGP,* XXIII (1924), 460–62. To illustrate the importance of *Gulliver's* relation to the authentic voyage, Secord shows that by a strategic choice of dates Swift makes a passage in Dampier corroborate Gulliver's departure on his first voyage. Dampier tells of meeting a ship named the *Antelope* rounding the Cape of Good Hope on June 3, 1699. Swift appropriates the name for Gulliver's ship and has it set sail from Bristol on May 4, 1699, thus allowing it sufficient time for its rendezvous with Dampier's ship at the Cape.

[18] Swift's relation to Holberg is discussed by James McNelis, Introduction, *Journey of Niels Klim to the World Underground,* ed. McNelis, Lincoln, Neb., 1960, pp. vii–xxxi.

[19] Frantz, *MP,* XXIX (1931), 49–57.

[20] The best discussion of Gulliver as impostor is James R. Wilson's "Swift's Alazon," *Studia neophilologica,* XXX (1958), 153–64.

[21] To Vanessa, July 13, 1722, *Corresp.,* ed. F. Elrington Ball, London, 1910–14, III, 134. To Ford, July 22, 1722, *Letters of Swift to Ford,* ed. D. Nichol Smith, Oxford, 1935, p. 97.

[22] Herbert Davis, "Recent Studies of Swift: A Survey," *UTQ,* VII (1938), 277.

[23] Gilbert Chinard, ed., Baron de Lahontan's *Dialogues curieux*, Baltimore, 1931, pp. 60–62.

[24] That Swift succeeded here in vexing the world is evident in the long line of commentators who have seen fit to call attention to the "error" of this passage, pointing out that salt is necessary in the diet, that most animals, including horses, are fond of salt, and the like. Crusoe's Friday has a strong antipathy to salt. See *Robinson Crusoe*, Everyman's Library, London, 1945, pp. 154–55. For a provocative discussion of the Swift-Defoe relationship in which their differences rather than the customary similarities are stressed, see John F. Ross, *Swift and Defoe: A Study in Relationship*, University of California Publications in English, XI, Berkeley, 1941.

[25] The indebtedness to Tom Brown's *Amusements Serious and Comical*, suggested by Eddy, is slight at best. Eddy and others had called attention to Rabelais' Court of Queen Whim as a predecessor of the Grand Academy. For Swift's relation to Rabelais see Huntington Brown, *Rabelais in English Literature*, Cambridge, Mass., 1933, pp. 152–71. More than anything else, says Brown, Swift and Rabelais shared "teeming imagination."

[26] Marjorie Nicolson and Nora Mohler, "The Scientific Background of Swift's Voyage to Laputa," *Annals of Science*, II (1937), 299–334; "Swift's 'Flying Island' in the Voyage to Laputa," *Annals of Science*, II (1937), 405–30. The former study is reprinted in Marjorie Nicolson, *Science and Imagination*, Ithaca, 1956, pp. 110–54.

[27] On Swift see especially pp. 189–95, which incorporates the material offered in the earlier article on the Flying Island.

[28] *HLQ*, I (1938), 329–34.

[29] The "kinship" between Richard Sympson and William Symson may be confined to what perhaps should be called a "blurb" in Corolini's *Key* (1726), a wretched "explanation" of *Gulliver* published by Curll. In that volume Richard Sympson is given the following footnote: "Capt. William Symson, his near relation, hath published A New Voyage to the *East Indies*. Printed for Mr. Curll."

[30] Mackie Jarrell, "The Handwriting of the Lilliputians," *PQ*, XXXVII (1958), 116–19, suggests Temple's "Of Heroick Virtue" as an additional source.

[31] John R. Moore, "A New Source for *Gulliver's Travels*," *SP*, XXXVIII (1941), 66–80.

[32] Grennan, *ELH*, XII (1945), 188–202. A more modest and convincing argument that Swift's art has some Gaelic roots is offered in Vivian Mercier's "Swift and the Gaelic Tradition," *A Review of English Literature*, III (July 1962), 69–79. Mr. Mercier is particularly good on Swift's influence on later Irish writers. See also his *The Irish Comic Tradition*, Oxford, 1962, pp. 182–209 *passim*.

[33] *Works of Swift*, 1814, XII, 108.

[34] Harold D. Kelling, "Some Significant Names in *Gulliver's Travels*," *SP*, XLVIII (1951), 761–78. Some related studies are Frederick Bracher, "The Name 'Lemuel Gulliver,'" *HLQ*, XII (1949), 409–13, who finds a hint to Gulliver's character in the syllable *Gull;* John R. Moore, "The Yahoos of the African Travelers," *N&Q*, CXCV (1950), 182–85, who suggests Swift derived the name from Yahudis, Yahouris, Gugoos, or Sorhois

of North Africa, a degraded remnant of Jews and Coptic Christians in the region from Lake Chad to Timbuctoo; and Sheridan Baker, "Swift, 'Lilliputian,' and Catullus," *N&Q*, CCI (1956), 477–79, who traces the word back to the Roman poet.

[35] Clark, "A *Gulliver* Dictionary," *SP*, L (1953), 592–624.

[36] Morley had suggested " 'Grand, big, noble,' with the final *le* dropped out." Henry Morley, ed., *Gulliver's Travels*, Carisbrooke Library, London, 1890, p. 18.

[37] Harold Williams, ed., *Gulliver's Travels*, London, 1926, p. 469. The "Anagrammatick Method" is at III, vi; HD, XI, 175.

[38] Émile Pons, "Les Langues imaginaires dans le voyage utopique; un précurseur: Thomas Morus," *RLC*, X (1930), 589–607; "Les 'Jargons' de Panurge dans Rabelais," *RLC*, XI (1931), 185–218; "Les Grammairiens: Vairasse et Foigny," *RLC*, XII (1932), 500–32. Another valuable study is Edward Seeber, "Ideal Languages in the French and English Imaginary Voyages," *PMLA*, LX (1945), 586–97.

[39] In *Mélanges offerts à M. Abel Lefranc*, Paris, 1936, pp. 219–28; reprinted in *Cahiers du sud*, XLIV (1958), 31–39.

[40] Irvin Ehrenpreis, "Swift's 'Little Language' in the *Journal to Stella,*" *SP*, XLV (1948), 80–88, discussed in Chapter II.

[41] While Clark in several footnotes is at pains to point out his differences with Kelling, this fortuitous agreement, deserving at least a "Eureka," receives no comment.

[42] Roland M. Smith, "Swift's Little Language and Nonsense Names," *JEGP*, LIII (1954), 178–96.

[43] Kelling, avoiding reversal, found French *grand*, "big," in the first syllable and Latin *altrix*, "nurse," in the second: an ironic counterpoint for Gulliver's "little nurse" (p. 771).

[44] *JEGP*, LVI (1957), 154–62.

[45] *Proceedings of the British Academy, 1919–20*, IX, 237–59; reprinted in Firth's *Essays Historical and Literary*, Oxford, 1938, pp. 210–41.

[46] Firth, in spite of his access to contrary evidence in the Swift-Ford correspondence, persisted in associating *Gulliver* with the Scriblerus Club and dating its composition from 1714. For the most incisive and thorough discussion of *Gulliver's* compositional history see D. Nichol Smith's introduction to the *Letters of Jonathan Swift to Charles Ford*, Oxford, 1935, pp. xxxviii–xlii. Smith proves conclusively that the composition of Part I took place about 1721–22, Part II about 1722–23, Part IV in 1723, and Part III in 1724–25. That Part III and not Part IV was written last invalidates the nineteenth-century notion of progressive pessimism in Swift's life, often and erroneously traced to the so-called deepening gloom of the "successive" voyages. Ricardo Quintana, *Swift: An Introduction*, London and New York, 1955, pp. 144–49, attempts to maintain *Gulliver's* Scriblerian connections.

[47] William A. Eddy, ed., *Gulliver's Travels, A Tale of a Tub, Battle of the Books, etc.*, Oxford Standard edition, New York, 1933, pp. vii–viii.

[48] Ehrenpreis, "The Origins of *Gulliver's Travels*," *PMLA*, LXXII (1957), 880–899; revised and reprinted in Ehrenpreis' *The Personality of Jonathan Swift*, London, 1958, pp. 83–116. I quote from the latter.

[49] Fink, *ELH*, XIV (1947), 151–61. Deteriorationism as a theme in *Gulliver* is also discussed in Quintana, *Swift: An Introduction*, pp. 153–56.

[50] De Morgan, "Swift: *Gulliver's Travels*," *N&Q*, 2nd ser., VI (August 14, 1858), 123–26. The article offers a great many further quibbles directed at other so-called faults, inconsistencies, and the like, De Morgan's purpose being to indict Swift for carelessness and inaccuracy. While the incredible geography has distressed some readers, others have been troubled by an instance of unaccountable adroitness in astronomy. In 1877 a Washington astronomer, Asaph Hall, discovered that Mars did in fact have two moons as the Laputan astronomers had claimed, and found their strange behavior to agree quite closely with the Laputans' description (III, iii; HD, XI, 154–55). S. H. Gould, "Swift and the Moons of Mars," *JHI*, VI (1945), 91–101, explains how such lucky guesswork might occur and concludes that Swift was not really a great and profound astronomer.

[51] Quintana, *JEGP*, XLVI (1947), 323.

[52] Moore, *JEGP*, XL (1941), 214–28.

[53] "The Maps in *Gulliver's Travels*," *HLQ*, VII (1944), 59–74.

[54] *PQ*, XXIV (1945), 161–62.

[55] Sherburn, *YR*, XXXV (1946), 760–61.

[56] Elder, *MLN*, XXV (1920), 206–11. Elder's article occasioned a classic history-of-ideas study, A. O. Lovejoy's " 'Pride' in Eighteenth-Century Thought," *MLN*, XXXVI (1921), 31–37; reprinted in revised form in Lovejoy's *Essays in the History of Ideas*, Baltimore, 1948, pp. 62–68.

[57] Wedel, *SP*, XXIII (1926), 434–50.

[58] W. J. Courthope, *A History of English Poetry*, London, 1905, V, 123.

[59] See Chapter I.

[60] There are some anticipations of Wedel in Ernest Bernbaum's introduction to his edition of *Gulliver*, New York, 1920, but the gulf between Bernbaum and Wedel is clearly evident in Bernbaum's judgment that "Swift's inventiveness . . . failed him, especially in describing the Houyhnhnms," who are "unintentionally grotesque" (p. xviii).

[61] McKenzie, *Five Studies in Literature*, University of California Publications in English, Vol. VIII, No. 1, Berkeley, 1940, 101–29.

[62] K. Williams, "Gulliver's Voyage to the Houyhnhnms," *ELH*, XVIII (1951), 275–86. " 'Animal Rationis Capax,' A Study of Certain Aspects of Swift's Imagery," *ELH*, XXI (1954), 193–207. The substance of these articles has been incorporated in Miss Williams' *Jonathan Swift and the Age of Compromise*, Lawrence, Kan., 1958. On *Gulliver* see especially pp. 154–209.

[63] Tuveson, *UTQ*, XXII (1953), 368–75.

[64] Samuel H. Monk, "The Pride of Lemuel Gulliver," *SR*, LXIII (1955), 48–71. First delivered as a public lecture at the University of Minnesota in 1952. Reprinted in *Eighteenth-Century English Literature: Modern Essays in Criticism*, ed. James L. Clifford, New York, 1959, pp. 112–29.

[65] Ehrenpreis, boldly employing a biographical approach in "The Origins of *Gulliver's Travels*," also associates the Houyhnhnms with Bolingbroke.

[66] Roland Mushat Frye, "Swift's Yahoo and the Christian Symbols for Sin," *JHI*, XV (1954), 201–17, relates the Yahoo to a tradition found in the Bible and the homiletic literature of Christianity in which sin and

depravity are suggested metaphorically by filth and deformity. The subsequent criticism of Frye by W. A. Murray (*JHI*, XV [1954], 599–601) deserves note if only to record Murray's conclusions that "Swift's Houyhnhnms are perhaps closer to being deists than he [Swift] realized" and they bring Gulliver "within sight of salvation." For a more reliable note on Frye see Tuveson, *PQ*, XXXIV (1955), 316–17.

[67] For an extended discussion of Swift's attitude toward science see George R. Potter, "Swift and Natural Science," *PQ*, XX (1941), 97–118. Potter needs to be corrected with two penetrating reviews by Louis Landa: *MP*, XXV (1937), 203 (of *Mind and Art*); and *PQ*, XXI (1942), 219–21 (of Potter). Both Potter and Landa rightly stress that it is the abuse of science rather than science itself that Swift attacks.

[68] Richard J. Dircks, "Gulliver's Tragic Rationalism," *Criticism—A Quarterly for Literature and the Arts*, II (1960), 134–49, explores these hostilities more fully and argues that the satire in the fourth voyage "is particularly, although probably not exclusively, directed against the extension of the political and social philosophy of John Locke, as implemented by the Whigs" (p. 145).

[69] Ronald S. Crane's recent demurrers to these conclusions will be discussed below.

[70] Quintana, "Situational Satire: A Commentary on the Method of Swift," *UTQ*, XVII (1948), 130–36; reprinted in *Studies in the Literature of the Augustan Age: Essays in Honor of A. E. Case*, ed. R. C. Boys, Ann Arbor, 1952, pp. 259–65.

[71] Several studies have attempted to deal with the allegory in Swift: H. E. Greene, "The Allegory in Spenser, Bunyan, and Swift," *PMLA*, IV (1889), 145–92; H. M. Dargan, "The Nature of Allegory as Used by Swift," *SP*, XIII (1916), 159–79; but most ambitious is the work of Ellen Douglass Leyburn, who, in *Satiric Allegory: Mirror of Man*, New Haven, 1956, attempts to stake out a new genre, satiric allegory, in which she places *A Tale of a Tub* and *Gulliver* (pp. 22–33, 71–91). R. C. Elliott offers an incisive review in *MLN*, LXXII (1957), 453–56. Leyburn's earlier article, "Certain Problems of Allegorical Satire in *Gulliver's Travels*," *HLQ*, XIII (1950), 161–89, is a preliminary exploration of the problem carried forward in *Satiric Allegory*. The primacy of the comedy over the allegory is rightly stressed by Quintana in *Swift: An Introduction*: "The allegorical elements, whatever they are and however they came there, have not been allowed to encroach on the comedy or break up the form" (p. 152).

[72] Leavis, whose championing of D. H. Lawrence led him to declare himself "on the side of life," expressed a singular disenchantment with the Houyhnhnms: ". . . they may have all the reason," said Leavis of the Houyhnhnms, "but the Yahoos have all the life." "The Irony of Swift," *The Common Pursuit*, London, 1952, p. 84. This article first appeared in *Scrutiny*, II (1934), 364–78, and was reprinted in Leavis' *Determinations*, London, 1934, pp. 79–108.

[73] Another defense of the third voyage appears in John H. Sutherland's "A Reconsideration of Gulliver's Third Voyage," *SP*, LIV (1957), 45–52. The best discussion of the unsatisfactoriness of the third voyage is in R. B. Heilman's introduction to the Modern Library *Gulliver*, New York, 1950, p. xi.

[74] In his review of Eddy, *RLC*, IV (1924), 154.

[75] On the use of biography see Louis Landa, "The Critical Significance of Biographical Evidence: Jonathan Swift," *English Institute Essays, 1946*, New York, 1947, pp. 20–40; reprinted in *Studies in the Literature of the Augustan Age*, pp. 177–97.

[76] John B. Moore, *MP*, XXV (1928), 469–80.

[77] Ross, *Studies in the Comic*, University of California Publications in English, Vol. VIII, No. 2, Berkeley, 1941, 175–96. See also Ross's introduction to the Rinehart *Gulliver*, New York, 1948.

[78] Horrell, *SR*, LI (1943), 476–504.

[79] Kliger, *MLQ*, VI (1945), 401–15.

[80] Stone, *MLQ*, X (1949), 367–76.

[81] Stone, pp. 369–70; Boas, pp. 10, 56. Churton Collins had associated the theriophily of the *Apology* with the voyage to the Houyhnhnms in *Jonathan Swift: A Biographical and Critical Study*, London, 1893, pp. 210–11.

[82] Kelling, *UTQ*, XXI (1952), 362–75.

[83] Elliott, *ELH*, XIX (1952), 49–63.

[84] W. B. C. Watkins, " 'Absent Thee from Felicity,' " *Southern Review*, V (1939), 346–65; reprinted in his *Perilous Balance: The Tragic Genius of Swift, Johnson, and Sterne*, Princeton, 1939, pp. 25–48. Watkins offers a biographically oriented interpretation in which the Houyhnhnms are a symbol of Swift's yearning for perfection. He finds in the last voyage "the heartbreaking despair of a man who has had a vision of perfection from which he awaked to sordid reality"; here the "satire passes over into tragedy" (p. 23). A similar interpretation has been offered by R. S. Crane in "The Rationale of the Fourth Voyage," first read before the Classical Period Group of the Modern Language Association in 1955, and published in *Gulliver's Travels: An Annotated Text with Critical Essays*, ed. Robert A. Greenberg, New York, 1961, pp. 300–7.

[85] Elliott's "Gulliver as Literary Artist" evidently appeared too late for Price to take account of it. Price acknowledges general indebtedness in his treatment of *Gulliver* to Ross, Horrell, and Quintana.

[86] Irvin Ehrenpreis, "Swift and Satire," *CE*, XIII (1952), 312. On the betrayal of the reader through Gulliver (and other putative authors) see also Henry W. Sams, "Swift's Satire of the Second Person," *ELH*, XXVI (1959), 36–44.

[87] This same concern is central in a lively and penetrating article by John Traugott, "A Voyage to Nowhere with Thomas More and Jonathan Swift: *Utopia* and *The Voyage to the Houyhnhnms*," *SR*, LXIX (Autumn 1961), 534–65. Traugott argues that a non-programmatic utopian ideal was retained by More and Swift "in the back of their heads" as a kind of necessary foolishness in their complex moral vision. As their apprehension and expression of this utopian ideal was always ironic and dramatic, they were saved from both involvement in the feast of fools and exile in Utopia or Houyhnhnmland by simply "playing the fool and not being one, by keeping utopia a city of the mind, where Raphael Nonsense [Hythloday, that is] and Lemuel Gulliver can live" (p. 564). The conceptualism of this interpretation (in which moral ideals exist for mind only) has one wholesome though perhaps unintentional result: Swift is saved from Platonism.

[88] Calhoun Winton, "Conversion on the Road to Houyhnhnmland," *SR*,

LXVIII (1960), 20–33. Martin Kallich, "Three Ways of Looking at a Horse: Jonathan Swift's 'Voyage to the Houyhnhnms' Again," *Criticism—A Quarterly for Literature and the Arts,* II (1960), 107–24. On the Struldbruggs as an exposure of freethinking see J. Leeds Barroll, III, "Gulliver and the Struldbruggs," *PMLA,* LXXIII (1958), 43–50. For a survey of critical opinion on the Struldbruggs see R. G. Geering, "Swift's Struldbruggs: The Critics Considered," *Journal of the Australasian Universities Language and Literature Association,* No. 7 (November 1957), pp. 5–15.

[89] Ricardo Quintana, *PQ,* XXXVII (1958), 354–55. George Sherburn, "Errors Concerning the Houyhnhnms," *MP,* LVI (1958), 92–97. Ronald S. Crane, *PQ,* XL (1961), 427–30. Crane's "The Houyhnhnms, the Yahoos, and the History of Ideas," in *Reason and the Imagination: Studies in the History of Ideas, 1600–1800,* ed. J. A. Mazzeo, New York and London, 1962, pp. 231–53, discounts the now dominant interpretation of the fourth voyage, largely the achievement of historians of ideas, as an unprovable hypothesis. His own hypothesis is less an interpretation than it is an unexceptionable statement about Swift's intention, namely, that the voyage is "in considerable part at least, an anti-Porphyrian satire" meant to discredit the common logicians' definition of man as *animal rationale.* While this is irrefutable, it is hardly something one would want to prove upon his pulses. A similar interpretation, evidently influenced by Crane, is found in Ehrenpreis' "The Meaning of Gulliver's Last Voyage," *A Review of English Literature,* III (1962), 18–38, which does indeed, as Ehrenpreis points out in a note, "differ fundamentally" from his earlier pronouncements. For an extensive discussion of the present issues from a point of view sympathetic toward Sherburn and Crane see Edward Rosenheim, Jr., The Fifth Voyage of Lemuel Gulliver: A Footnote," *MP,* LX (November, 1962) 103–19, and Rosenheim's *Swift and the Satirist's Art,* Chicago, 1963.

[90] George Sherburn, "Swift," *A Literary History of England,* ed. A. C. Baugh, New York, 1948, p. 865.

[91] George Sherburn, Introduction, *Gulliver's Travels,* Harper's Modern Classics, New York, 1950, pp. xiv–xv.

[92] Charles H. Peake, "Swift and the Passions," *MLR,* LV (1960), 169–80.

[93] These have usually been ascribed to Pope, but Sherburn has argued that they are more likely joint productions of the Scriblerians and ought not to be attributed to Pope alone, at least not all five of them. See "The 'Copies of Verses' About *Gulliver,*" *Texas Studies in Literature and Language,* III (Spring 1961), 3–7.

[94] Dyson, *Essays and Studies,* n.s. XI (1958), 53–67.

V

SWIFT THE MAN

[1] Alfred Ainger, "Swift—His Life and Genius," *Lectures and Essays,* London, 1905, I, 188–272.

[2] More, *Nation,* CI (August 5, 1915), 171–73; reprinted in *Shelburne Essays,* Tenth Series (*With the Wits*), Boston, 1919, pp. 101–21. I quote from the latter.

[3] Whibley, *Jonathan Swift,* Cambridge, 1917; reprinted in *Literary Studies,* London, 1919, pp. 343–70. I quote from the former.

[4] Boyd, "A New Way with Old Masterpieces," *Harper's,* CL (1925), 584–94; reprinted as "Jonathan Swift," *Literary Blasphemies,* New York, 1927, pp. 74–105. I quote from the former.

[5] Huxley, "Swift," *Do What You Will,* Garden City, N.Y., 1929, pp. 97–112. Huxley is more temperate in *On the Margin,* New York, 1923, pp. 83–93, where in an essay on *Polite Conversation,* he finds many of its clichés more vital than Swift gave them credit for (p. 88). The presence of two Struldbruggs in *After Many a Summer Dies the Swan* (1939) and numerous pale reflections of Swiftian satire in *Brave New World* (1932) do not really suggest a softening of Swiftophobia in this pursuer of "higher utilitarianism," "the perennial philosophy," and "nonattachment." D. H. Lawrence, who evidently influenced or was influenced by Huxley's Swiftophobia, has no extended comments on Swift, but repeatedly reveals an *idée fixe* on the subject of Celia: "Think of poor Swift's insane *But* of horror at the end of every verse of that poem to Celia," Letter to Lady Ottoline Morrell, December 28, 1928; the same theme also in introduction to *Pansies* (1929), where Lawrence's inaccuracy in describing the offending line as a refrain strongly suggests that he did not read the poem carefully (*Selected Literary Criticism,* ed. Anthony Beal, New York, 1956, pp. 26, 29). Recent Lawrence studies perpetuate Lawrence's view of Swift. See Mark Spilka, *The Love Ethic of D. H. Lawrence,* Bloomington, 1955, pp. 186–87; and F. R. Leavis, *D. H. Lawrence: Novelist,* New York, 1956, p. 151, where Lawrence is described as one "whose genius is to be the antithesis of the inventor of the Houyhnhnms and the Yahoos."

[6] Read, pp. 80–99. This essay first appeared unsigned in *TLS,* October 28, 1926, pp. 729–30, and was augmented with two notes on Swift in *Collected Essays in Literary Criticism,* London, 1938, pp. 196–219, published in the United States as *The Nature of Literature,* New York, 1956. The two notes, which stand as introductory and concluding sections to the original essay, deal with Swift's habits of composition and with his status as poet and are less hostile than the material they surround. I quote from *The Nature of Literature.*

[7] Leavis, *Scrutiny,* II (1934), 364–78. Reprinted in his *Determinations,* London, 1934, pp. 78–108. I quote from the same essay in his *The Common Pursuit,* London, 1952, pp. 73–87.

[8] Knight, "Swift and the Symbolism of Irony," *The Burning Oracle,* Oxford, 1939, pp. 114–30.

[9] Willey, "A Note on Swift," *The Eighteenth Century Background,* London, 1940, pp. 100–109.

[10] Eliot, "Cyril Tourneur," *Selected Essays, 1917–1932,* New York, 1932, pp. 166–67. There is a ghost of Swift—with associations with Yeats—in "Four Quartets," *Complete Poems and Plays of T. S. Eliot,* New York, 1952, pp. 140–42. See Maurice Johnson, "The Ghost of Swift in 'Four Quartets'," *MLN,* LXIV (1949), 273. In " 'Ulysses,' Order, and Myth," *Dial,* LXXV (1923), 481, Eliot, disagreeing with Thackeray, praised the conclusion of the voyage to the Houyhnhnms as "one of the greatest triumphs that the human soul has ever achieved."

[11] Leslie, *The Skull of Swift,* Indianapolis, 1928.

[12] Mario M. Rossi and Joseph M. Hone, *Swift, or the Egotist*, London, 1934.

[13] Murry, *Jonathan Swift: A Critical Biography*, London, 1954. Worthy of mention among the *better* critical studies is W. D. Taylor, *Jonathan Swift: A Critical Essay*, London, 1933.

[14] Students of Swift and the eighteenth century eagerly await the three-volume biography promised by Irvin Ehrenpreis, *Swift: The Man, His Works, and the Age*. Volume I, *Mr. Swift and His Contemporaries* (London 1962), concentrates on family background and the influence of such mentors as St. George Ashe and Sir William Temple.

[15] G. Bernard Shaw, Postscript to *Back to Methuselah*, World's Classics Edition, New York, 1946, p. 260.

[16] Quintana, "Recent Discussions of Swift," *CE*, II (1940), 12.

[17] *The Letters of W. B. Yeats*, ed. Allan Wade, London, 1954, p. 680, by permission of the publisher, The Macmillan Co.

[18] W. B. Yeats, "Bishop Berkeley," *Essays by W. B. Yeats, 1931 to 1936*, Dublin, 1937, p. 30. This essay apppeared originally as the introduction to Rossi and Hone, *Bishop Berkeley, His Life, Writings and Philosophy*, London, 1931.

[19] W. B. Yeats, *Collected Poems*, New York, 1951, p. 236, by permission of the publisher, The Macmillan Co.

[20] Jacques Barzun, Introduction, *Gulliver's Travels*, New York, 1947, pp. vii–xix. Revised and reprinted as "Swift, or Man's Capacity for Reason," *The Energies of Art*, New York, 1956, pp. 81–100. I quote from the former.

[21] Letter to Wyndham Lewis, *The Letters of W. B. Yeats*, p. 776. *Wheels and Butterflies*, New York, 1935, pp. 13, 40.

[22] *Wheels and Buterflies*, pp. 1–56.

[23] F. M. Darnall, "Old Wine in New Bottles," *SAQ*, XLI (1942), 53–63.

[24] Kronenberger, "Swift," *Kings and Desperate Men*, New York, 1942, pp. 140–52.

[25] Landa, "The Critical Significance of Biographical Evidence: Swift," *English Institute Essays, 1946*, New York, 1947, pp. 20–40; reprinted in *Studies in the Literature of the Augustan Age*, ed. R. C. Boys, Ann Arbor, 1952, pp. 177–97. I quote from the former.

[26] Camille Looten, *La Pensée religieuse de Swift et ses antinomies*, Lille, 1935. Hans Reimers, *Jonathan Swift: Gedanken und Schriften über Religion und Kirche*, Hamburg, 1935. Max Armin Korn, *Die Weltanschauung Jonathan Swifts*, Jena, 1935. Charlotte Dege, *Utopie und Satire in Swifts Gulliver's Travels*, Frankfurt (Oder), 1934. Lilli Handro, *Swift, Gulliver's Travels: Eine Interpretation im Zusammenhang mit den geistesgeschichtlichen Beziehungen*, Hamburg, 1936. Hans Glaser, *Jonathan Swifts Kritik an der englischen Irlandpolitik*, Breslau, 1932. Adolf Heidenhain, *Ueber den Menschenhass: Eine pathographische Untersuchung über Jonathan Swift*, Stuttgart, 1934. I take up here only Looten, Reimers, Korn, and Heidenhain.

[27] Pons too had found no place for the mysteries in what he regarded as Swift's pervasive rationalism. *Swift*, pp. 332–33.

[28] Kathleen Williams, in her *Jonathan Swift and the Age of Compromise* (1958) and in her earlier articles (see Chapter IV above), draws upon recent scholarship and adds her own keen critical sense to bring this empha-

sis to its fullest development. The human, contradictory, unadjusted (or at best precariously balanced) Swift who emerges from the work of Miss Williams is to be contrasted with the sternly moral, uniformitarian, Olympian and often Platonistic Swift of the early Quintana and the recent R. S. Crane. For Swift as Platonist see Crane, "The Rationale of the Fourth Voyage" (Chapter IV above, note 84) and Jeffrey Hart, "The Ideologue as Artist: Some Notes on 'Gulliver's Travels,'" *Criticism—a Quarterly for Literature and the Arts,* II (1960), 125–33.

²⁹ Jones, "The Background of the *Battle of the Books,*" *Washington University Studies,* Vol. VII, Humanistic Series 2 (1920), 99–162, Abridgment in *The Seventeenth Century,* Stanford, 1951, pp. 10–40.

³⁰ Lovejoy, "The Parallel of Deism and Classicism," *MP,* XXIX (1932), 281–99.

³¹ Crane, "Anglican Apologetics and the Idea of Progress," *MP,* XXXI (1934), 273–306, 349–82.

³² See R. S. Crane, "Anglican Apologetics."

³³ See "On Burning a Dull Poem" and "Directions for a Birthday Song," *Poems,* ed. Harold Williams, Oxford, 1937, II, 460–70.

³⁴ Landa, *University of Texas Studies in English, 1944,* Austin, 1945, pp. 239–56. Landa carefully traverses the same ground in the introduction to his Riverside edition, *Gulliver's Travels,* Boston, 1960, especially pp. xxi–xxv. See also John A. Yunck, "The Sceptical Faith of Jonathan Swift," *Personalist,* XLII (1961), 533–54.

³⁵ Landa rightly insists that Swift shows nothing of predestination, election, and the other doctrines which buttressed Calvinism. Introduction to the Riverside edition, p. xxii.

³⁶ Søren Kierkegaard, *Either/Or,* Princeton, 1944, II (trans. Walter Lowrie), 283.

³⁷ Smith, *Essays by Divers Hands: Transactions of the Royal Society of Literature,* XIV (1935), 29–48.

³⁸ For this tendency in Quintana, see *Mind and Art,* pp. 69, 72.

³⁹ Landa, "The Critical Significance of Biographical Evidence," p. 31.

⁴⁰ W. B. C. Watkins' chapter, "Vive la Bagatelle," in his *Perilous Balance,* Princeton, 1939, pp. 25–48, is a modest but perceptive comparative study of Swift and Johnson. *Perilous Balance* has been reissued as a Boar's Head Book, Cambridge, Mass., 1960.

⁴¹ G. A. Aitken, *Life and Works of John Arbuthnot,* Oxford, 1892, pp. 435–42. Lester M. Beattie, *John Arbuthnot: Mathematician and Satirist,* Cambridge, Mass., 1935, pp. 376–82.

⁴² Pons, "Swift et Pascal," *Les Langues modernes,* XLV (1951), 135–52.

⁴³ Tuveson, *JHI,* XI (1950), 54–74.

⁴⁴ Brown, *PQ,* XXXIII (1954), 368–87.

⁴⁵ Ong, *MLQ,* XV (1954), 208–21.

⁴⁶ The attempt by A. E. Case to minimize the ingratitude is far from successful. See his "Swift's Supposed Ingratitude Toward his Uncle Godwin: A Surmise," *Pope and His Contemporaries,* ed. James L. Clifford and Louis A. Landa, Oxford, 1949, pp. 129–34.

⁴⁷ Maynard Mack in "The Muse of Satire," *YR,* XLI (1951), 80–92, has a good deal of value to say about the satirist's use of fictional artifice

and his conventional habit of raising his ethos in the minds of his audience. Reprinted in *Studies in the Literature of the Augustan Age,* ed. R. C. Boys, Ann Arbor, 1952, pp. 219–31.

[48] Maurice Johnson, "Swift and the Greatest Epitaph in History," *PMLA,* LXVIII (1953), 914–27, discusses the epitaph and its tradition and attempts to relate Swift's indignation to the righteous anger of the Old Testament prophets. Johnson calls attention to Juvenal, *Satire,* i. 79, upon which Swift draws in his epitaph. Horace Gregory suggests that Yeats often failed to recognize the mock heroic in Swift, especially in the epitaph: "On William Butler Yeats and the Mask of Jonathan Swift," *The Shield of Achilles: Essays on Belief in Poetry,* New York, 1944, pp. 136–55.

[49] By Whibley, for instance, in *Jonathan Swift,* p. 37.

[50] *Miscellaneous Criticism,* ed. T. M. Raysor, Cambridge, Mass., 1936, p. 407.

[51] The best study of irony is Norman Knox, *The Word* Irony *and Its Context, 1500–1755,* Durham, N.C., 1961, in which Swift's use of "blame-by-praise" and other ironic stances enjoys thorough and sensitive attention. Ian Watt's "The Ironic Tradition in Augustan Prose from Swift to Johnson," in *Restoration and Augustan Prose,* William Andrews Clark Memorial Library Seminar Papers, 14 July 1956, Los Angeles, 1957, pp. 19–46, is a more modest but equally incisive treatment. See especially Watt's discussion of irony and the bifurcated audience, pp. 21 ff.

[52] Phelps, "A Note on Gulliver," *YR,* XVII (October 1927), 92–98.

[53] Redinger, *American Scholar,* XV (1946), 221–26.

[54] Ehrenpreis, *CE,* XIII (1952), 309–12.

[55] [Mark Van Doren], "Two Hundred Years of *Gulliver,*" *Nation,* CXXII (March 17, 1926), 274.

[56] Babcock, *University of Michigan Publications in Language and Literature,* VIII, Ann Arbor, 1932, 133–49. Swift's subsequent efforts for the Tories and the consequent break with Addison and Steele are meticulously set forth in Bertrand Goldgar's *The Curse of Party: Swift's Relations with Addison and Steele,* Lincoln, Neb., 1961.

[57] Landa, "Swift's Economic Views and Mercantilism," *ELH,* X (1943), 310–35.

[58] Landa, "Swift and Charity," *JEGP,* XLIV (1945), 337–50.

[59] Ehrenpreis, *JHI,* XIII (1952), 131–46. See also R. C. Churchill, *He Served Human Liberty: An Essay on the Genius of Jonathan Swift,* London, 1946, where a somewhat uncritical sympathy for Swift leads Churchill to see in *Gulliver* a reaffirmation of "the notoriously old-fashioned doctrine of the four freedoms" (p. 31).

[60] Firth, *RES,* II (1926), 1–17.

[61] R. W. Jackson's *Jonathan Swift: Dean and Pastor,* London, 1939, published by the Society for the Propagation of Christian Knowledge, is a popular and pedestrian biography concentrating on Swift as churchman.

[62] Bernard, *Prose Works of Jonathan Swift,* ed. Temple Scott, London, 1908, XII, 85–106. See also Bernard's "Dean Swift in Dublin," *Blackwood's Magazine,* CLXXX (1906), 676–93.

[63] See also Joseph Manch, "Jonathan Swift and Women," *University of Buffalo Studies,* XVI (Monographs in English, No. 3), Buffalo, 1941, 135–

214, who defends Swift generally against charges of misogyny; George Hand, "Swift and Marriage," *Essays and Studies by Members of the Department of English*, University of California Publications in English, XIV, Berkeley, 1943, 73–92, argues sensitively and persuasively that Swift had a lifelong antipathy to marriage.

[64] New impetus is given to the old story that Swift and Stella were consanguineous in Denis Johnston's "The Mysterious Origin of Dean Swift," *Dublin Historical Record*, III (1941), 81–97, and in his lengthy and petulant *In Search of Swift*, Dublin, 1959. Johnston first accepts the common gossip claiming Stella to be a natural daughter of Sir William Temple, and then enriches Swift legendry by asserting that he was the natural son of Sir John Temple, the father of Sir William. Oliver St. John Gogarty supports and amplifies Johnston's theories in "Dean Swift as a Human Being," *Atlantic Monthly*, CLXXXVI (October 1950), 54–56, reprinted as "The Enigma of Dean Swift," in Gogarty's *Intimations*, New York, 1950, pp. 81–97. Johnston's views are strongly challenged by Harold Williams, *TLS*, November 29, 1941, p. 596, and by Herbert Davis, *Stella*, pp. 1–8. Notable twentieth-century affirmers of Stella's illegitimacy are Pons (*Swift*, pp. 147–48 n.), Shane Leslie (*The Script of Swift*, London, 1935, p. 4), and Rossi and Hone (*Swift, or the Egotist*, pp. 234–35).

[65] According to Yeats, one of the reasons Swift avoided marriage was his fear of madness. The other reason, somewhat contradictory of the first, is revealed in a question asked by Yeats's imaginary Swift: "Am I to add another to the healthy rascaldom and knavery of the world?" John Macy, in "Swift's Relations with Women," *The Critical Game*, New York, 1922, pp. 163–72 (earlier in *The New Republic*, XXVIII [1921], 354–55), suggests fear of insanity as deterrent to marriage in Swift, an element also in Edith Sitwell's novel, *I Live Under a Black Sun*, London, 1937, which renders the Swift-Stella-Vanessa story in a twentieth-century setting including World War I, cigarettes, and ragtime.

[66] Gold, drawing upon Krafft-Ebing (*Psychopathia Sexualis*, trans. F. J. Rebman, Brooklyn, 1929, p. 64), attempts to explain much of Swift's conduct, or lack of it, on the basis of "Anaesthesia sexualis" (*Swift's Marriage to Stella*, pp. 126–46).

[67] Mencken, rev. of Van Doren's *Swift*, *NYHTB*, October 19, 1930, p. 1.

[68] Yost, *Florida State University Studies*, No. 11, Tallahassee, 1953, pp. 25–55.

[69] Sigmund Freud, "On the History of the Psychoanalytic Movement," *Collected Papers*, Vol. I, London, 1946, 321.

[70] Ferenczi, *International Journal of Psychoanalysis*, IX (1928), 283–300.

[71] W. Cooke Taylor, ed., *Gulliver's Travels*, Philadelphia, n.d., p. 64. Dr. Karpman (see note 72, below) describes Taylor's edition as having "a publisher's note by Richard Simpson [sic], who seems to have been a contemporary of Swift" (p. 26 n.).

[72] Dr. Benjamin Karpman, "Neurotic Traits of Jonathan Swift as Revealed by *Gulliver's Travels*: A Minor Contribution to the Problem of Psychosexual Infantilism and Coprophilia," *Psychoanalytic Review*, XXIX (1942), 26–45, 165–84. One typographical error deserves mention: a Brobdingnagian breast (p. 168) has a "dung" instead of a "dug," indicating

that Swift's coprophilia may be contagious. Louis A. Landa, *PQ*, XXII (1943), 177, was the first to see a truly Swiftian catalog in these conclusions of Dr. Karpman. My debt to Landa will be apparent. See also his Riverside edition of *Gulliver*, Boston, 1960, pp. xi–xii, and his "Jonathan Swift: The Critical Significance of Biographical Evidence," *English Institute Essays, 1946*, New York, 1947, p. 26, for the suggestion that psychoanalytic criticism of Swift is "a logical development of the disordered-intellect theory of the nineteenth-century critics."

[73] I. F. Grant Duff, "A Onesided Sketch of Jonathan Swift," *Psychoanalytic Quarterly*, VI (1937), 238–59.

[74] Barrett, *Partisan Review*, XIV (1947), 5–22.

[75] D. S. Savage, "Swift," *Western Review*, XV (1950), 25–36.

[76] Roberts, "A Freudian View of Jonathan Swift," *Literature and Psychology*, VI (1956), 8–17.

[77] Critics are all too apt to miss Swift's delicious fun with Gulliver in this incident, especially in Gulliver's unguarded admission that "her Countenance did not make an Appearance altogether so hideous as the rest of the Kind" (IV, viii; HD, XI, 251).

[78] Ehrenpreis, *PMLA*, LXX (1955), 706–16; reprinted in *The Personality of Jonathan Swift*, London, 1958, pp. 11–28.

[79] J. Wickham Legg, Letter, *Academy*, XIX (June 25, 1881), 475. J. C. Bucknill, "Dean Swift's Disease," *Brain: A Journal of Neurology*, IV (January 1882), 493–506, quoted by Craik in an appendix to his *Life*, has sometimes been credited with the original diagnosis.

[80] Wilson, *Irish Journal of Medical Science*, ser. 6, No. 162 (June 1939), pp. 241–56; reprinted in *Annals of Medical History*, ser. 3, II (July 1940), 291–305. I quote from the latter.

[81] Brain, "The Illness of Dean Swift," *Irish Journal of Medical Science*, ser. 6 (August–September 1952), pp. 337–45; reprinted as "Jonathan Swift: L'Enfant Terrible" in his *Some Reflections on Genius and Other Essays*, Philadelphia, 1960, pp. 23–33. See also chapters VI and VII of Ehrenpreis' *The Personality of Jonathan Swift*: "Madness," pp. 117–26; "Old Age," pp. 127–47.

SOURCE BOOKS OF SWIFT CRITICISM

Some of the critical works cited in this book have been reprinted, in whole or in part, in anthologies of selected Swift scholarship. The three such "source" books now available are listed below, together with the names of critics and works represented. Selections marked with an asterisk are excerpts from, or abridgments of, the original work.

Gulliver's Travels: An Annotated Text with Critical Essays (Norton Critical Edition), ed. Robert A. Greenberg, New York, 1961. Includes brief excerpts from the work of John Lawlor, G. Wilson Knight, Bonamy Dobrée, Kathleen Williams, J. Middleton Murry, W. B. C. Watkins, Henry W. Sams, Ricardo Quintana, Basil Willey, F. R. Leavis, and Herbert Davis, and the following essays:

> * Louis A. Landa, "The Critical Significance of Biographical Evidence: Jonathan Swift."
> Samuel Holt Monk, "The Pride of Lemuel Gulliver."
> R. S. Crane, "The Rationale of the Fourth Voyage."
> A. E. Dyson, "Swift: The Metamorphosis of Irony."

A Casebook on Gulliver Among the Houyhnhnms (Crowell Literary Casebook), ed. Milton P. Foster, New York, 1961. Includes excerpts from Orrery, Deane Swift, Thomas Sheridan, Sir Walter Scott, Edmund Gosse, and William Makepeace Thackeray, and the following essays:

> * T. O. Wedel, "On the Philosophical Background of *Gulliver's Travels*."
> John B. Moore, "The Role of Gulliver."
> * D. Nichol Smith, "Jonathan Swift: Some Observations."
> * Ricardo Quintana, "Critical Notes on *Gulliver's Travels*" (from *The Mind and Art of Jonathan Swift*).
> John F. Ross, "The Final Comedy of Lemuel Gulliver."
> * A. E. Case, "The Significance of *Gulliver's Travels*" (from *Four Essays on "Gulliver's Travels"*).
> Samuel Kliger, "The Unity of *Gulliver's Travels*."
> * Louis A. Landa, "The Critical Significance of Biographical Evidence: Jonathan Swift."
> * Herbert Davis, "Moral Satire" (from *The Satire of Jonathan Swift*).
> Edward Stone, "Swift and the Horses: Misanthropy or Comedy?"
> Kathleen Williams, "Gulliver's Voyage to the Houyhnhnms."
> * F. R. Leavis, "The Irony of Swift."
> Roland M. Frye, "Swift's Yahoo and the Christian Symbols for Sin."

189

Samuel H. Monk, "The Pride of Lemuel Gulliver."

* Irvin Ehrenpreis, "Gulliver" (from *The Personality of Jonathan Swift*).

Ricardo Quintana, Note on Ehrenpreis' "The Origins of *Gulliver's Travels*."

George Sherburn, "Errors Concerning the Houyhnhnms."

* Louis A. Landa, Note on Ehrenpreis' *The Personality of Jonathan Swift.*

Calhoun Winton, "Conversion on the Road to Houyhnhnmland."

Charles Peake, "Swift and the Passions."

Discussions of Jonathan Swift (Heath Discussions of Literature), ed. John Traugott, Boston, 1962.

* Samuel Johnson, "The Life of Swift."

* William Makepeace Thackeray, "Swift."

* W. B. C. Watkins, "Absent Thee from Felicity."

F. R. Leavis, "The Irony of Swift."

A. E. Dyson, "Swift: The Metamorphosis of Irony."

* Martin Price, "Swift's Symbolic Works" (from *Swift's Rhetorical Art*).

William Butler Yeats, "Preface" to *Words upon the Window-Pane.*

George Orwell, "Politics vs. Literature: An Examination of *Gulliver's Travels*."

Norman O. Brown, "The Excremental Vision" (from *Life Against Death*).

Arthur E. Case, "Personal and Political Satire in *Gulliver's Travels*" (from *Four Essays on Gulliver's Travels*).

J. C. Beckett, "Swift as an Ecclesiastical Statesman" (from *Essays in British and Irish History*).

index

The manuscript was edited by Faith S. Schmidt. The book was designed by Richard Kinney. The text type face is Linotype Caledonia, designed by W. A. Dwiggins in 1940. The display face is Baskerville based on a face originally designed by John Baskerville between 1750 and 1758.

This book is printed on Olde Style Antique White Wove paper made by the S. D. Warren Company and bound in Holliston's Kingston Linen. Manufactured in the United States of America.